PASSION
CONNEMARA

Published in 2023 by
Potential Architecture Books
7253 Berri
Montreal, Quebec, Canada
H2R 2G4

Includes bibliographic references.

ISBN: 978-1-988962-07-8 (softcover)

The author and publisher apologize for any misattribution
and will correct any future printings as soon as they are informed of any such error.

In this book, the author pays tribute to Pat Lyne and her book *Shrouded in Mist*. Every effort has been made to contact the current copyright holder of *Shrouded in Mist* in order to inquire about the policy regarding the reproduction of short passages and the use of illustrations to no avail. This task was further complicated by the fact that Orphans Press was unable to obtain the contact information of the current publisher of the book.

Cover images
_Front cover:
Two Connemara mares owned by John J Mulkerrins on the beach in Callowfeenish,
September 2019. Photo: Jeannine Marolleau.
_Back cover:
Daniel Chupin and Balia de Briacé,
Laval in 2020. Pho: Jeannine Marolleau.

Daniel Chupin
Connemara Pony breeder
www.elevage-de-briace.com

DANIEL CHUPIN

PASSION
CONNEMARA

THE TUMULTUOUS HISTORY OF THE
WORLD'S FIRST SPORT PONY

To my father who passed on to me his passion for breeding.

Daniel Chupin
December 11, 2021

ACKNOWLEDGEMENTS

This book owes much to the careful reading, advice and unfailing support of my companion Jeannine Marolleau.

This English version would never have been possible without the involvement of Helena de Belloy, Maria Mahon and Emmanuelle de Monléon.

I thank with gratitude for their collaboration: Isabelle and Stéphane Jault, Louis-Marie Philibert, Hubert Laurent, Pascal Wandon, Sébastien Thilvert, Leatitia Bernard, Nelly Groene and Sophie Soulez Larivière, Sigrid Gilet.

Jean-Pierre Chupin, Mathilde Thierry, Louis-Marie Philibert, Aurélien Jault, and Sophie Soulez Larivière had the tedious task of reading the manuscript, correcting it and criticizing it. I thank them for the time they devoted to this project.

By providing me with numerous photos to document this work, I would like to thank the following people: Louis-Marie Philibert, Isabelle Jault, Jeannine Marolleau, Hubert Laurent, Emmanuelle de Monléon, Sophie Soulez Larivière, Willem Goedhart, Pascal Wandon, Françoise Clémenceau, Gilles Le Mouellic, Didier Merlet, Sorcha Foley, Valérie Wilmot and Marguerite Brassens.

This book is also the result of many meetings I had in Ireland in the early 1980s: Mrs. Maria Levinge, Mrs. Elizabeth Petch, Mrs. Pat Lyne, Mrs. L. Hemphill, James Jones, John Daly, Michael J. Clancy, Graham Tulloch, Joe Gorham, Michael King, Joseph Conroy, Padraic Hynes, Mrs. Brooks, Eddie Madden, Paddy Lally, Bartley O'Malley, Festy Mulkerrins, Mr. Ormsby, Stephen Heanue, Bobby Bolger... these breeders explained to me with passion and simplicity what they were looking for in the Connemara pony.

TABLE OF CONTENTS

INTRODUCTION

In 1981, I discovered Ireland and Connemara. My father had been breeding this breed of pony since 1976 and the need to discover this island had become essential. After several stays, I met Pat Lyne in Ireland in 1986, then in Stoneleigh in 1987. Her book *Shrouded in Mist* will be an important support to understanding the Connemara pony. That same year, I began translating Shrouded in Mist. In many ways, I underestimated the magnitude of the task. My job in the industry and the workload of a pony farm left me little time. In March 2020, I went back to my handwritten notes and began an analysis of Connemara stallions with offspring in France.

Historical documents on the Connemara pony are almost non-existent. So, I continued my analysis based on two other books: *Connemara Pony Breeders' Society 1923-1998* written by Mrs. Petch, and the beautiful book *Seahorses* written by Stephanie Brooks and Karen Mannion.

After all these years dedicated to breeding and equestrian sport, the need to share my experiences and knowledge about this pony, this beautiful region, and Ireland in general, became obvious to me.

Originally from Connemara, a region in the west of Ireland, the pony has been shaped by the history of Ireland, the people who have used it, and by its environment. The Irish folklore with the legends surrounding the pony remains alive in Connemara and the hearts of many people in Ireland. Cuchullain, Fionn, Finn, and Oisin are names that the Irish give to their stallions. These names refer to characters from Irish mythology. It seemed to me essential to approach the Irish legends and myths through some examples.

Invasions, conquests, colonizations, revolts, bloody repressions, food shortages, famines. One may wonder if Ireland was not an island condemned to misfortune? I have therefore tried to include a chronology with some major historical events. This subject is very well treated in many books of which you will find some references in the bibliography. I have chosen to resume the main dates and historical events to allow you to better understand the Irish, the difficulties of the breeders, and the evolution of breeding in Connemara.

Connemara and Ireland are open-air museums. By developing several paragraphs on the archaeology and the origins of the horse in Ireland, I present to you a synthesis of the archaeological discoveries which will give you indications on the use of the equids, their harnessing, their size, and globally their utility.

In the chapter "The Connemara", we go back to the heart of the matter by discussing the origins of the Connemara pony, the reasons for its decline, its revival, and especially its development.

The study on French stallions will allow you to discover the different bloodlines used by French breeders to produce high-level sport ponies.

You will discover the breeding of the Connemara pony in France, its evolution, and the axes of development.

The Connemara pony is now represented by 12 breed associations and present on four continents. I will tell you, its history.

This book is intended for lovers of this pony, for people who wish to discover it.

GENERAL

Before telling you about the Connemara pony, I think it is appropriate to make some reminders about Ireland.

Ireland is an island located in the northwest of the European continent in the North Atlantic. It is a member of the European Union since 1973. It is a republic divided into two parts: the island of Ireland (EIRE or commonly called Southern Ireland) and Northern Ireland which is part of the United Kingdom also called ULSTER.

In total, it includes 32 counties (regions): 26 for Eire and 6 counties for Northern Ireland. The official symbol of the country is the Celtic harp. This symbol appears on the Euro coins used only in Southern Ireland. But there is another symbol, notably used by the Irish rugby team, symbolizing St. Patrick's Day, celebrated on March 17 it is the shamrock.

The capital of Northern Ireland (ULSTER) is BELFAST. Its surface area is 14 139 km² for approximately 1.77 million inhabitants. The official language is English. The currency is the pound sterling. The country is ruled by King Charles III of England. The religion is divided between 45% Protestants and about 41% Catholics.

Southern Ireland covers 84% of the island with only 16% belonging to Northern Ireland. The island consists of a central plain surrounded by mountains and hills, lakes, and rivers. In the southwest, cliffs overlook the Atlantic Ocean, but almost all around the island, there are many sandy beaches.

It is an independent state since 1937 and its capital is Dublin. The surface area of Southern Ireland is 70,273 km2 with a population of approximately 4.46 million. The official and majority language of the country is English, but there is another language, Irish Gaelic. The religion is 89% Catholic.

The climate is oceanic temperate: summers are generally mild (about 25°C) and winters are cool and rainy (about 0°C). Winds can reach speeds of around 160 km/h in the western counties. The prevailing winds are from the southwest, so rainfall is particularly heavy in the western part of the island. Throughout the country, about 60% of the annual rainfall occurs between August and January.

The highest point of the island is Carrauntuohill which rises to 1,041 m above sea level. It is located in the Macgillycuddy's Reeks in County Kerry in the southwest of Ireland. Irish mountains are not very high. Only three peaks exceed 1,000 meters in elevation and the other 457 are 500 meters in elevation. The largest river on the island is the River Shannon, which is 386 kilometers long.

Ireland is divided into 4 provinces: Ulster, Munster, Connacht, and Leinster.

Figure 1. Map of Ireland. Source Andrein, CC BY-SA 3.0.

During my research, I found only a few elements on the origins of this pony in Ireland. After reading many scientific works. Here is a synthesis of some books and scientific articles that I have translated, on the origins of the horse in Ireland. This information seems interesting because it deals with archaeological discoveries and gives us indications of the use of horses, their harnesses, their size, and globally their usefulness.

PREHISTORIC IRELAND

Around 7,000 BC, the first traces of human activity were discovered by archaeologists. They must have been men hunting wild boar, gathering wild plants, collecting shells, and fishing in lakes, rivers, and the sea.

Around 3700 BC the first traces of agriculture appear. These farmers raised cattle, sheep, goats, and cultivated cereals such as wheat and barley. These farmers lived in rectangular wooden houses. They also used flint tools. Remains from Shandon Cave, Co. Waterford, show that the wild horse was present in Ireland about 28,000 years ago. Subsequently, an increase in ice cover led to their extinction in Ireland.

THE BRONZE AGE (AROUND 2300-500 B.C.)

Horse bones from Newgrange have been found mixed with food waste from other domesticated animals. Finbar McCormick in "The Horse in Ancient Ireland" suggests that while the horse was primarily used for transportation, it was also eaten. Some horses were quite old, up to fifteen years, which might suggest that they were only killed and eaten after a useful life of transport or traction.

There is no factual evidence for the use of horses for purposes other than food in the Bronze Age.

THE IRON AGE (ABOUT 500 B.C. - 500 AD)

Horse bits are the most common metal objects found in the Early Iron Age in Ireland. A large number of horse bits suggests an expansion of horse breeding in Ireland during the Iron Age. Most of the horse bones found at Tara were from adult animals that would have been used for riding or pulling.

PAGAN IRELAND

THE CELTS

The Celts began to settle in Central Europe around 1000 BC. A great Celtic civilization will develop from the 6th century BC in Ireland.

As summarized by Stéphane Verger, a specialist in protohistoric societies, there are two ways to approach the beginning of the Celtic era:

> *"The first, positivist, consists in going back in time beyond the second Iron Age, or even the beginning of the Metal Ages, in the regions supposed to have been occupied by Celtic populations to determine, according to the archaeological data, from which moment and in which zone of Europe the cultural characteristics traditionally attributed to the Celts can be highlighted. The second, hypercritical, is the one that consists in considering that the notion of Celts is a modern construction."*

According to this thesis, the Celts would not have existed before their conceptualization in the 17th century. The historian Jean-Louis Brunaux, a specialist of the Gauls, is quite close to this second vision. He doubts the reality of Celtic civilization. In his eyes, the idea of a Celtic language is an unproven postulate. The similarities between Breton, Gaelic, and Welsh...would be explained more by contacts and influences between neighboring peoples than by the existence of a mother language. Jean-Louis Brunaux agrees with the idea put forward by Tolkien:

> *"The Celts [...] are a magical bag into which you can put anything you want and out of which you can get just about anything."*

This is all the easier since they have left almost no written records. The Celts would have spread throughout Europe, not from central Europe, but the center south of Gaul. This extension would have been done in the form of colonization and not of migrations. This interpretation is the opposite of the work of most specialists of the Celtic world, who like Wenceslas Kruta emphasize on the contrary the existence of a specific civilization, immediately identifiable by its language, the material remains it has left, the beliefs and myths that specialists in comparative mythology have been able to reconstruct.

For Myles Dillon (the Celtic kingdoms), it is a civilization very structured by a system of clans that is directed by a supreme king of Ireland. A discernible feature of the Celtic civilization is to have made springs, rivers, and sacred trees, objects of worship, under the patronage of gods and goddesses.

Pierre Joannon in his work *History of Ireland and the Irish* makes a description of the Celtic society:

> *"On the organization of the Gaelic society of this Insula Sacra, one is informed by a whole series of texts of transcription certainly late since writing, related to magic, was proscribed in the 'heroic age', but which do not reflect less the archaic character of the uses, customs and social structures of the pre-Christian time. Among these texts, it is appropriate to quote the Senchus Mor or law of the Brehons, and the Ulster epic, of which the Tain Bo Cualnge which constitutes the heart was admirably translated into French and annotated by the great Celtic scholar Christian-J. Guyonvarc'h. These texts give us the image of a pastoral community, subdivided into a multitude of principalities, where priestly, warlike, and productive activities provide a perfect illustration of the functional tripartition highlighted among the Indo-European peoples by Georges Dumézil.*
>
> *Based on wealth and birth, a distinction was made between serfs, freemen, and nobles, of whom the king was only the primus inter pares[1]. However, the law of the Brehons[2] showed great flexibility by allowing certain social mobility. It was also possible to fall from one's rank just as it was possible to rise to the top. Falling into the hands of the enemy and being condemned to pay a fine without being able to pay it led to servitude.*
>
> *The power of the sovereign, precarious and always contested, was deployed within the geographical framework of the tuath, equivalent to our cantons. Ireland had up to one hundred and fifty of them. They were bounded by artificial limits, furrows, dry stone walls, or ditches, the imprecision of which fueled incessant quarrels. Threatened by the extension of rival sovereignties, the king's power was coveted and held in check even within the group over which it was exercised.*
>
> *The political organization of the Gaels, with its jumble of tiny principalities, bristling against each other, and its indefinite*

---

[1] The Latin phrase *primus inter pares* refers to a person who presides over an assembly without having powers of his own.

[2] The *Dlíthe na mBreithiúna* or 'laws of the judges', or *Brehon Laws* in English, are statutes that governed daily life and politics in Ireland until the Norman invasion of 1171 (the word 'Brehon' is an English adaptation of *breitheamh*, an Irish word meaning 'judge').

subdivision of quasi-independent, mobile, and turbulent cells, was one of the great weaknesses of this society.

The social organization of the Gaels was so tightly constituted that it took several centuries for foreign influence to erode it and break down its amazing resistance. The three pillars of this social organization were the family, the semi-collective ownership of land, and that singular Celtic Christianity.

A particular institution of the Gaelic family, probably borrowed from the pre-Celtic inhabitants of Erin, singularly reinforced the cohesion of the social milieu and later favored the assimilation of foreigners. This was the custom of fosterage, whereby children were not brought up by their parents but entrusted to a friendly home from an early age. Whether it was a duty of affection or a paid service of up to eighteen cows for a king's son, fosterage obliged the host family to provide for the child's education according to very demanding criteria. Failure to do so resulted in the imposition of a heavy fine. The experience lasted until the age of seventeen for boys and fourteen for girls. The child who became an adult owed, throughout his life, help, and assistance to the family that had taken him in. With his adoptive parents, the ties were as strong as those between him and his natural parents. Many Norman invaders entrusted their children to Irish families in fosterage; this custom was a powerful force for assimilation that the English government quickly took umbrage with, to the point of forbidding it on pain of high treason. It continued until the end of the 18th century: this is how the 'Liberator', Daniel O'Connell was entrusted to a herdsman and his wife for fostering, which seemed so natural to him that his two sons would have the same fate.

Within the family, although the Senchus Mor[3] recognized the pre-eminence of the man, the woman enjoyed a status that made her more or less equal to her partner. The married woman remained the owner of her property; she could inherit and sue.

How land was appropriated also reinforced the cohesion of Gaële society. A certain portion was the private property of the king and the nobles or flaith, to whom it was given as a reward for services rendered to the community. The rest of the land,

---

[3]   The Senchus Môr is a treatise on jurisprudence written in Old Irish.

which made up most of the territory, belonged collectively to the tribe and to those of its members, shepherds, peasants, and artisans, to whom the productive functions were devolved. The land was divided among the different septs, no part of it was privately owned. It was occupied by temporary owners. Each free man was entitled to his share of the land for two or three years, after which a new distribution took place. When he returned a piece of land, he always received another in exchange.

The non-arable land, the mountains, the forests or marshes were common goods that could not be privately appropriated: every free man had the right to graze, the right to estovers[4] or to hunt.

The memory of the right of co-ownership of clan lands remained surprisingly vivid among the Irish peasant despite conquests and confiscations. The feudal law had a lot of difficulty in replacing the collective property right of the ancient Gaelic system.

The new Anglo-Norman mode of appropriation, by reducing it to nothing, generated a powerful feeling of frustration.

The Gaelic Ireland offered a landscape of subdivided lands, cut by hedges, pits, and earthen levees. The dispersed and fortified habitat of the Gaels sometimes took the form of wooden huts protected by a palisade of logs, sometimes that of Caiseal[5] when the residence and the rampart were out of stone, or still crannogs, lake houses posed in the middle of a lake or a peat bog. Cities and villages will only appear in the 9th century of our era. More than the work of the fields, it was the breeding that occupied the producers, a consequence of the wet climate favorable to the grass. The wealth of Celtic Ireland was the livestock. In the Tain Bo, the Irish Iliad, the raids on herds legitimized most of the warlike activity. Tributes, royalties, and fines were payable to cattle.

The tight and strong fabric of the Gaelic family and society contrasted sharply with the total absence of cohesion on the political level. Of unity or semblance of unity, there was no

---

[4]   The right to estovers is the possibility given to reserve a part of the woods of the communal forest for the domestic use of the inhabitants.

[5]   Circular stone construction.

question until the 8ᵗʰ century. The kings of Tara,[6] , whose conquests were the talk of the town from the 6ᵗʰ century onwards, remained provincial kings with powers contained and limited by the other dynasties.

Figure 2. Stone huts, Dingle Peninsula. Photo Daniel Chupin.

The Turoe Stone is a granite stone decorated in a Celtic style located in the village of Bullaun, County Galway, Ireland, 6 km north of Loughrea. It probably dates from the period from 100 BC to the present day.

*Figure 3. The Turoe stone.
Photo Daniel Chupin*

---

6   Kingdom of Tara was the place of coronation of the powerful kings of the island, the hill of Tara is located in the valley of Boyne (County Meath).

THE IRISH INVASIONS IN GREAT BRITAIN

The Celts seem to have been well-equipped to travel by sea. The Annals of Tighernach tell us that in the year 222, Cormac's fleet sailed the sea for three years. We are told that Niall took his fleet with him when he invaded Britain; he sailed it around the British coast and then carried his army to France. And Cormac's Glossary says that Breccan, Niall's grandson, had a trading fleet of 50 currachs sailing between Ireland and Scotland. It was after the destruction of Emania (AD 331) that the Irish and Pictish invasions of Britain took their most serious form. The royal house of Connaught and its family were by then firmly established over most of Ireland. They conducted their British operations so successfully and threateningly that in 343 the emperor Constantine had to take personal charge of repelling them.

Other invasions followed. Irish records say that Crimthann the Great ruled Britain (which means, of course, a major part of Britain) for 13 years, from 366 to 379. The Roman general Theodosius, the father of the emperor of that name, led the Roman legions against this Irish king. He defeated him and drove him out of Britain.

The Christian faith that the Irish people as a whole so willingly absorbed from Patrick during the 5th century brought about a radical change in their character.

After this century, there are no other recorded cases of military raids abroad.

FROM CONMAICNE TO CONNEMARA

The Conmaicne were a tribe. They claimed to be the descendants of Conmac, son of the legendary Maeve, Queen of Connaught. They settled in several districts of Connaught, and those who lived west of Lough Corrib were known as the Conmaicne Mara, the Comaince of the Sea, to distinguish them from the other branches of the Conmaicne tribe living further east. The district they occupied was in the northwestern part of Galway, and as was the custom at the time, the main local tribe gave its name to the place.

This is how the region came to be known as Conmaicne-Mara, or Connemara as we know it today.

LEGENDS AND MYTHOLOGIES

The sea creeps far inland in many of Connemara's bays, coves, and gulfs. The hinterland valleys and bogs are dotted with lakes and rivers. Water is everywhere, so it's not surprising that it features in many stories and tales of Irish Celtic mythology and folklore.

In pagan Celtic Ireland, there was no clear distinction between the natural and the supernatural, between the real world and the other world (often considered the land of happiness, beyond the water, in the west of Ireland).

Horses enjoyed an even more important position in old Irish society. In a pre-Christian country where water was believed to be the gateway to the Other World, there was an oral tradition throughout Ireland linking the horse to this Other World.

Fables tell of horses that mysteriously emerge from the sea, lakes, and rivers, spend some time with a man and then disappear again into the misty depths... It is said that these fairy animals leave the human world when their master dies.

In Irish folklore, the beautiful underwater-dwelling stallion known as the 'each uisce' or water horse would emerge from the lake on full moon nights to graze on the shores and, on occasion, to cover the local mares and produce high-quality foals for the lucky farmers.

The mystique that surrounded the horse has faded, but the esteem and affection that the people of Connemara felt for their little native ponies is still present today in the hearts of many people in Ireland and around the world who love the pony.

IRISH MYTHOLOGY

Cuchullain, Fionn, Finn, Oisin, are names that the Irish give to their stallions. These names refer to characters from Irish mythology. Seumas Macmanus, in his book *The Story of Irish Race, a Popular History of Ireland*, relates a panoply of characters from this Irish mythology that embody the essence of the hero. They are portrayed in the writings as demi-gods, endowed with superhuman physical forces, as well as with magical powers transmitted to them by the Gods.

I have extracted a few short passages from his book, selecting only three of these heroes: Cuchullain, Cormac Mac Art, and Fionn and the Fianna. As often in Irish writings, the link between history, tale, and mythology is close.

CUCHULLAIN

The Reign of Conor MacNessa, on the throne of Ulster, was a brilliant one in Irish history. It was a heroic period in Ireland - the period of chivalry, mainly created by the famous Red Branch Knights of Emania. However, two other famous bands of Irish warriors gave additional lustre to this period: the Gamanraide of the West (who were Firbolgs) and the Clanna Deaghaid of Munster led by Curoi MacDaire. But the most glorious of all the heroes of this heroic age was Cuchullain, whose life and wondrous exploits, real or imagined, are the subject of hundreds of stories. His legendary story is told in many stories in the greatest of Irish epics, The Tain Bo Cuailgne' – the raid on the cattle of Cuailgne.

The plan of the very great and ancient epic of The Tain Bo Cuailgne is roughly as follows: Queen Maeve of Connaught, secured by a second marriage to the kingdom of Connaught, and by a third marriage, she had Ailill, of Leinster. Queen Maeve and her king Ailill began to count and compare their material possessions. In the course of a long and careful tally of these possessions, it was clear that neither had an advantage over the other in material wealth - until it was finally discovered that Ailill, in his herds, possessed a valuable bull. Moreover, in all of Ireland, no bull could match him, except for the famous brown bull of Cuailgne (in present-day County Louth).

Maeve sent a messenger to the chief of Cuailgne, asking him to lend her his precious animal so that her herd could outnumber Ailill's. He refused. Then Maeve, furious and determined, mobilized a great army to invade Ulster and to take by force the brown bull of Cuailgne.

She had all the forces of Connaught at her disposal. With this powerful army, she marched into Ulster and met the formidable Cuchullain. Cuchullain defended Ulster against Maeve and the four-fifths of Ireland. He became the hero and the great central figure of Tain. After long wars and acts of bravery on both sides, Queen Maeve obtained the coveted brown bull and returned to Connaught with this rare prize.

Cuchullain died heroically, as he should, on a battlefield, with his back to a rock and his face turned towards the enemy, the shield on his arm, and the lance in his hand. He died standing in an attitude of defiance (supported by the rock). He had been dead for several days before the enemy dared to venture close enough to make sure he was dead. This they did only when they saw the vultures alight on him, and, undisturbed, peck at his flesh.

CORMAC MAC ART

Of all the ancient kings of Ireland, Cormac, who reigned in the 3rd century, is undoubtedly considered the greatest by poets and chroniclers. A noble and illustrious king, says a parchment preserved in the Book of Ballymote, took sovereignty and power over Eire (Ireland). The world abounded in all that was good in his time: the food and fat of the earth and the gifts of the sea were in abundance under the reign of this king. There were no injuries or robberies in his time, and everyone enjoyed his property in peace.

Cormac rebuilt the palace of Tara, with great magnificence. He built the Teach Mi Chuarta, the great banquet hall, which measured 232 m by 14 m, and 14 m high. Until very recently, the outline of the foundations of this great hall and the traces of its fourteen doors could still be seen on the hill of Tara. He also built a grianan (house of the sun) for the women and the house of the thousand soldiers. He gave to the office of Ard-Righ a magnificence that it had not known before.

When Cormac reached an advanced age, he resigned from the throne, thus ending one of the most successful and illustrious reigns. He was the greatest king Ireland had ever known. During his reign, no one needed to lock the door, no one needed to herd the flock, and no one in all of Ireland was afflicted by a lack of food or clothing. He retired to Cleite Acaill, on the Boyne, where he devoted himself to study and good works.

FIONN AND THE FIANNA

Fionn MacCumail (Finn MacCool) or Finn is a pseudonym which means blond (about the color of his hair), handsome and of good race, but also white, the Whiteness, the Purity. Fionn, chief of the Fianna (Fen-ians), at the time of Cormac MacArt, is the great central figure of these tales.

It was during the reign of Conn, at the end of the second or beginning of the 3rd century, that the Fianna was founded, a great standing army composed of bold warriors, specially trained and selected, whose duty was to carry out the mandates of the great king.

They were soldiers in wartime and a national police force in peacetime. But Fionn, being a full-fledged chief himself, had a residence on Allen's Hill (Almuin) in Kildare.

The Fianna recruited at the great fairs, especially at Tara, Uisnech and Taillte. The greatest discretion was used to select eligible candidates from the crowd of applicants, which included many sons of chiefs and princes. But no candidate was considered unless he, his family, and his clan were willing to accept for him all the daily risks of a perilous career. The tests were many and difficult for the one who wanted to be part of the noble body.

One of the first tests was literary: no candidate was accepted if he or she had not mastered the twelve books of poetry. With this condition in mind, it is not surprising that the Fianna has bequeathed to posterity ten thousand tales. In a trench, knee deep, the candidate, equipped only with a shield and a hazel stick, must protect himself from nine warriors who throw javelins at him from nine ridges. If he is given the start from a single tree, in a thick wood, he must escape his pursuers without being hurt. He must be so adept at running through the woods, and so agile, that none of his braids will become attached to a branch in his flight. His step must be so light that he does not break any dry branch under his feet. In his run, he must leap over branches as high as his forehead, and stoop under others as high as his knee, without delaying, nor leaving behind him a trembling branch. In the most difficult situations, the weapon should not tremble in his hand.

When a candidate had passed the tests and was found suitable to be a member of this heroic troop, four geasa (vows of chivalry) were imposed as a final condition of admission:

- He will marry his wife without sharing, choosing her for her manners and her virtues.
- He will have to be gentle with all women.
- He will never reserve for himself what another person needs.
- He will fight against all odds, up to nine to one.

Difficult, then, was the task of one who entered the ranks of the noble Fianna. Wandering and roaming from one end of the island to the other, hunting and fighting, feasting and making love, the Fianna made legend every day of their lives. In time, during the reign of Cairbre Lifeachar, son of Cormac, they rebelled against the Ard-Righ. Fionn and his Fianna joined Breasil, king of Leinster, to resist Cairbre's levy of the Boru tribute. Cairbre suffered a crushing defeat at the battle of Cnamros, where he is said to have left nine thousand dead on the battlefield. In 280 AD, the two sides fought to the death at the Battle of Gabra, one of the fiercest battles of ancient times. Oisin, the son of Fionn led the Fianna. Oisín's son, Oscar, the most powerful fighter of the Fianna, was killed in single combat by Cairbre. The Fianna, who had for so long occupied such a brilliant place in the history of Ireland, were annihilated.

In every corner of Ireland, to the remotest promontory, the stories of the Fianna arouse the admiration and excite the emulation of the Irish people. The best of the Fianna stories are preserved in the poems of Oisín, the son of Fionn, the chief bard of the Fianna in a book of poems. The Agallam na Seanorach (The Colloquy of the Ancients), by far the finest collection of Fianna tales, is said to be an account of the great deeds of the Fianna, handed down to Patrick by Oisín and Caoilte, over 150 years later."

The Gaels were breeders. Herd raids were commonplace in this country where wealth was measured in cattle. Brave in war, and good talkers, they were easily carried away and had a very high sense of honor. They were arrogant in victory and so downcast in defeat that they would kill themselves. The impression they leave on historians is that of a people with a great artistic and religious sense, brave and cheerful, with great physical strength, surprisingly successful, but surprisingly resistant to any unifying initiative.

These warrior shepherds wrote one of the most beautiful pages of early Christianity, transforming Ireland into the 'Island of Saints'.

CHRISTIAN IRELAND

Unlike Great Britain, Ireland was not colonized by Rome. From the 4th century, the country was Christianized, but certain Celtic rites continued until the 12th century. From its conversion to Christianity until the Viking invasion, Ireland shone in Europe.

THE ISLAND OF SAINTS AND SAGES

Ireland never belonged to the Roman Empire. The Latin merchants landed there and were evangelists. According to tradition, Green Eire was evangelized by Saint Patrick between 432 and 461. The secret of this lightning conversion is probably the decline of Druidism. The numerous contacts with insular Brittany and Gaul, the skill of Patrick who undertook to win over the great ones in this very aristocratic society, invariably led to the conversion of the whole clan. Without violence and martyrdom, the country was covered with churches. The success of Saint Patrick is surprising because his apostolate was based on a Roman conception of religion, very different from the Celtic temperament. This is probably one of the reasons why the orthodox heritage of St. Patrick did not survive him.

From being episcopal and Roman, it had become Celtic and monastic. The monastery corresponded better to the rural and tribal framework of Irish society.

Its organization was modeled on that of the family, its life was linked to that of the tribe. It was strongly aristocratic: the abbot, all-powerful, often belonged to a noble family. The monks simply transposed the religious traditions of the Celts to the Christian mode. People from all over the world flocked to the Irish monastic schools: Breton nobles, kings of Northumbria[7] , Merovingian princes, and scholars from the continent flocked to Clonard[8] , Clonmacnoise[9], Armagh, Glendalough.[10] For two centuries, the monks of Ireland were the tutors of barbarian Europe.

---

[7]   Northumbria originally referred to the lands that were invaded by the Angles around 500 and which lay north of the River Humber, between what is now northern England and southern Scotland.

[8]   Clonard Abbey (Gaelic: *Cluain Eraird* or *Cluain Iraird*, the "meadow of Erard") is an important Irish religious foundation of the 6th century, located in County Meath.

[9]   The monastery of Clonmacnoise (in Irish *Cluain Mhic Nóis*) is located in County Offaly, on the banks of the River Shannon and south of the town of Athlone. The monastery, which is also called the *seven churches*, was founded in 544 by Saint Ciarán.

[10]   Located in County Wicklow, south of Dublin, Glendalough is home to one of the most important monastic sites in Ireland. This early Christian monastic settlement was founded by St. Kevin in the 6th century and it is from there that the "Monastic City" developed. Most of the buildings that remain today date from the 10th to the 12th century. Despite Viking attacks over the years, Glendalough flourished as one of the great ecclesiastical foundations and schools of learning in Ireland until the Normans destroyed the monastery in 1214.

Grace Neville writes:

> *"It was the monks of Ireland who, in the Middle Ages, after the fall of the Roman Empire, re-exported Christianity and the taste for knowledge to a Europe devastated by successive invasions.*

More precisely, these monks crisscrossed continental Europe, founding monasteries everywhere along the way.

> *By the way, to have the oldest written vestige of the Gaelic language (Celtic language, of course), one would have to go not to some grandiose library, but to the small municipal library of the town of Cambrai lost in the mists of the flat country of northern France. There, a bible, perhaps left behind by an Irish monk on his journey to central and southern Europe, contains a passage that linguists hail as the world's oldest surviving record of a text written in Gaelic."*

But, pagan or Christian, warlike or monastic, Ireland remained divided against itself. Its insularity did not protect it from the Vikings. Rising from the fog on their light Drakkar, they plundered the coasts of Ireland, established strongholds, and sailed up the rivers, sowing death and desolation in their wake.

Figure 4. Glendalough, a monastic site in County Wicklow, Photo Jeannine Marolleau.

THE FIRST MEDIEVAL PERIOD (AROUND 500-1170)

With the emergence of the early medieval period from 500 AD, zooarchaeological evidence comes from archaeological sites where the horse is found in association with the food waste of other domestic animals. Their presence probably reflects periods of acute food shortage. Monastic rules assigning penances for various sins made it clear that the church frowned on the consumption of horse flesh, at least among clerics. The Irish canons state that "the penance for eating horse flesh, is four years on bread and water." Despite this, horse bones were found among the food waste at most sites of the time, including ecclesiastical sites such as Church Island in County Kerry. Around 732, Pope Gregory wrote to St. Boniface, the apostle of the Germans, that eating the flesh of wild and domestic horses was "a repugnant and abominable practice" and should be forbidden.

In early medieval Ireland, horses were used for riding and light traction. Horses could only be used for heavier traction after the introduction of the breastplate, which was soon replaced by the collar.

Early Irish sources make a clear distinction between horses used for riding and those used for work. Riding was the prerogative of the nobility and the wealthy class of free farmers. Thus, a typical lord would own one saddle horse and four others for less important tasks.

The early medieval Irish did not use stirrups or saddles. The spur and horseshoe also made their first appearance in Ireland in the early 11th century.

There was a wide variety of horse coats, white, black, gray, dark gray, isabella, and orange.

A large amount of metric data is available for the early medieval period. The range of sizes is much wider than in the Iron Age, with a peak for horses of 130-134 cm.

CHURCH ISLAND: A 19TH CENTURY CHURCH ON AN ISLAND

Figure 5. Church Island, Lough Currane, County Kerry. Three photos by Daniel Chupin (this page and illustration at the top of the next page).

This interesting site is one of the least visited in Ireland. It is located in the county of Kerry. Church Island is located in the middle of Lough Currane (Lake Waterville) and can only be reached by renting a boat on-site. If the season permits, I encourage you to take advantage of this trip to do a day of fishing. On the island, you will find the remains of an ancient Irish monastery dating from around the 12th century. Also located on the island, the cell of St. Fininas is believed to be associated with the 6th century saint known as Fionan Cam. An early Christian monastery is said to have been founded here by St. Finán Cam in the 6th century. As we sailed across the lake, after a few hours of fishing, the island came into view with its 12th-century Romanesque church of St. Finán. One enters the church through a round-headed door on the western gable. The four orders of the jambs are richly decorated in the Romanesque style. Unfortunately, these sculptures

are very damaged over time. In total,
11 decorated slabs. Two of these slabs have
inscriptions. The cross-shaped slab on the far
right has a double-rimmed ringed cross with
a tapered shaft. It also bears the Greek
symbols alpha and omega. A rectangular
block of sandstone bears a sculpture from the
12th century representing a musician playing
a bowed lyre. It is thought that bowed lyres
arrived in Europe in the 11th century. This is
the only known representation of this
instrument in Ireland. The third leacht is a
low, rectangular, stepped mound lined with
stone slabs. Reputed to mark the grave of
St. Finán, this leacht is located northwest of
the church. St. Finán's cell is a large dry-stone
structure known as a clochán. The remains

of another dry-stone hut are located in the center of the island, between the cell of
St. Finán and the cemetery. The remains of two rectangular huts are located at
the southern end of the island. The cell of St. Finán is a rectangular dry-stone
structure with rounded outer corners. Inside, it is about 5.25 meters long and
5 meters wide. St. Fínán Cam is said to have been born in Kerry in the 6th century.
It is believed that he studied under the guidance of St. Brendan of Clonfert before
founding a monastery at Kinnity in County Offaly. Fionain (light-haired) returned
to Kerry and founded the small monastic settlement on Church Island.

Figure 6. Kilmalkedar Monastery, County Kerry, Photo Daniel Chupin.

IRELAND SUBMITTED

In the 8th century, Ireland was the victim of murderous Viking expeditions, the Vikings even set up fortresses on the territory. From the 12th century, the Normans and then England undertook to conquer the island, and in 1494 the British crown declared its domination over all of Ireland. In 1541, Henry VIII took the title of King of Ireland. A revolt broke out in 1641, but it was broken by Cromwell in 1649. For five centuries, the old Celtic Ireland groans in the convulsions of indescribable anarchy. Wars, murders, pillaging, betrayals, and famines are the common currency of an era marked by the clash of two irreconcilable peoples.

Regarding the arrival of the Normans (1169), Grace Neville states:

> "The 12th century in Ireland saw the arrival of the Normans. Significantly, in Ireland, there is some hesitation between the terms 'arrival' and 'invasion' to describe this event: it is that, in the space of only three generations, the Normans, eternal chameleons, became (to use the Latin phrase of the time) 'more Irish than the Irish'.

> They conquered most of the country through 'soft power': alliances, marriages of convenience, and other contracts rather than through more conventional strike forces. They who originally spoke and wrote in French in Ireland converted within three generations, not to English but Gaelic.

> If the Normans quickly became more Irish than the Irish, the same could not be said of the English who transformed Ireland into a colony in the 16th century.

> As in any colony, the culture of the natives was quickly attacked: the Gaelic language, prized by the Normans and the Irish, was gradually marginalized (pushed towards the Atlantic coast) by English, the language of power, administration, and commerce; the economic survival of the natives was threatened: see as an example among many others the suffocation of the flourishing Irish wool trade in the 17th century destroyed by tariffs imposed by the English to prevent any competition with the equivalent English trade, tariffs that triggered the fury of the great writer, Jonathan Swift, then Dean of St. Patrick's Cathedral in Dublin. Cathedral of Dublin.

The religion of most Irish people, Catholicism, was also attacked by penal laws that prohibited, with varying degrees of success, the practice of the Catholic religion.

In this context, the Catholics of Ireland clung to their religion as a lifeline, a reality that differentiated them from the English; and the Catholic priests, present everywhere, in every parish, on every street corner, presented themselves as the defenders of the people, especially the little people who lived on land belonging to large landlords, those 'absentee landlords' who lived in London where they lived (literally) the life of a castle thanks to the rents paid by their miserable tenants in Ireland."

LATE MEDIEVAL PERIOD (AFTER AROUND 1170)

The occasional presence of horseshoes and other horse paraphernalia at medieval urban sites attests to the presence of horses in cities. The accounts of Holy Trinity Priory, Dublin, for the years 1337-1347, record the different types of horses held and the expenses associated with their maintenance. They refer to cart, farm, and plow horses that can be considered work horses. They also refer to Hackney horses, which can be considered general-purpose horses but are primarily used to pull light carriages. Palfrey horses, i.e. saddle horses, often associated with women, are also mentioned.

King John's Pipe Roll, dating from 1212-1213, refers to 'hobbles', battle horses for light troops as well as war horses for men-at-arms which must refer to horses for more heavily armored troops. The technological advances in the saddle and stirrup introduced to Ireland during the Viking period were considered the norm by the Anglo-Normans, but do not seem to have been adopted by the native Irish.

Cavalry charges were extremely rare and incursions, raids, skirmishes, and the taking of fortified positions were far more common than pitched battles. Perhaps the particular nature of warfare in Ireland did not justify the adoption of the stirrup and saddle.

Irish infantry mounted on fast, light horses were very effective in medieval warfare and it may well be that the Irish never used cavalry to any great extent. Horses were used to move into battle, but on the battlefield, the war was fought on foot, which is why it is called mounted infantry. Irish infantry mounted on small horses, the hobblebones, were known to be extremely effective in harassing heavily armed knights, so much so that these horses were hired by the English king Edward I for his campaigns. The first reference to the use of these 'hobbler' infantry horses dates back to 1296 when Edward imported 150 of them to help him in his war against the Scots.

While the absence of saddles, stirrups, and spurs might imply a military disadvantage, the Irish experience clearly shows that this was not the case. Indeed, the Irish light infantry mounted on their relatively small hobbled horses played an important role in the disappearance of the use of heavily armored cavalry in medieval warfare.

Irish horses were also in high demand. In 1171, it is reported that 100 horses were sent at one time from Ireland to England. Some horses went farther. In 1330, Irish horses were sent to royal studs in France.

The average height of horses around the 12th and 13th centuries is also greater, with an average height of 134.8 cm compared to 130.7 cm in rural Ireland in the early Middle Ages. A more pronounced increase in horse height, however, can be seen in the horses of the 14th and 15th centuries. Horses smaller than 122 cm have disappeared and horses of 153.6 cm are present when the average size is 137.4 cm. This increase in size can probably be attributed to the demand for large horses needed for plowing. The size of horses increased slightly in the 16th century, with horses measuring up to 156.7 cm.

It is difficult to understand why the Irish refused to adopt technological improvements such as the saddle and stirrup. Ireland was much slower than elsewhere to adopt these developments, but this may be due in large part to the particular nature of warfare in Ireland at the time.

In 1565, Blundeville wrote his book *The fowre Cheifest Ofyces Belonging to a Horseman* and it contains an interesting paragraph about the Irish Hobby[11]:

> " The Iryshe Hobby is a pretty fine horse, havening a good head, and a body indifferently well proportioned, saving that many of them be slender, thin buttocked, they be tender mouthed, nimble, light, pleasant and apt to be taught and for the most part they be amblers and therefore very meet for the saddle and to travel by the way, yea and the Iryshe men both with darts and light spears to use to skirmish with them in the field. And many of them prove to that use very well, by means they be so light and swift: notwithstanding I take them to be very neashe and tender to keep, and also to be somewhat skittish and fearfull, partly perhaps by nature and partly for lack of good breaking at firste. "

In 1562, Queen Elisabeth Ire started religious persecutions and then had to face several revolts in Munster. These revolts were violently repressed. The massive colonization of Ulster by settlers from Yorkshire and the Scottish Lowlands began in 1608. They shared the land, which was then sublet to Irish farmers who were reduced to the condition of miserable tenants. Anglo-Saxon Anglican or

---

[11]   The Irish Hobby: the Celtic/Hobby horse arrived in Ireland and was crossed with native Irish horses; a superior breed, the Irish Hobby, was developed and used for racing and light military work.

Presbyterian farmers gradually replaced a population of Celtic and Catholic shepherds and breeders. Revolts justified land confiscations, but the substitution of seigneurial law for Celtic law made most Irish property titles questionable.

Charles Ier had Catholic worship banned in 1629.

1641 was a pivotal year, the year of the General Revolt in Ireland, whose population was exasperated by the spoliation of land and anti-Catholic measures. Cromwell landed in 1649 with his "Iron Coast" and called his troops to massacre the Irish. The towns of Drogheda and Wexford were plundered, and their populations put to the sword.

Within a decade, more than 500,000 Irish died as a result of this colonial enterprise. The carnage spread across the country.

Under this ruthless regime, the rebellion quickly died out. But there were still far too many "Irish savages" for the taste of the Protector, who wanted to give Ireland to his army to create a colony of small Puritan landowners, guarantors of the English presence. No matter what. It was decided to push the Irish back into Connaught[12] and Clare and to isolate this native reserve from the rest of the colony by a military cordon. "Go to hell or go to Connaught" was the choice offered at swordpoint to the remnants of the Gaelic race.

1652. The Act for the Settlement of Ireland confiscated three-quarters of Irish land. The Irish deemed hostile were forced into exile or deported to the Caribbean where they were sold as slaves. The property passed into the hands of the Protestants, who set up a colonial-type system.

1784. Foundation in Ulster of a secret society, the Peep O'Day Boys, which will become in 1795 a strongly structured politico-religious movement, better known under the name of Orange Order.

1789. The beginnings of the French Revolution met with a favorable response from Catholics who formed clubs in Dublin and Belfast. The two French expeditions to Ireland, led by Generals Hoche and Humbert under the Directory, ended in two fiascos.

---

[12] After the capture of the town of Drogheda in September 1649 by Cromwell's troops, 3,000 of its inhabitants were massacred and the survivors deported to the west of Ireland. Cromwell is said to have uttered the words: 'To Connacht or to Hell'. The province includes the five counties of Galway, Leitrim, Mayo, Roscommon and Sligo.

GALWAY, THE CITY OF THE TRIBES

Galway was built in 1124 by the Connacht king Turlach O'Connor. During the Anglo-Norman invasion of Connacht in the 1230s, the fort of Galway, which was still a small fishing village, was captured by Richard de Burgo, led the invasion. Richard de Burgo was King of Connaught and even Lord Justice of Ireland. His descendant Walter de Burgo, Earl of Ulster, died in Galway Castle in 1271.

From 1200 onwards, it seems that Galway was ruled by an oligarchy of large families - the de Burgos, the Lynches, and the O'Flahertys. The O'Flahertys were the most powerful of the tribes. With them Granuaile[13], the female pirate considered the Irish Boadicea[14] , is legendary.

Grace was born in 1530 to the great O'Malley family. She married Donal O'Flaherty around 1546. The O'Flaherty family-built castles in Moycullen, Bunowen, Renvyle, and Ballinahinch. When Donal and Grace married, they settled in Bunowen. Grace was a thorn in the side of Queen Elizabeth I for many years and they finally met in 1593.

Grace was a dominant, picturesque, and ruthless character and her story is well told by Anne Chambers in 'The Life and Times of Grace O'Malley'. Her possessions were substantial. On the death of her husband, she gathered her followers and, with 1,000 heads of cows and mares, moved to Burrishore. Her son Owen, who continued to reside at Bunowen Castle, owned 4,000 cows, 500 mares, and a thousand sheep. In due course, they were all confiscated by Captain Richard Bingham (Governor of Galway for Queen Elizabeth) to pay for the campaign he was conducting.

To quote Anne Chambers[15]:

> " The lifestyle of a Gaelic chieftain's household was geared to outdoor activities, a fact reflected in the buildings of the time which were primarily shelters and defences rather than luxurious and stately homes. Owen O'Malley (Grace's father) lived in a stone fortress of Belclare with his family and household. Around the outskirts of his castle nestled the thatched mud and stone cabins of his followers, while in front lay the sea, on which his livelihood mainly depended. In the nearby fields grazed the clan's herds of cattle and sheep and the small but

---

[13] Granuaile: Gaelic translation by Grace O'Maley.

[14] Boadicea (spelled variously) was the legendary queen of the Iceni, a Celtic tribe that resided in Britain. Her reign corresponds to the Roman occupation of Britain, and although her leadership was brief, it is so memorable that historians are still talking about it 2,000 years later.

[15] Anne Chambers is an Irish biographer, novelist and screenwriter who lives and works in Dublin. She is best known for her biography of Grace O'Malley, the Irish pirate queen of the 16th century.

hardy Irish horses, used for ploughing and for the few excursions made inland. By custom in the summer months, they left their permanent castle or fortress to live in a temporary summer dwelling called a 'booley' for the purpose of grazing their cattle in the uplands. The 'booleying' custom had its origins back in Celtic times and survived in O'Malley country into the 20th century."

In 1549, an inscription was placed over the west gate of Galway City, which read:

"From the fury of the Flaherties Good Lord deliver us".

Galway had an important trade with the continent and Spain in particular. It was considered the capital of the West and its bay, one of the most beautiful in the world, was described as a magnificent natural funnel for ships from all over the world.

In 1652, after a nine-month siege led by Sir Charles Coote, the city surrendered. Not only was it sacked, but the remaining citizens were driven into the bogs. In the 17th century, the entire territory of Iar Connaught was confiscated and those O'Flaherty's who survived the war and famine were dispossessed of their land and scattered throughout the world.

The area was broken up and assigned to several families. These principal landowners were called English merchants and are now better known as the "Galway tribes" named: Athy, Blake, Bodkin, Browne, Deane, D'Arcy, Fant, French, Joyce, Kirwan, Lynch, Martin, Morris, Skerrett. Many of them were the entrepreneurs of their time and it was largely due to their wealth and entrepreneurial spirit that Connemara became more accessible in the 19th century.

It was not until the 19th century that Galway regained its former glory.

CONNEMARA

Today, the name Connemara refers to the larger area west of the city of Galway, with the Corrib and Mask lakes, the Twelve Bens, and the Maumturk mountains. Connemara is bordered on the west by the Atlantic Ocean. It is a wild and beautiful land of mountains, bogs, and lakes, with a rugged and deeply indented coastline whipped up by the Atlantic gales. There is little arable land, and the small fields are strewn with stones and rocks.

For countless generations, a breed of ponies has existed in this remote region, living off the sparse grazing of the bogs and mountains and enduring the harsh winter conditions with little shelter from the rain and gales from the Atlantic.

This harsh environment produced, by natural selection, robust ponies resistant to all weather and renowned for their strong constitution. Indeed, only the strongest could survive. From birth, they learned to make their way through bogs and rocks, over rocks and seaweed on the seashore, or on steep mountain paths, and they developed sure-footedness that made their reputation.

Figure 7. Village Laura and Village Colleen in Ballinafad, October 1987. Photo by Daniel Chupin.

MAP OF CONNEMARA

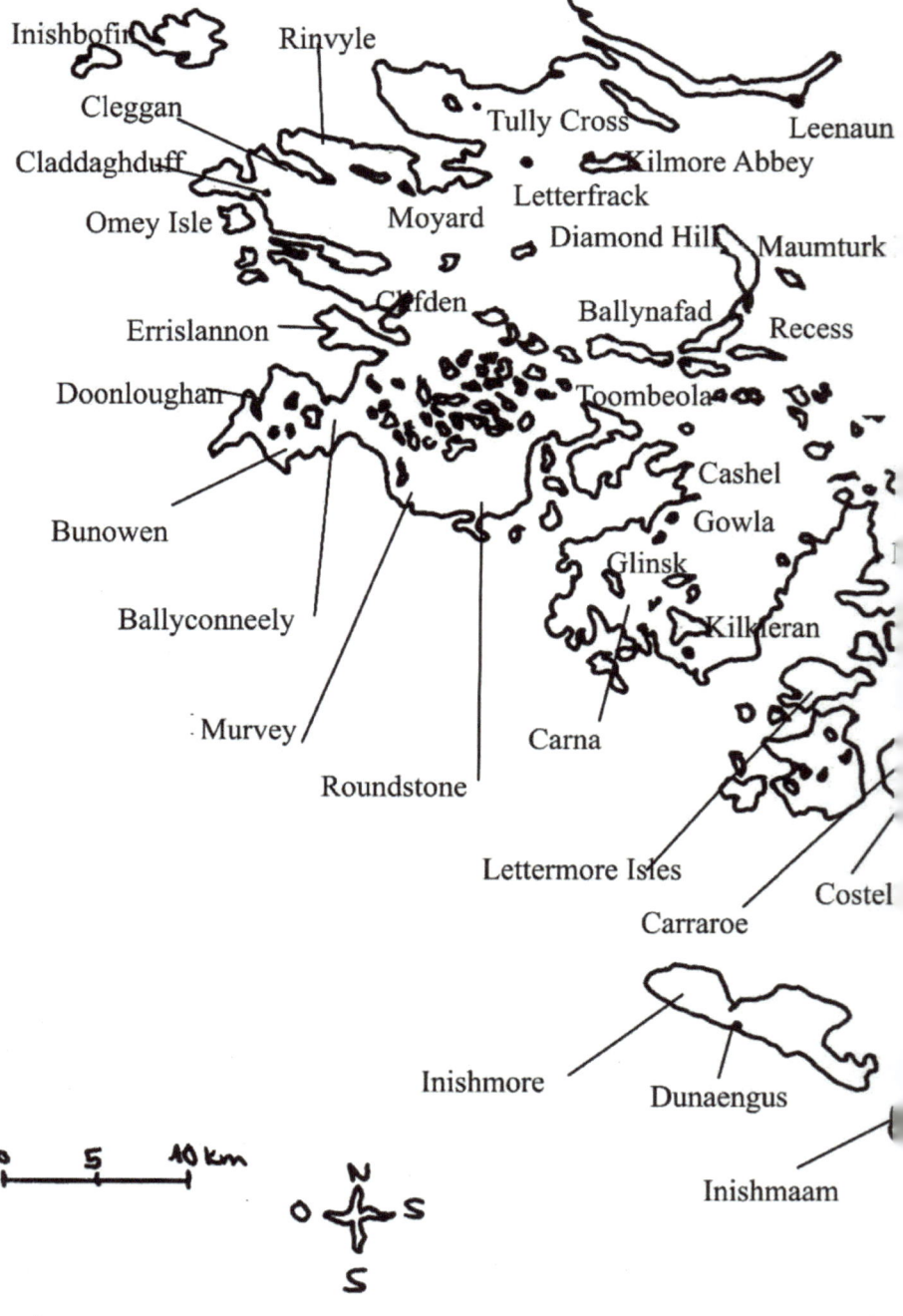

Figure 8. Map of Connemara. Daniel Chupin.

The Burren

GEOLOGY OF CONNEMARA

I won't bore you with scientific terms, but from the map below you can see that Connemara's bedrock shows a wide variety of rock types that were formed at different times in geological history.

- Metamorphic rocks such as gneiss and schist.
- Plutonic rocks such as granites and gabbros.
- Sedimentary rocks such as sandstone, limestone, clay.

Limestone also covers much of the country, especially in the Midlands and in areas such as the Burren in County Clare.

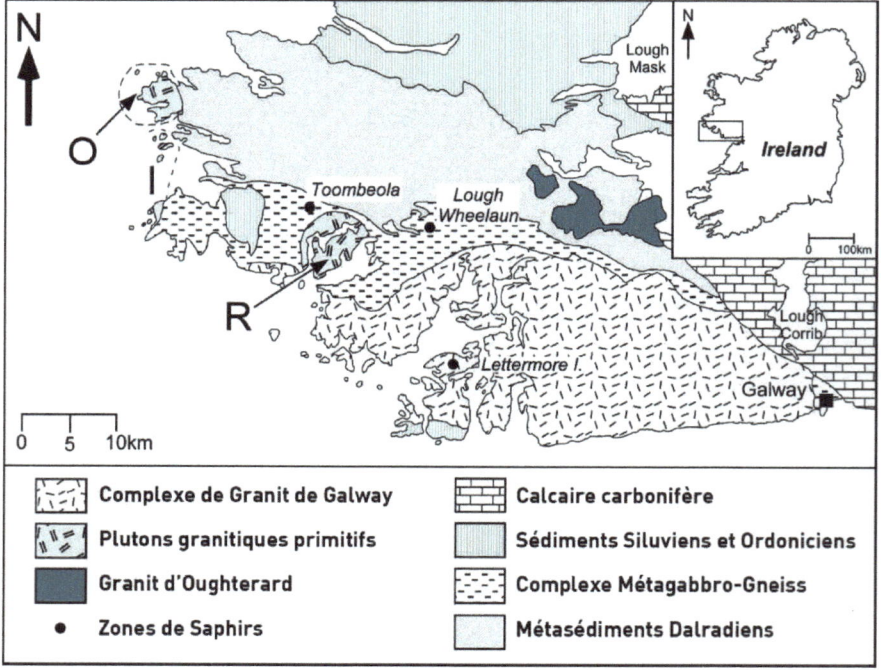

Figure 9. Geological map of Connemara extracted from: Sapphire Occurrences in Connemara, *M. Feely et al, Irish Journal of Earth Sciences 35:45, 2017.*

Figure 10. Inishmore, the largest of the Aran Islands, with Dun Aengus Fort in the distance. Two photos by Daniel Chupin.

Figure 11. Between Carna and Glinsk Photo Daniel Chupin.

Figure 12. Village Colleen in the vicinity of Lough Fadda. Photo by Daniel Chupin.

Figure 13. Between Oughterard and Rossaveel. Photo Daniel Chupin.

Figure 14. Four broodmares on the beach at Knock, Ballyconneely. The mares were hobbled.
Photo by Daniel Chupin.

Figure 15. Village Star with Castle Dama on the heights of Clifden.

Figure 16. In the Toombeola area. Photo by Daniel Chupin.

Figure 17. Between Carna and Kilkieran. Two photos by Daniel Chupin.

Figure 18. Finisklin, between Moycullen and Spiddle. Photo Daniel Chupin.

Figure 19. Errislannon. Photo Daniel Chupin.

40

Figure 20. From left to right: Shamboolard Hill, Ballynakill Harbor, Tully Mountain. View from Diamond Hill. Photo by Daniel Chupin

Figure 21. The Twelve Pins as seen from Diamond Hill. Photo by Daniel Chupin.

41

Figure 22. Diamond Hill, in the heart of the Connemara Natural Park. Photo by Daniel Chupin.

Figure 23. Clifden in 1982. Photo by Daniel Chupin.

Figure 24. On Callowfeenish beach near Carna. Two photos by Jeannine Marolleau.

Figure 25. View from Costelloe, bottom left Errisbeg 987 meters. Opposite Kilkieran. Photo Daniel Chupin.

Figure 26. Between Errislannon and Ballinaboy. Photo Daniel Chupin.

44

Figure 27. Murvey, Roundstone, in the distance The Twelve Pins. Photo by Daniel Chupin.

Figure 28. Rusheeny, near Oughterard. Photo by Daniel Chupin.

Figure 29. Carna is the historical heart of the Connemara pony, Photo Daniel Chupin.

Figure 30. The Twelve Pines, view taken from the Toombeola road toward Ballinaboy. Photo by Daniel Chupin.

Figure 31. Errisbeg, Roundstone, view taken from the Toombeola Road toward Ballinaboy. Photo by Daniel Chupin.

Figure 32. The port of Roundstone. Photo by Daniel Chupin.

Figure 33. View from the top of Errisbeg, Roundstone. Photo by Daniel Chupin.

Figure 34. Landscape near Cong, Joyce Country, Photo Daniel Chupin.

THE ORIGINS OF THE CONNEMARA PONY

The history of ponies in Connemara may date back to the arrival of the Celts, but there are no sources to support this.

The Celts would have arrived with their herds of horses through Northern Europe, passing through England, Scotland, Wales, and finally Ireland.

The old Connemara dun ponies are perhaps the most typical of their Celtic ancestors.

Figure 35. Dun pony. Photo Daniel Chupin.

THE SPANISH INFLUENCE

Even today, many writers tell the romantic story of the Andalusian stallions that swam ashore and ran with the native herds from the ships of the Invincible Armada, which was wrecked off the rocks of the Galway coast in 1588.

This story refers to the mythical fables about water horses from the other world in an earlier era, but in reality, many Spanish and Arabian horses had arrived on Irish soil before the disaster of the Invincible Armada[16]. Indeed, many historical sources show that the city of Galway prospered through international trade and gradually became the main trading port with Spain, Portugal, and France.

---

[16] The Spanish fleet consisted of 130 ships, mostly galleons, carrying 30,000 men, including about 20,000 soldiers. At first, faced with an agile and determined English navy, it was unable to engage in combat during the battle of Gravelines. Then, faced with very difficult weather conditions and the absence of any friendly port of call, it had no choice but to abandon the invasion project. It was during the return voyage, while rounding Great Britain by the north, that a violent storm led to the shipwreck on the Irish coast. The crews that reached the coast had varying fortunes, being helped, captured or massacred.

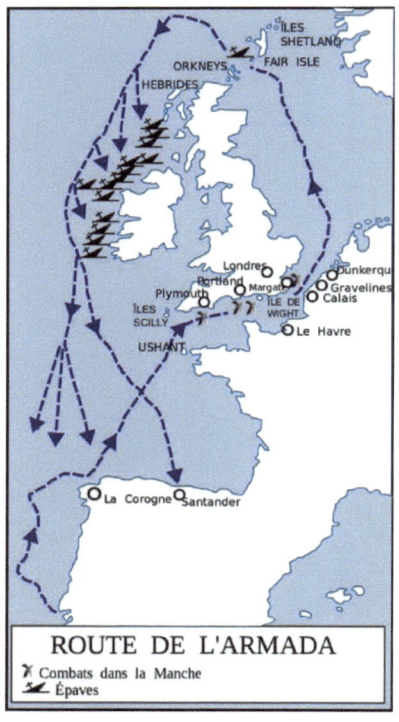

ROUTE DE L'ARMADA

✗ Combats dans la Manche
⚓ Épaves

Figure 36. The Spanish Armada shipwreck on the Irish coast. Source Rogilbert.

Professor Low, in his 1842 book on the breeds of domestic animals in the British Isles, has a stronger opinion on the strong Spanish influence in the Connemara region:

> *"The horses of Spain have notoriously helped to create all the breeds of the British Isles: but it is not generally known that a breed of horses of almost pure Spanish origin exists in this country in considerable numbers. They live in the Connemara region of County Galway. Tradition has it that from the wreckage of some of the ships of the Spanish Armada on the west coast of Ireland in 1588, several horses and mares survived the sinking, reproduced in the rugged and desolate country. But it is not necessary to refer to tradition to prove the origin of these horses since all their characteristics are essentially Spanish. They are between 122 and 142 cm tall, generally with the chestnut coat of the Andalusian horses, light in their underside, they have the characteristic head of the Spanish breed. They are abandoned. They live in the wild in what has become their habitat, a territory made up of rocks and peat bogs, where they can be seen galloping in herds in this rugged country of*

limestone rocks. When they have to be captured, usually at the age of three or four, they are driven to the peat bogs and taken by halter. They are robust, dynamic, with very sure feet and retain the amble so particular to the Spanish Gennet. Any selection can be made from the wild herds. After having been hunted in the peat bogs, these animals could be obtained at little cost. That these horses have been able to retain the characteristics of their breed for such a long time in a country so different from the one from which they originated is quite incredible. They have simply become smaller than the original breed, a little rounded in the rump, and are covered in their natural state with shaggy hair, a consequence of one of the most humid climates in Europe. Through simple negligence in the selection of breeding stock, many of these small horses are extremely ugly, but still conform to the original characteristics... "

THE PONAIDH

PONAIDH, the Gaelic translation of pony, simply means small. A ponaidh native to Connemara has probably existed for many centuries. It has needed certain characteristics to survive in an often very austere environment. Progress has improved people's lifestyles and the pony no longer does farm work. Connemara remains a land of moors, mountains, bogs, coasts exposed to the Atlantic wind, and small paddocks with only low stone walls. This is where the Connemara Ponaidh continues to live and breed.

Historical documents on the Connemara pony are almost inexistent and photographs are rare. Also, I relied on three books written by an English breeder Mrs. Pat Lyne (*Chiltern Stud*), an Irish breeder Mrs. Petch (*Coosheen Stud*), and the book *Sea horses Connemara and Its Ponies* written by Stephanie Brooks (Errislannan Stud) and Karen Mannion.

The ponies were used for travel and warfare, but more importantly, they were an essential staple food supply for the natives living in this coastal wilderness of western Ireland. They were part of the landscape and always seemed to have been exploited in one way or another.

For Pat Lyne, there is strong evidence that a smaller, more robust breed of pony than the one that came from Spain existed for many centuries before Galway appeared. For her, it would be unwise to suggest that one breed had more influence than another in the composition of the Connemara pony.

Sir Walter and Mr. Low suggest that the Connemara breed deteriorated when the Spanish influence disappeared. This probably occurred as a result of Galway's decline as a trading port.

Hely Dutton's 'Survey of County Galway'[17] was written in 1824 and his observations on horse breeding in Connemara are of great interest. He writes:

"The Connemara pony had to pull the farmer's small cart, take it to market, and perform all other necessary tasks. Malnourished and harried, they were surprisingly strong and hardy."

In the 18th century, in hilly and mountainous regions, the wheelless cart, known in Connemara as a loadeen or slide, was widely used. It was ideally suited to transporting loads over wet, marshy ground, where cartwheels would have become bogged down, and on steep slopes where a pony would have been thrown and perhaps crushed by its burden.

Figure 37. Sketch of a Loadeen. Daniel Chupin.

The loadeen was made of wood or basketry attached to two long stretchers, connected by a few crossbars on which it was supported. It was used to carry peat, seaweed, etc., and could move at a surprising speed.

The loadeen could be built for a few shillings. But once the public roads were built, they became unusable. They damage the roads and fines are imposed on those who continue to use them. With the disappearance of the loadeen, the ponies carried the various loads on their backs and the straddle was designed for this purpose. The straddle is very simple to build and consists of two flat boards, sometimes resting on mats placed on each side of the pony's back. The straddle, which can be translated as a packsaddle, is attached to the pony by a belly rope, usually made of twisted hay or straw. The ponies were overloaded, carrying peat, fish, cabbage, potatoes, or other marketable goods.

---

[17] *A Statistical and Agricultural Survey of the County of Galway* by Hely Dutton was published in 1824. It covers all aspects of the economy and society of County Galway in the early[e] 1800s. This work provides a revealing insight into the dire economic and social circumstances that contributed to the Great Hunger.

TOWARDS THE DECLINE OF THE CONNEMARA PONY

Connemara ponies were considered "inferior" by the leaders who conducted the Victorian policy. This irrational, unwise and harmful policy under English rule was one of the causes of the decline of the Connemara pony.

In 1800, Great Britain proclaimed the Union Act which united Ireland completely with the United Kingdom. The 19th century is marked by terrible famines, a massive emigration to America, the peaceful Catholic resistance expressed by O'Connell[18] , and the national feeling that animates the members of Young Ireland and the Fenians of the Irish Republican Brotherhood.

JOHN D'ARCY, AN ATTEMPT TO DEVELOP IN A DIFFICULT CONTEXT.

I will now introduce you to John D'Arcy, a man who contributed to the development of Clifden.

John D'Arcy was descended from an illustrious Galway family, the D'Arcys of Kiltullagh. This family, of Anglo-Norman and Gaelic origin, had been prominent in Galway since the 16th century. John was young and ambitious and quickly became involved in local politics. He was appointed High Sheriff of the county in 1811. This was a prestigious position that conferred power and influence in the county. John overstepped his powers however, when, in April, he released from Galway jail three Connemara men who were serving a sentence that included three public whips. John was partly responsible for their arrest, but perhaps he considered the punishment too severe for the crime committed. In any case, his action brought him into conflict with Dublin Castle and led to his removal as High Sheriff. After his disgrace, John D'Arcy seems to have devoted his energies to the development of his estate in Connemara and, in particular, to the creation of a town, which he named Clifden.

In 1812, John D'Arcy obtained permission to hold markets and fairs in Clifden. When he arrived in Clifden in 1812, the coastal people who lived in the surrounding hills were struggling to survive. John provided work for these people and gave them the opportunity for a better life. He built himself a crenellated house with a beautiful lawn that sloped down to the bay. With the

---

[18] In 1813, the Catholic lawyer Daniel O'Connell became the spokesman for the Irish people. During the first half of the 19th century, secret societies were formed in the countryside and attacked the farms and crops of Protestant landowners. In 1841, O'Connell was elected mayor of Dublin, and, in 1843, he gathered his supporters in Tara, a place of historic Ireland. England reacted by arresting O'Connell, even though he had always remained within the law. The time of non-violent action was over. The Young Ireland movement intended to give priority to the cultural struggle: "A nation must preserve its language more than its territories. It is a safer barrier and a more important frontier than fortresses and rivers. To lose your mother tongue and learn that of the stranger is the worst mark of conquest: it is the soul that is burdened with chains.

help of the famous engineer Nimmo[19] , he built a wharf where ships carrying loads of up to 200 tons could dock. He built a beautiful Protestant church, other houses, stores, and a spacious hotel. Twice a week he organized a market where potatoes, peat, fish, etc. could be sold. Fairs were organized in June, September, October and December for the sale of livestock. A huge scale was erected and tolls per animal were collected. Much of the swampy land, consisting of bogs, was reclaimed and produced particularly fine oats. In many ways, because of his ambitions, John D'Arcy was ahead of his time.

Hely Dutton had very complimentary comments about John D'Arcy's horse breeding activities and stated:

> *"Mr. D'Arcy had acted more judiciously. He procured a very beautiful small sire, who I am informed has left a very improved small breed in Connemara."*

Throughout the 1820s, Clifden developed rapidly under the leadership of John D'Arcy. By granting generous leases at low rents, he was able to attract merchants, tradesmen, and artisans to his estate. Recognizing that the newcomers came from many parts of the country, he was always concerned with fostering social unity. Over the years, John's even-handed approach to his duties as landlord and magistrate made him popular with his tenants. But this did not mean that his tenants were 'submissive', for because of their diversity, they had a more independent mindset.

In 1835, 800 tons of oats were exported to London and Liverpool from the Clifden wharf. By 1843, the number of dwellings had increased to 182.

John D'Arcy was known throughout the county as a hospitable man inclined to live beyond his means. Like many of his contemporaries, he borrowed heavily from his estate and, upon his death in 1839, left little to his wife and large family. His son and heir, Hyacinthe, was finally declared bankrupt and the entire D'Arcy estate was sold by the Court of Encumbrances in 1850. It was a sad day for his tenant farmers when he went bankrupt.

The same cannot be said of all the owners who succeeded Mr. D'Arcy, who inflicted much hardship and suffering. There were evictions and injustices when the tenant farmers could not keep up with the increase in their rents.

THE GREAT HUNGER

To understand the causes of the great famine of 1845 to 1852, we must go back to the revolt of Irish Catholics in 1649 against Oliver Cromwell, which led to

---

[19] The Scottish engineer Alexander Nimmo planned the modern roads of Connemara and founded the port of Roundstone in the 1820s.

brutal repression and the implementation of the Penal Laws intended to discriminate them.

Among other measures, the Inheritance Act of 1703 instituted that the lands of Catholics, instead of being passed on to the eldest son, were to be divided among all the sons of the same family, which led to a splitting of inheritances, a significant decrease in the size of farms and increasing vulnerability of their operators. To survive, the Irish began to grow mainly potatoes (the staple food for the majority of the population), a nutritious tuber that required little space to cultivate. Moreover, many farmers did not own their land and had to pay rent to a British Protestant landlord.

At the beginning of the 19th century, the relative prosperity of the countryside with a mild climate allowed a plot of land to feed a family adequately, and the population, which in 1801 was between four and five million, rose to nine million forty years later. The plots proved too small to feed a family on the overcrowded island of Ireland.

In 1845, blight from continental Europe, combined with the wet climate, caused a sharp drop in potato production of about 40 percent and led to a massive famine. In contrast to the famine of 1780, Irish ports remained open in 1845-46 under pressure from Protestant traders and, despite the famine, Ireland continued to export food. While whole families in parts of the island were starving, convoys of food belonging to the landlords, escorted by the army, left for England. Nevertheless, in 1845, the shortage was no greater than previous regional crises. It was the destruction of the potato crop in three of the next four years that led to famine and epidemics.

Several charitable initiatives were taken. As early as 1841, the pope urged the archbishops to raise funds throughout Europe and America. This movement of Catholic solidarity resulted in a large number of donations, the total amount of which is difficult to evaluate. The Archbishop of Dublin, Paul Cullen, estimated £14,000 to £15,000. In 1845, the Ottoman Sultan Abdülmecit I declared his intention to donate £10,000 to the Irish peasants, but Queen Victoria requested that the Sultan send only £1,000, as she had given only £2,000. So the sultan sent £1,000 and three ships full of food, which the British soldiers tried to block.

In Connemara the situation was catastrophic, Here are some paragraphs, directly concerning the Connemara region, that I selected from the book *The Great Hunger*, Ireland 1845-1849 written by Cecil Woodham Smith in 1962.

> *"On September 5, 1845, Sir James Dombrain, Inspector General of the Coast Guard Service, informed Routh that his officers had found it necessary to make free distributions of meals. For Coast Guard officers, making rounds of inspection in the Killeries[20],*

---

[20] Killary Harbour Fjord. Leenaun for memory is located at the edge of the Fjord.

Clifden and Ballinakill, remote districts in the far west, had found the population dying, due, according to the local dispensary doctor, to a total lack of food. Sir James Dombrain decided that the people should not starve and that, under the circumstances, Her Majesty's Government would justify the distribution of food to the people. Her Majesty's Government would justify the distribution of small amounts of food on the certificate of the dispensary doctor, which was done free of charge. For this action, Sir James received a public and severe reprimand in a Treasury minute. He had no authority, he was told, to provide free meals to every locality in distress, to form a relief committee, and to raise a fund by private contribution, which might be augmented later by a government donation. On September 18, Sir James replied briefly: "No committee could have been formed. There was no one for miles around who could contribute a shilling..." People were dying.

"At Clifden, W. E. Forster was soon surrounded by a crowd of men and women, looking more like starving dogs than other creatures, whose figures, looks, and cries all showed that they were suffering from the agony of hunger. When we enter a village," writes W.E., "our first question is: how many dead? Everywhere they shouted, 'The hunger is upon us,' and involuntarily we found ourselves looking at this hunger as an epidemic, looking at the famine as a disease. In England," he writes, "we thought the newspaper accounts of the state of Ireland were exaggerated, but no amount of coloring can deepen the darkness of the truth."

"The unnatural severity of winter drove people to huddle together for warmth; a fire or even a light in a shack attracted neighbors and passersby; the traditional hospitality of the Irish poor welcomed them, and all lay down to sleep warmly, side by side, on the floor of the shack. A crowd of beggars and homeless people roamed the roads, going from place to place with no fixed destination. Dirty, hungry, and infested with lice, they often had a fever. Whole families were seen lying feverishly by the roadside; the contemporary name for the epidemic was road fever. Yet the poor Irish, even if they were themselves in distress, never refused admission to the poorest beggar. The Central Board of Health writes, "The Irishman thinks himself cursed if he refuses to help a begging stranger." Once the infection had

been introduced into a district, it spread with lightning speed among the crowds gathered for relief. Huddled together, they waited for hours for their food, and still waited, sometimes all night, at soup kitchens. The fever-transmitting louse or its dusty droppings could be passed on to a new victim with a slight touch, and one person with a fever could spread the infection to a hundred others in a day. A crowd of paupers was something to run away from. In early 1847, people were in such a state that the smell of a crowd of starving paupers was intolerable."

Figure 38. A thatched cottage near Roundstone. Photo by Daniel Chupin.

A well-known and humane physician, Dr. Phelan, found himself unable to stand the smell of a crowd in Clifden, although in the practice of his profession he was accustomed to exhalations.

The courage of those who came to the aid of the population during the epidemic is beyond praise. Among physicians in 1847, deaths were formidably high. Losses were similar among the clergy, especially Catholic priests. In Connemara, where for 45 km the small villages and isolated huts along the coast were almost depopulated, two doctors out of three died; four died between Clifden and Galway, three between Oranmore and Athenry, and four between Anadown and Kilmaine.

The French government sent two physicians to study the epidemic. They were accompanied by a professor of medicine from Dublin; two died, including the professor.

The main epidemic of 1847 was typhus and relapsing fever, but other diseases also afflicted starving Ireland. On January 18, 1847, W. E. Forster wrote that "the most common form of the famine plague" in Westport was dysentery, which carried off people by ten or twenty a day. Two types of dysentery appeared in Ireland during the famine, and the two were confused. Dysentery produced diarrhea among people who had survived for months on a diet of old cabbage leaves, raw turnips, seaweed, and Indian flour, either semi-cooked or raw. But, though painful and exhausting, it was not generally fatal, except to children; its danger lay in the fact that it opened the way to infection by the terrible disease of bacillary dysentery, and bacillary dysentery became epidemic in Ireland.

"Ireland was facing a winter of total failure, bankruptcy, and starvation, with nine-tenths of the population of Clifden, for example, receiving relief in the open air..."

The minute book of the coastguards between March 13, 1848, and May 25, 1850.

While there is no official count of the number of deaths between 1846 and 1851, various recent estimates put the total number of victims at one million. The famine lasted until 1851, but had a longer-term impact, particularly on demographics.

This decline in the population of Ireland was not only due to famine, but also nearly two million emigrants, mainly to the United States, Britain, Canada and Australia.

The Irish population fell by almost a quarter in ten years, from eight to about six million. Emigration became a structural phenomenon and continued until 1911 when the Irish population fell to 4.4 million, its level in 1800.

Culturally, the famine was also a factor in the decline of the Gaelic language, spoken by more than 90% of the Irish people before 1845, whose vitality was the main sign of resistance of the Irish people and which the British were unable to eradicate. Many of the famine orphans received the English language as a legacy in the orphanages. The Gaelic language never recovered from the great famine of 1845-1851 and today only 2% of the Irish people speak the language of their ancestors in everyday life.

This catastrophie was the origin of a revival of Irish nationalism, resulting in the birth of the 'Young Ireland' movement. John Mitchel, one of the leaders of the movement, wrote in 1860:

"The Almighty did indeed send the blight, but the English created the famine."

Life in Connemara was a struggle for those who survived the famine years, and extreme poverty meant that many people were forced to sell their ponies, reducing their numbers. In some districts, poor-quality foals were abandoned in the hills and bred freely with the mares. Many large estates went bankrupt, leading to a general feeling of despair.

Alongside this misery, a wealthy financier and surgeon, Mitchell Henry, designed and built Kylemore in 1852 for his beautiful French wife. The castle and grounds covered an area of 3642 hectares. Mr. Henry famously had an Andalusian stallion in his stable. All the great landowners roamed the sandy and stony trails on horseback. Mr. Butler of Moyard was seen daily on his horse making the rounds of his tenant farmers. Mr. Eastwood of Kylemore "often rode by on horseback so fast that it would have been difficult to stop him."

Figure 39. Kylemore Abbey is located in an area called Kylemore Pass, on the shore of Pollacappull Lake. Photo Daniel Chupin.

The Martin family, who ruled over an immense territory of nearly 100,000 hectares, is certainly the most feudal and the best known. Richard Martin, in the 1830s, lived in the style of Ballinahinch Castle[21] (once a stronghold of the O'Flaherty's) and entertained sumptuously. He was often called the King of Connemara. His mail was brought to him three times a week by small letter carriers who ran for a day and a night and then slept for a day and a night. Maria Edgeworth wrote:

> " I remember seeing one of these post boys leaving Ballinahinch with his leather bag on his back, across the heath and across the bog, leaping every now and then, running and fast, his bare white legs thrown up among the brown heather."

Hely Dutton notes:

> " A few years ago I saw some stallions in the stables of Mr. Martin at Oughterard that were sufficient to destroy the breed of any country, especially Connemara."

The word Arabian is not used, but at the Horse Breeding Commission in 1897, Mr. Usher Roberts testified that Arabian blood was introduced by Colonel Martin in 1883.

It is difficult to make hay in a region as humid as Connemara (1986). As for the wheat harvest, it is another matter (1987).

The *Congested Districts Boards* (or C.D.B.) for Ireland was created by Arthur James Balfour (1848-1930), 1er Earl of Balfour (Prime Minister of the United Kingdom and leader of the Conservative Party), in 1891 to alleviate poverty and overcrowded conditions in the West and parts of the Northwest of Ireland.

---

[21] Ballinahinch Castle is located between Recess and Toombeola.

Figure 40. Above, Haying in Connemara. Below, Barna. Two photos by Daniel Chupin.

THE CONGESTED DISTRICTS BOARD, 1891-1903

The *Congested Districts Board* was part of the Conservative policy of killing Home Rule with kindness. It aimed to reduce poverty by subsidizing public works, such as the construction of jetties for small harbors on the west coast to help fishing, the modernization of agricultural methods, and the redistribution of land by allowing farmers to buy land (on average the loan allows them to buy 0.3 to 0.6 hectare) or sponsoring local crafts to create jobs and stop emigration from Ireland. In the Aran Islands, a knitwear industry was created, and, to this day, supplies Aran knitwear on a commercial basis using skilled local knitters and designers.

Following the Land Purchase (Ireland) Act of 1903, the C.D.B. was authorized to purchase additional land from large estates to expand the small holdings of tenants. In 1909, it obtained powers to authoritatively purchase land and began to redistribute more than 1,000 estates totaling 8,100 km2.

The C.D.B. was strongly criticized by the nationalist Frank Hugh O'Donnell in 1908. O'Donnell considered that the C.D.B., which was run by local Catholic priests, was not properly supervised by the British government, and was used to fund projects such as craft schools where young workers were underpaid.

Irish historian Joseph Lee, in his book *The Modernization of Irish Society*, pointed out that the C.D.B. invested heavily in unprofitable projects in the west of Ireland and in County Donegal in western Ulster. Projects that failed once they were no longer subsidized. As a result, the flow of people from the west and northwest of Ireland was not converted into internal migration to the more developed east, as might have been expected.

The opening report of the C.D.B. on horse breeding by the Commissioner, Frederick Wrench, J.P., describes the horse population at that time:

> *"Diminutive horses and ponies sadly deteriorated and apart from the rare occasions where the Arab or Thoroughbred had been introduced no attempt at improvement had been made."*

Some authorities on horse breeding such as the Lord Lieutenant, Mr. Chaplin, Lord Harrington, Mr. Burdett Coutts, Sir Walter Gilbey, and Sir George Wombwell were consulted in the country, as well as other specialists abroad. In the end, it was decided that to produce cob, the introduction of the little Yorkshire Hackney would be the most suitable solution. In addition, the introduction of the Arabian or the Barb would meet the needs of the customers by producing Polo ponies. The small Thoroughbred stallions were not recommended by the best authorities. It was said that a small Thoroughbred was small only by accident and that he was likely to produce, from small mares, animal over 152 cm. It was also said that the Thoroughbreds had no extraordinary quality of hardiness and soundness, compared to other breeds they had decided to use. "It was therefore agreed to breed from a sire who possessed by heredity the tendency to produce strains of his size and character."

Some £60,000 was spent on the horse breeding program. In support of such a large sum, it was pointed out that a mare was essential to every family living near the coast for extracting seaweed, peat, and other foodstuffs. A mare, not a horse, was used because the sale of a foal every two years was an important source of income. It was expected that an improvement in the pony breed would bring higher prices for foals and provide better animals capable of doing more work.

Commissioner Wrench was responsible for the selection and purchase of stallions used in the *Congested Districts* and had close ties to English breeders. The Beard, Welsh, and Hackney stallions probably came from England. The Thoroughbreds were of Irish origin. In 1892, four stallions were sent to Connemara, one Beard, and three Hackneys[22]. In 1893, five were sent, one Beard and four Welsh Cobs. No reason was given for the decision to introduce the Welsh Cobs in 1893. From then on, they were used in counties Galway and Mayo.

In 1894, seven ponies were sent for the first time to the islands of Aran and Inishbofin.

The 1895 report of the Commission is brief and simply states that Welsh Cobs and two Arabs had been used, as well as Hackneys and Barbs. These Arabs were never actually sent to the Connemara district. The Council also bought several foals produced by their stallions in different regions, to verify the results of these experiments and to follow the development of the Hackneys and Welsh Cobs. These foals were placed at the Chantilly stud[23] owned by the Board.

The list of assignments for 1897 shows the return of the Barbe, the withdrawal of the Welsh Cobs, as well as four Hackneys to their breeding station. The report expresses some dissatisfaction with the inability of breeders to retain their best stock and states:

> *"But horses form no exception to the rule which appears to be followed by so many farmers of selling off, at the earliest possible moment, the best animals and keeping the worst to breed from."*

---

[22] The Hackney is a recognized British carriage horse breed. It is the heir of the famous Norfolk trotter and the Yorkshire carriage horse, famous trotting horses in the early 19th century. His studbook was established in 1883 in Norwich. It takes its name from the London district of Hackney, which first gave its name to the small horse-drawn vehicle that was manufactured there and was mainly used as a hire car. The name Hackney was given to the horses used to pull these carriages. A horse of average size 152 to 160 cm, it often moved at the amble, usually ridden by ladies. At first heavy and massive, with a heavy trot, the Hackney gradually became agile, vigorous and fast thanks to the contribution of the Thoroughbred and the Arabian towards the end of the 17th century. At the end of the 19th century, the Americans imported it and created the Hackney pony, which makes the Hackney one of the rare breeds that can be both horse and pony.

[23] According to my research, this stud farm was located in the suburbs of Dublin.

In 1898, a Hunter horse[24] named Borrisoleigh appeared in the Galway district for only one year and stood for the Beard in Clifden.

In 1899, Borrisoleigh's place was taken by a Thoroughbred called Golden Crescent stayed in Clifden for three seasons and was followed by another Thoroughbred called Punster in 1902.

From 1898 to 1902, a mixture of Hackney and Welsh Cob was used. In 1901 and 1902, a Norwegian pony called Norseman was introduced. Another pony of a similar breed named Oscar appeared on the Isle of Clare at a later date, but again, there is no record of the purchase or use of these two stallions.

In 1901, the annual report clearly describes the state of livestock in Connemara:

> *"The scarcity of the old type of pony found in Connemara and in the Barony of Erris has become so marked that the Board has thought it wise to make some attempt to preserve it; with this object, thirteen mares have been purchased and are being crossed with a high-class stallion, it being nearly impossible to obtain a native sire that is sound and worth using. From this experiment, it is hoped that an improved Connemara pony will become available and will help to maintain the supply of ponies which in many instances have formed such excellent foundation stock."*

---

[24]   In the past, the hunter was only bred for hunting. The Irish wanted a strong, powerful hunting horse that could gallop and jump behind the pack without flinching or tiring. In addition, it had to be pleasant to ride. The hunter is not originally a breed, but a type of horse, generally resulting from a cross between a Thoroughbred stallion and a mare of the Irish draft breed, or Connemara. Depending on the size and origins, there are several types of Hunters. Depending on the terrain and the rider, heavier or lighter horses were sought. The result of these efforts was the existence of four different types of hunters: light, medium, heavy and small.

The small hunter usually has Connemara ponies among its ancestors and is intended mainly for young riders, but it must also have all the qualities of a hunting horse.

The heavy hunter comes from an Irish Draught mare and a Thoroughbred stallion. It is distinguished by its strength and its large size and offers a great security to the riders on the heaviest grounds. In terms of character and temperament, the heavy hunter strikes by its calm and balance.

The medium and light hunters are more modern horses. Most of them come from the crossing of a hunter mare, therefore already the product of a crossing, and a thoroughbred stallion. In this sense, they are really refined very close to the blood.

In breeding competitions, male hunters are ridden by expert judges. On the one hand, the behavior of the horses on a hunting ground is of utmost importance and on the other hand, the examination is more complete and more objective. There are five criteria: *conformation, action, presence, manners,* and *ride.* By "conformation" we mean the stature of the horse, its exterior; we want horses that are harmoniously and powerfully balanced, with a solid base, but that are also capable of moving with elegance. The term "action" means the horse's gaits, and one will check above all that he has a good walk and a good canter; one appreciates a good trot, of course, but its importance remains secondary. The "presence" of a horse is the way he presents himself: if he looks noble and attentive or on the contrary indifferent and indolent. Manners" means his behavior. A hunter must show his good character, he must behave correctly towards other horses, otherwise, on the hunting ground, he would be anything but a good mount. Finally, the "ride" refers to the horse's ability as a mount, its ability to easily shorten or lengthen the canter; a hunter must show speed and stamina in the canter while being pleasant to ride and lead. Hunting requires independent horses that can be expected to take a lot of initiative, and they are most comfortable when allowed to move forward.

The result is that the first ten years of the board's life did little more than reduce the level of the most valuable native herd. By the end of the board's life, local ranchers had the desire to return to production close to their native herds. Perhaps for the first time, they became aware of the value of their pony and a certain patriotism was triggered in their favor?

Here are some stallions used by the C.D.B:

THE AWFULLY JOLLY BARB: chestnut, born in 1875, Height 142 cm. Pedigree unknown. Winner of many races. Imported from Tunis by the Earl of Harrington. A first-class Polo pony[25]. Registered by the Congested Districts Board. Sean Keane did a paper on the Connemara pony at the international conference held in Galway in 1970. He read some excerpts from the Irish Horse Breeding Commission and one-line mentions:

" *The Barb Awfully Jolly did very well at Cashel, Co. Galway.* "

He was last on the Council's list in 1898, when he would have been twenty-three years old. He seems to have given them very good service. He was stationed at Cashel in 1892 and 1893, at Carraroe in 1894, at Achill Sound, County Mayo in 1895 and 1896; then at Clifden in 1897 and 1898.

Figure 41. Awfully Jolly, Engraving from Volume I of the Polo Pony Studbook.

---

[25] Depending on the time and place, the size of polo ponies has varied from about 132 cm in the 16th century to modern horses of 152 cm and more. Today, most polo ponies stand around 155 cm. Although they are called 'ponies', this is a reference to their agility rather than their size.

More than one witness at the Horse Breeding Commission spoke well of him as a sire. The remark already quoted was made by Major Ruttledge-Fair. Questioned, Mr. Samuel Usher Roberts stated:

> "That was a very good Barb."

The comment from the reputable breeder in Connemara at the time, Mr. AJ Robinson of Roundstone stated:

> "The Barb that the Board had down in Connemara was, I think, a very good horse indeed, but not big enough for the District."

It was also said that the price of his foals increased with the demands coming from England, as he was famous as a sire of polo ponies.

THE HACKNEY LORD GO BANG 2D: born in 1882, brown bay, 155 cm tall. His sire Lord Derby 2d comes from an old and distinguished Hackney line.

The testimony given to the Horse Breeding Commission was overwhelmingly against the use of Hackney blood.

Mr. Harry M. Donnell stated:

> "The Hackney is condemned by the outer people altogether, they won't touch him, and say when they come to Connemara, they want to get a pony, they don't want to buy a horse."

Mr. Samuel Johnson, when asked, stated that he thought the use of Hackney stallions would weaken the blood. When asked why he replied:

> "I believe from their action and the way I have seen them get so heated in work, that they would hot have anything like the enduring power of our horses."

On January 5, 1897, Mr. Thomas Craddock, a member of the Ballinasloe Agricultural Society, states:

> "This Society has passed a resolution against the introduction of Hackney blood into the Congested Districts."

In December 1896, Mr. R. Malone V.S. was asked if he had seen any of the products of the Hackney stallions and he replied:

> "I could tell them the very minute I saw them, little pudgy foals with upright pasterns."

He goes on to talk about a Connemara mare that could pull a team for 100 miles. He sold her for 60 gns and her new owner sold her two weeks later for 80 gns. She had an accident and was sent to a Hackney stallion. Mr. Malone then bought his yearling. He kept her for three and a half years and said:

"I drove him out to a place three miles away and on the road, I thought he was sick. I left him at a farmer's house. I gave him another chance. He used to tire on the road and knock up, you might beat him with the butt end of the whip. I sold him at Enniscorthy two fairs ago for £10."

So Mr. Malone is quite clear about the production of the Hackney.

Mr. Robinson of Roundstone remarked that he had seen some of Hackney's descendants, but did not like them:

"They might make a trapper but not a Polo Pony."

The facts speak against Hackney as a sire in Connemara. It is difficult to draw any other conclusions, given the opinions expressed. The fact that they were removed from the area in 1903 suggests that they were producing bad stock or were rejected as stallions by local breeders. And if so, the question is, what damage did they do? Bartley O'Sullivan suggests in his article that few of them survived the harsh climatic conditions:

"We have yet to meet a specimen of any of the four breeds[26] of which mention is made in this paragraph, capable of living through a winter in the valley of the Twelve Pins."

THE WELSH COB PRINCE LLEWELLYN: The arrival of the Welsh Cob on the Commission's list of breeding stations was sudden and unexplained. Six were used in the Galway district between 1893-1903. Prince Llewellyn is the most important of the stallions used by the Congested Districts Board. He was the only one to provide a vital link to the C.P.S. Studbook when it opened in 1924. Prince Llewellyn was a Welsh Cob born in 1904. He was small and chestnut.

In the 1939 article, Bartley O'Sullivan states:

"The most famous Connemara stallion of recent times — Cannon Ball No. 1 in the Connemara Pony stud book — was descended from a Welsh sire. Early in the 1890s the C.D.B., having decided to locate Welsh stallions in the Connemara District, approached the late Mr William Lyons of Bunakill near

---

[26] Thoroughbred; Half bred; Hackney ; Clydesdale.

Maam Cross and offered him a stallion. Mr Lyons chose the
Welsh Cob Prince Llewellyn . . . Cannon Ball was by Dynamite
out of a Connemara mare. Dynamite also out of a native mare
by Prince Llewellyn."

O'Sullivan notes that some of the Welsh strains have performed very well.

Powder, another Prince Llewellyn contribution out of a native mare, also proved to be a good sire and some of the best-aged mares in the Maam area, circa 1939, are said to be out of this pony and Cannon Ball.

Dynamite received a mention at the first C.P.S. meeting in 1923. Its owner, Mr. John Lyons, stated:

"He was a remarkable pony who had taken first place in every
show at which he was exhibited for style and action. He was sold
for 80 gns. on his own doorstep when horses were as cheap as
now."

Dynamite was certainly a fine example of the product of a Welsh stallion used on a good native mare. This cross was by no means guaranteed to produce such favorable results. It is fortunate for the future of the Connemara breed that, in this case at least, the best of both worlds fed the studbook a generation later with the illustrious sire Cannon Ball.

In 1901, the Congested Districts Board admitted in an annual report that the old Connemara pony type had become very rare. During the twelve years of the Board's existence, a varied introduction of blood from outside the native stock was made into the Connemara region. Bartley O'Sullivan considers that this has been done indiscriminately.

The termination of the Board's livestock business is presented in a very simple statement by Mr. Micks:

"Under the Wyndham Land Act of 1903 an arrangement was
arrived at between the Irish Government and D. O. A. by which
the operations relating to Agriculture and Livestock should be
transferred to the department."

The C.D.B. was dissolved in 1923 by the new Irish Free State government and its staff was absorbed into the Irish Land Commission when its functions were assumed by the Department of Fisheries and Rural Industries. Unfortunately, it must be said that the next ten or more years under the D.O.A. were a period of blindness.

68

The end of the 19th century witnessed a major land reform, led by Michael Davitt's Land League, demanding what is known as the 3 Fs: fair rent, free sale, and fixity of tenure.

The British Parliament passed acts in 1870, 1881, 1903 and 1909 that allowed most tenant farmers to purchase their land and reduced the rents of others. Beginning in 1870 and following the agrarian war unrest and the Plan of Campaign of the 1880s, the *Wyndham Land Purchase Act* of 1903 was enacted. This act set the conditions for the division of large properties. It ended the era of absentee landlords.

The Ewart report has caused a lot of excitement among some breeders outside Ireland. Mrs. Petch says:

> *"The Ewart Report was a lengthy document of thirty-four pages with twenty-one photographs, but much of the report is irrelevant today, and its "five types" tend to be confusing for contemporary breeders of Connemara ponies."*

Bartley O'Sullivan was convinced that Professor Ewart may have seriously underestimated the number of Connemara ponies running around the mountains. He suggested that the report was based on only a small portion of the native breeding herd and that there were hundreds of ponies in the remote valleys of Connemara that had never been seen by Ewart during his visit.

The report went unheeded for many years, but when the Connemara Pony Breeders' Society was formed in 1923, one of Ewart's suggestions for improving the breed was implemented by the new committee when it decided to select the best mares and stallions in the breed to form the basis of the Stud Book.

THE EWART REPORT

Professor J.C. Ewart, M.D., of the University of Edinburgh, was commissioned by the Department of Agriculture and Agricultural Technical Training for Ireland to visit the West of Ireland, and with some local experts, to study the Connemara pony. He submitted a report dated September 20, 1900, which was published by the Department of Agriculture. There is strong evidence to support my belief that his visit to Connemara was made four years before the report was published.

Printed by the Department in Journal form, it was the first in-depth report ever made on the breed, consisting of thirty-four written pages and twenty-one illustrations.

The report was divided into two parts, the first entitled "The Different Types of Ponies" and the second "The Environment of Ponies." The latter was subdivided into sections that discussed the recent ancestry of the ponies, their size, work, character, and abilities. Soil texture and structure, climate, and food available to the ponies are also described.

Pat Lyne analyzed the professor's report, contrasting it with Bartley O'Sullivan's article on the Connemara pony written forty years later.

While in Connemara, professor Ewart was struck by the strength, stamina, and lose gaits of the ponies, by their intelligence, docility, and ability to work under conditions that would quickly prove disastrous for horses bred under less natural conditions. The professor points out the total lack of uniformity in size, production, coats, and in conformation.

From the ponies seen between Maam Cross and Leenane and towards Cashel, Carna, Clifden, and other areas, he came to the conclusion that the Connemara pony, instead of forming a breed, would be defined by five Types with quite distinct characteristics named:

- Andalusian
- Oriental (Eastern)
- Cashel
- Clydesdale
- Clifden.

THE ANDALUSIAN TYPE

This group includes the ancient Connemara breed. Resembling the Andalusian ponies. From 125 to 132 cm, they can be black, grey, or chestnut, but the most characteristic subjects are dun (yellowish). They appear to be slightly roach-backed, so perhaps Connemara's inherited this trait from their Spanish ancestors, they have a relatively shorter neck and limbs, a deeper chest, shorter ears, and are equipped with stronger jaws.

THE ORIENTAL TYPE

The Oriental Type is related to the Arabian, the Barb being an African variety of the Arabian breed. Arabian horses were probably introduced into Connemara towards the end of the 18th century and further introductions were made in the 20th century. In the distant past, most of the ancestral Connemara may have been chestnut, but today, grays are much more common. That the gray coat persists once introduced is widely recognized, especially when it comes to the spotted gray of Arabian horses.

The Cashel Type

These ponies were descendants of an old grey stallion living in Cashel. He can be considered a good type of Connemara pony. He does not look like an Arabian horse, nor a Barb, nor the Clifden Type which has short legs. Robust, strong, and practical for driving, he is also pleasant and safe when ridden. The Cashel Type was more like an Irish hunter than an Arab.

THE CLYDESDALE TYPE

This type of Cob combines the characteristics of a pack pony for transporting game and horses of the "Douglas breed" [27], now almost extinct. One has been seen in Joyce country and another in Clifden. They are said to be descended from Clydesdale stallions. Three such animals were seen, and all were nearly black and about 142 cm long with a girth of 177.8 cm. Those from Joyce and Clifden country would probably have influenced the Connemara.

THE CLIFDEN TYPE

The Clifden-type ponies, have beautiful head and evokes intelligence. They undoubtedly belong to old stock and can be considered as representing the good Connemara type. Their origin will probably remain a mystery, but Professor Ewart suggests their foreign ancestors differed from the imported Andalusian ancestors, and that there was a large and rather homogeneous herd of wild horses in the west of Ireland from which the native ancestors of the Clifden Type.

Pat Lyne suggests that:

> *"Although the professor was a recognized authority of his time, it seems strange that someone from Edinburgh would be asked to conduct the investigation. Was it possible that the policies of the C.D.B.[28] were already being questioned and the opinion of an independent outsider deemed desirable? Or was it simply that Connemara might be a potential source of hitherto untapped supplies for British infantry remounts? Under the heading of his report, it was written "the results of his investigations and the practical implications thereof will be fully reported by the Departmental Horse Breeding Commission." The Commission opened in October 1896 and closed in March 1897. Some 13,760 questions were asked during these six months. I was not able to study all of them, but I did try to read what was related to Connemara. I found that Mr. Wrench, Mr. Micks, and various Connemara breeders were interviewed. I did not come across any reference to the Ewart report. From those who testified about the situation in Connemara, we heard conflicting reports. The Hackney found favor with one witness but was condemned by*

---

[27] Stagecoach or streetcar horse, light draft, referring to the type of horse-drawn vehicle.

[28] Congested Districts Board 1891-1903.

most. *Some spoke well of Welsh Cobs, while others recommended the use of Thoroughbred or half-blood stallions. One witness described the Connemara breed as "destroyed and reduced to a state of absolute scrub", others named various stallions that had been used with some success in the past. Mr. Harry Donnell mentioned Tearaway, a half-blood horse imported from County Meath. Colonel Blake's stallion Ballinafad was mentioned more than once as a good sire. I believe he was a Thoroughbred.*

The fact that the C.D.B. and the Royal Dublin Society had stallions operating in the same area at different stud fees was considered disappointing.

No doubt for the D.O.A.[29] it was very wise to choose someone from outside Ireland, an authority on horses, who would provide an impartial report. This, I am sure, is what Professor Ewart did. His mandate was to ascertain whether Connemara could provide a herd of horses that could remount the mounted infantry which was unfortunately depleted at the time."

Bartley O'Sullivan had reservations about this report. One paragraph reads:

"Professor Ewart seems to have underestimated to a very large extent the number of native Connemara ponies that roam the mountains. The same mistake could be made by any visitor, and indeed by people living in this area who are mistaken on this point... I am convinced that on the occasion of Professor Ewart's visit there were, roaming the remote mountains and valleys of Connemara, hundreds of ponies of which he was not aware."

Bartley is more emphatic in his article that this was not the case:

"There is nothing that can be described as the Clydesdale pattern except for a few crossbred horses, encountered near Galway City. There is no Clydesdale blood west of the Corrib and certainly no ponies with even remotely Clydesdale-like characteristics ... with the exception of an area near Galway City, which is really not part of the pony breeding area, the writer can find no evidence of the introduction of Clydesdales. In fact, careful investigation has confirmed that no one in Connemara has ever heard of it. If Clydesdales had been used, it is certain that the offspring would not have survived the local conditions. Occasionally mares with

---

[29]   Department of Agriculture.

Clydesdale blood were brought in, but they were primarily for heavy driving work and were almost never used for breeding."

Pat Lyne thinks it's more reasonable to trust Bartley's word rather than the professor's conclusions. And she thinks that the Clifden type is surely the closest to what breeders today call the traditional Connemara pony type.

Bartley faults the professor for suggesting that the ponies were light in their limbs and again I quote:

> *"Given that the average Connemara today has limbs with real bone, in abundance and whose quality, in all likelihood, cannot be beaten by any breed of pony or horse in the world, one wonders what could account for the lack of bone forty years ago implied in the "bone deficient" statement."*

Sir Alfred Pease, who wrote in *Horse & Hound* after a recent visit to Connemara:

> *"I have seen some of the cleanest, flattest, hardest limbs, measuring 7 to 8 inches (17.78 to 20.32 cm) below the knee, that it is possible to find."*

CONCLUSIONS ON THE EWART REPORT

The Ewart Report is an interesting historical document. However, it is not taken seriously by Irish breeders. It is therefore unfortunate that it is regularly used to support fanciful theories about the existence of Connemara types. The types that were presented may never have existed or, as Louis Marie Philibert thinks, have completely evolved.

The existence of specific types would have implied compartmentalization of these types in the areas concerned. Before the advent of fences in Connemara, pony herds moved, and they sometimes moved very fast over long distances. The types proposed do not seem very realistic to me. When one analyzes the geographical situation of Connemara it seems obvious. But for that, one must take a step back.

In 1984, I observed that a free-ranging herd of mares took a maximum of two days to move between Carna and Glinsk. If you talk to the sheep farmers, they will explain to you that if you release a flock of sheep on the outskirts of Clifden, the farmer regularly has to recover some of them eight days later in the Maam Cross area!

Louis Marie Philibert remembers seeing ponies between Oughterard and Costelloe move 15 km in 2 days!

During this period, which I describe as a decline, the various foreign stallions that were introduced into the region to improve the livestock such as the English

Thoroughbred, the Hackney, the Welsh Cob, the Barb, and the Arabian were regularly stationed in different areas of Connemara to service the local mares.

This breeding policy did not work. It was not accepted by the Irish breeders, and it had negative effects on the development of the native pony. It is surprising to expect an improvement when you know Hackney's high trotting gait. The Hackney's trot is particularly unsuited to the rocky, wet terrain of Connemara.

Figure 42. The author is in a discussion with a sheep farmer. Don't hesitate to reach out to the Irish. Photo by Jeannine Marolleau.

The great famine, the political choices in the selection of the stallions, and the total absence of coherence to lead this breeding policy, unfortunately, pushed, at the beginning of the 20th century, the traditional breed of the Connemara pony towards extinction.

1895-1938, A PERIOD OF PROGRESS

During this period, several extraordinary events took place in Connemara. Some of them may seem insignificant but put in the context of the period they constitute improvements and real progress for a stricken region.

1895. The railway line connecting Galway to Clifden was opened.

1899. Arthur Griffith became the advocate of Sinn-Fein (which can be translated as: "*We Alone"*). He demanded the withdrawal of Irish representation in the Commons and advocated a general boycott of English institutions. The Land League's most effective method was the boycott, named after a militant campaign in 1880 when an unpopular landlord, Charles Boycott, was ostracized by the local community in south County Mayo. The boycott was also applied to tenants who wanted to pay their rent, to the police, and to stores and other businesses that traded with boycotted individuals. Boycotts were often extremely effective, since they were legal under the common law, non-violent, and truly punitive. There could be no legal recourse against them since the right not to participate in trade, socialization, or friendship is implicit in the right to engage in them. This proved to be an extraordinarily effective remedy against abuse, using non-violent and lawful means.

1903. A new agrarian law liquidated the system favorable to the landlords. That same year, King Edward VII visited Connemara.

The independence movement strengthened and in 1905 Sinn-Fein, the independence party was created.

1907. The first radio signal was transmitted from Clifden to Canada.

1912. Michael O'Malley took two ponies from Rosmuc to Olympia, England.

In 1916, the Easter Rising broke out, it was crushed by British forces, but the popularity of Sinn-Fein was growing.

In 1918, Sinn-Fein won the elections and formed an Irish parliament. It proclaimed independence, but the parliament was dissolved by the British. A new uprising broke out.

1919. Alcock and Brown made the first non-stop transatlantic flight and landed near Clifden.

In 1921, the Treaty of London made Ireland, cut off from part of its territory, a dominion of the British Empire. This treaty was ratified, but it was very unpopular, the Irish civil war broke out between supporters of the fight for independence and supporters of the compromise of 1921.

1923. The Connemara Pony Association was created.

In 1937, the President of the Council had a new constitution adopted that proclaimed Ireland's independence. A treaty was concluded with the United Kingdom in 1938.

Figure 43. Dolan. Photo Daniel Chupin.

RACES IN CONNEMARA

Why race in Connemara? It's hard to imagine a more unlikely place to race than Connemara, given the nature of the landscape. However, from 1900 to 1950, racing in Connemara was an integral part of people's lives. They were joyful and festive events. The season was short, and the meetings were held only in July and August. They were topics of discussion long before and after the event. The races were a day out for everyone and an opportunity to meet up with friends for betting and to participate in sporting activities. The races contributed to the preservation and development of the Connemara pony until 1950.

These family race meetings were unlike any other in the world. They were organized with a minimum of formality. No or few rules, no silks, colors, no grandstand, and no presentation ring. For the start, a line drawn in the sand with a stick or, on the grass with a line of lime. The handicap[30] and an armband were sufficient. The saddle and bridle were a luxury. Many horses were ridden bareback with a simple rusty bit, held in place by rope reins. Races were run in laps, not miles or furlongs[31]: two, three, or four laps of a course marked by flags. Flags planted in the sand at irregular intervals marked the course. The crowd dispersed as it pleased.

Sean O'Faolain, who visited the Oughterard races, puts us in the mood:

> "If you can, don't miss the races at Oughterard. They are typical of western skullduggery, and if you win money, you are a financial genius. But I doubt anyone goes to the Oughterard races to do anything other than participate in wild betting and see the colorful characters who attend, because it's a great day of gathering for tinkers and shell players[32] and all the scoundrels that roam the plains of Galway and Mayo, from Derg to Erris."

Many of the ponies we breed today are direct descendants of those that ran on the beach at Omey[33] or on the winding course at Clifden or perhaps on the beaches at Roundstone.

Cannon Ball was rightfully the king of Oughterard races for many years and he couldn't be beaten in the Farmers Race. A report on the Oughterard races of

---

[30] The handicap, in horse racing, is a penalty system that aims to give all starting horses a chance. It can be done by weight, recoil, rope, etc.

[31] Anglo-Saxon unit of length equal to 220 yards, or 201 meters, used mainly in horse racing.

[32] A game in which one person hides a small object under one of three nutshells, thimbles or cups, then shuffles them on a flat surface while the audience tries to guess the final location of the object.

[33] Omey is a tidal island, located near Claddaghduff.

August 27, 1921, from the Connaught Tribune, reads as follows: in the Ladies Plate, run over a distance of 2.4 km, it is stated:

"From the start, Cannon Ball took the lead and was followed by Little Lizzie. Cannon Ball won by a length and a half."

In the 1930s and '40s, many of the ponies with familiar names such as Rebel, Inchagoill Laddie, and Adventure competed in these races. The Thoroughbred stallions used in Connemara had an obvious influence. The association's stallions, Winter and Little Heaven, were used successfully on local ponies. Many breeders turned to breed race ponies rather than the Connemara pony. A good racing pony could more than make a living.

One of the best courses was provided by the Omey Strand. Omey Island lies off the coast and is approached at low tide across a wide sandbar from the village of Claddagh-duff on the mainland. A line of painted markers indicates the correct route for motor vehicles to cross when the tide is out and the sand is firm. This is where the Omey races are held.

The Roundstone races did not boast a firm, clean shoreline like Omey's, and the dunes posed a considerable danger. The course was hilly and the deep sand made the racing very difficult. It was here that the Thoroughbred horse Buckna won his only race in 1935. Owned by Marty Mannion, he was not a great racehorse, but he was the sire of Carna Dolly. A few seriously trained their animals for racing, but unorthodox methods abounded. Trial gallops were held in the Tullochs' fields on Sunday afternoons below Shanbolard Lake. But no one allowed their animal to show its true form on these occasions. Garnet rode to Omey and back to train his horse. 35 km on the road was a good way to get her animal in shape.

For many Connemara men involved in racing, the maxim was "a fit horse is a lean horse that carries as little flesh as possible." To achieve this, their feeding program was: lots of oats, but only as much hay as a chicken can eat.

Most of the riders were local boys with little talent and only one thing on their minds: going hard. Those who could ride a race were in high demand as jockeys. Tommy Grogan was a professional, while Garnet Irwin was the only girl to compete alongside the boys. These two often fought for a close finish. "Happy" Mulkerrin of Thievalough was a regular jockey who had weight problems that were partly solved by riding without a saddle. One of Happy's favorite mounts was Sucking Bottle, a fast little bay mare by Adventure, who had been bottle-fed after losing her mother at birth.

When the English Thoroughbreds left Connemara in the 1950s, the racing fever seemed to die down. The value of registered ponies began to improve and the Stud Book had achieved its goals.

Louis Marie Philibert is convinced that racing has saved the Connemara breed. They made the Connemara pony evolve. It is the crossing with Thoroughbreds that made the strong, rustic working pony evolve into an elegant animal with sporting qualities. It is from this time that the Connemara were sold internationally. The Irish made an intelligent cross between mass and blood, without the products losing their primary qualities. And to continue:

> *"The English have gone too far in their quest for breed purity. The Fell[34] , the Dales[35] , and the Highlands[36] have kept the original type, but these animals do not meet any market anymore. They are no longer of interest to anyone. That's the danger of keeping a breed in isolation."*

PONY RACING IN FRANCE

In France, pony races are organized under the auspices of the National Association Les Poneys au Galop and the FFE.

I asked Sigrid Gilet Moisson (qualified race trainer, specialist, and commercial of horse feed at Horsebreed) to present us pony races in France:

> *"There are three disciplines: flat, hurdles (the obstacles are identical), and cross-country. Ponies cannot participate in races before the age of 4. Children must have a minimum of a Galop 2 and must participate in a course organized by the association Poney au Galop to be able to participate in a race of index 1. In the first year, they will only be able to ride the pony they have presented in the course. After two victories in Indice 1, they will be able to race in Indice Elite. The 16 best couples, by pony size (A, B, C, and D), are selected to participate in the French Elite Championships organized for each discipline. The world of racing is an environment of excellence, the health protocols are identical to the protocols of the Thoroughbreds, and ditto for the care and shoeing.*

---

34 The Fell is a breed of pony measuring 1.38 m at the withers. It takes its name from its original region, the fells of Northern England. It is used as a pack pony and lives in semi-freedom.

35 The Dales is native to the northeast of England, bordering Scotland. This pony almost became extinct in the 1950's and was considered an endangered species.

36 The Highland is a breed of pony originating from Scotland. Raised in a semi-wild manner, it is very hardy. It has long been used as a working pony and as a pack animal by Scottish farmers and hunters who appreciate it for its strength and agility.

Margaux and her brother Calix (the Sigrid's children) explained to me why they were so passionate about riding ponies. They both answered that the sensations they felt with their pony were very strong. And Sigrid, their mother, concluded:

"During training I have them work on their stance of course, but they work a lot with speech to reassure and encourage the pony, it's very important."

Having attended several days of races organized by the PONEYS AU GALOPS, a day of races usually runs from 11 am to 6 pm. 13 races of ponies A, B, C, and D in flat, hurdles, and cross-country follow each other every 20 to 30 minutes. Activities are organized for children who do not participate directly in the races. A parade of old cars sometimes completes the event. The atmosphere is incomparable to showjumping or 3 day eventing. The gifts are abundant and all the competitors participate in the group photo at the end of the afternoon. The icing on the cake is that France Sire provides parents and children with free photos and videos of each race.

I had been planning for some time to prepare one of my mares for racing. With Jeannine, we knew Sigrid Gilet. She had bought for her daughter Margaux, Quinquina d'Aze a son of Gill de Briacé. But this project had to mature.

At the end of 2021, I introduced Daphné de Briacé to Sigrid, her daughter Margaux and her son Calix. After having tried her, they fell in love with her. But we still had to verify Daphné's ability to evolve quickly in this discipline. Physically and mentally, I had no doubt. Daphné had been preserved. She was only broken at 5 years old. In 2019, she started eventing and ranked 4th in the 3-day eventing at the Chp de France Poney 1 D Minime and - Excellence. She evolved upto 115 cm show jumping.

Daphné de Briacé is a Palomino Connemara mare 147 cm high. She is the daughter of Mistral de Briacé and Frow Frow by Icare. Her inbreeding coefficient is 3.57%. She has about 10% of Thoroughbred and 3% of Arabian.

Daphne's results in races from her first season speak for themselves:

- 2nd place in D1 Flat in Chantilly.

- Winner over 2800 meters in D Elite Cross at Senonnes.

- Winner over 1600 meters in D Elite Hurdles in Nort-Sur-Erdre.

Figure 44. Daniel, Sigrid, and Margaux under the colors of the breeding of Briacé and Pierre.

Figure 45. Daphné de Briacé is one of the rare Connemara mares able to race with results.

THE FAIRS

Fair days in Connemara were a regular and unmissable event. They provided the main opportunity to sell livestock and other goods. It was an excuse to interrupt the monotonous and uneventful daily life, to check on your neighbors whom you rarely met. Fair days followed the same pattern as race meetings in that the dates were mostly regular appointments, year after year.

To date, three fairs have survived in Connemara, at Spiddal on the second Wednesday of October, at Maam Cross on October 26, and at Clifden on the second Tuesday of November.

The quality of the Irish fair lies in the informal way in which business is conducted. It's man-to-man, without intermediaries. And that is certainly one of the riches of what so often appears to be a poor way of life.

That the fair remained a monthly event in Clifden until the 20th century is certain from a description Mrs. Pat Lyne found in the Connaught Champion of October 1st, 1904:

> *"The first Saturday of the month is the fair day. As soon as the day breaks, the town begins to fill up, one after another can be seen coming down from the hills, the Connemara horsemen, each mounted on his steed with baskets on either side of him, while the woman walks and carries her baby. The only time she can be carried is when she returns home and the contents of the basket have been sold! Around 10 o'clock, the islanders themselves arrive."*

The islanders are those who lived on the islands of Inishbofin, Inishturk, Turbot, and Omey. They arrived by currach[37] a few hours after those who lived on the mainland and formed a wild crowd ready to feast. After a pot or two, it was not very difficult to fall out with someone from the mainland and a colorful picture of a fight that ensued is contained in the same newspaper article. The monthly fair was an opportunity to buy and sell products such as eggs, potatoes, peat, butter, and other goods.

The regular livestock fair in Oughterard did not include the sale of ponies. Therefore, local breeders took their cattle to the Galway Horse Fair which was held in early September.

Mark Geoghegan's memories of fair days are most vivid. He and Jack Bolger would get together and drive a group of eighteen-month-old fillies and wild colts taken straight from their Dames' sides out off the mountains and take them

---

[37] A currach (also written curragh) is a light boat from the west coast of Ireland. Its length varies from 4 to 7 meters and its width between 1 meter and 1,50 meters.

down the Oughterard Road to Galway. One old mare served as a leader; another was in the rear. By the time they made it the 26 km to the city center, the young were less wild. Once in Galway, they were lined up behind an iron railing in front of the Bank of Ireland and it was from there that they were sold. Mark, by blowing on his cheeks and making a soft whistling sound with his lips, could stop the wildest of them, so Jack told to Pat Lyne.

Mrs. Pat Lyne continued:

> *"It is worth telling Mark's own story of the day he bought a filly at Clifden Fair for £1. He just missed the train to take the filly back to Oughterard. Earlier in the day, he had traveled in a pony-drawn cart and had already purchased five piglets. For the return trip, the filly and the five piglets travelled in the back of the cart at his feet. What strange companions!"*

The October Foal Fair at Maam Cross has a special place and has stood the test of time. Mark Geoghegan remembers going with his father when he was 8 years old. They bought two fillies at weaning and walked them back to Oughterard. That night the foals were locked up in different buildings at his father's house in Lettercraff near Oughterard. The next morning, one of them was missing: it had escaped and swam across the Corrib at its narrowest point to join its Dame in a field at Cornamona on the opposite bank.

Figure 46. The Clifden show was also a fair that allowed children to participate in a céilí (Irish folk dance competition). 1986. Photo Daniel Chupin.

Michael O'Malley was the key figure in the revival.

He was born in Rosmuc in 1884 and died at the age of 83 in 1967. As a young man, he left his native Connemara to study to be a veterinarian. Upon his father's early death, he returned home to support the family. He was a true patriot who believed passionately in Connemara products, including the Connemara pony itself. This multi-faceted man was a personal friend of Patrick Pearse[38]. He founded the Rosmuc Irish College in 1933 intending to preserve Gaelic among the youth of his region. This tiny portion of Connemara is known to this day for its Gaelic-speaking people. Michael was a successful beekeeper and an avid amateur photographer. He felt that the land in Connemara was not being fully utilized and needed to be cultivated more, especially by planting trees.

---

[38] Patrick Pearse (1879-1916) is one of the most emblematic figures of Irish history in its struggle for independence. A man of action, Patrick Pearse was one of the main leaders of the Easter Rising of 1916, which failed a few days later. After the revolt, the British authorities decided to make an example of him and executed many insurgents, including Patrick Pearse, on May 3, 1916.

THE REVIVAL OF THE CONNEMARA PONY

The Connemara pony revival began when a public debate about the pony was started by Michael O'Malley, a pony breeder in Rosmuc in southern Connemara. Like all farmers, he used them as a means of transportation to get around wherever his business took him. All trips were made on the back of the ponies or by carriage. Michael O'Malley was so convinced of the need to preserve the traditional type of pony that he accepted an invitation from a London doctor and rider. He had befriended Michael while on a fishing vacation at Screeb. He encouraged him to present his ponies at the 1912 Olympia Horse Show rare breed parade in London, England.

Figure 47. Michael O'Malley.
Source Shrouded in Mist.

Michael then embarked on an incredible journey with two of his ponies. He chose to take his four-year-old grey stallion, Irish Dragoon, and a six-year-old cream mare, Eileen Alanna. He and his assistant, Pat Walsh, walked the two ponies to catch the train at Maam Cross. At the Galway station, they transferred them to the Dublin train. In Dublin, they walked them through the city to the docks to board a boat for England. Once they arrived in England, they boarded the train to London. The same for the return trip to Connemara. The hardships of the journey took their toll and they had to deal with a very sick pony who had contracted tetanus on the way back due to the confined travel conditions. News of the long journey by land and sea to London sparked new interest in the breed.

O'MALLEY'S LETTERS

Mrs. Pat Lyne, in finding the last copy of the compilation of O'Malley's letters, helped to understand the concerns of some Irish people to save the Connemara breed.

By making the Ministry of Agriculture aware of the imminent actions to be taken, with an extraordinary will and dynamism, Michael O'Malley became the key figure in the revival of the Connemara pony.

Michael's visit to Olympia in 1912 gives us a real insight into the man's character. He felt he had to show the Connemara pony to as many people as possible, as he was convinced that it was the best pony in the world. His attempts to form a society in 1911 had failed, but undeterred, on his return from England, he wrote a letter to the Irish Farming World. This letter set off a chain of correspondence on the merits and plight of the Connemara breed. It undoubtedly drew attention to the situation as it then was throughout Ireland. Not content with this, Michael had the letters compiled into a booklet. They were printed by the Connaught Tribune at his expense and sold as a Brochure.

This one is long out of print and only one or two copies still exist today, including the one owned by Mrs. Pat Lyne.

In his preface, Michael says:

> "My aim in compiling this booklet is to show people, but especially Connemara pony breeders, in a handly form, what others think of our ponies, with a view, and in an ardent hope, that they will, even at the eleventh hour make an effort to save the breed."

His first letter to the press is entitled: A plea for the Connemara pony.

> " Sir, might I venture to ask you if you could find room to do that neglected and unjustly treated animal, the Connemara pony, some justice, by inserting some views and opinions on the havoc rendered among that valuable breed of ponies by the seeming misunderstanding of the Department of Agriculture's officials who have charge of our horse breeding schemes, and by the apathy and indifference of the Connemara breeders in allowing the gradual extinction of their famous pony?
>
> As you are aware, the Department of Agriculture has spent thousands of pounds on what, no doubt, they thought the "improvement" of the Connemara pony. What is the result of their labours and expense? I regret I must sorrowfully admit, as

much as every other breeder in Connemara, that the result is everything but satisfactory. Instead of our hills and our mountains being now dotted over, as of old, with that pleasant looking animal with the short, stout legs, the strong thick neck and wide chest, the powerful back and deep barrel, and the full and intelligent looking eye, we have only to be content with a smaller number (quantity, as well as quality, having been reduced) of animals which, if not inferior to the old type, will arrest nevertheless, the passerby's attention; for their sleepy and languid appearance is almost sure to cause any thinking man to stand and put himself the question: who is or are, responsible for such an awful change from the old type?"

In one of his letters, Michael describes the authentic type of the Connemara pony.

"A Connemara pony should be intelligent, active, enduring, presenting the outline of a long, low, powerful animal covering a lot of ground. The action should be good and straight. The hobby[39] should be of a yellow dun, grey, or bay colour, from 132 to 142 cm high, having the croup as high as the withers; the head should be larger than fine, with large jaws, the ears small and pointed; the distance from the occipital crest to the eyes relatively great, and the distance between the eyes from 19 to 20 cm. The neck should be strong and of medium length, the shoulders somewhat straight, the withers of moderate height, the body long and deep (girth 160 to 178 cm) mounted on short, stout legs (foreleg measuring from 79 to 84 cm from elbow to ground), a good back; powerful loins, slightly drooping, rounded quarters; well-developed breech, short below the knee, with flat hard bone (measuring 16.5 to 19 cm under the knee), wide, open and well-formed hooves."

He went on to say that he thought there was a great future for the Connemara pony as foundation stock for breeding polo ponies. He had just returned from his trip to London, where he was no doubt made aware of the problems in England in keeping the polo pony under 147 cm.

Hugh Deady of County Cork, in his letter, tells stories of Connemara ponies that he knew. He remembers a bay pony, 132 cm, that pulled the butcher's trade cart,

---

[39] The Hobby, Irish Hobby or Celtic/Hobby is crossed with native Irish horses; a superior breed, the Irish Hobby, was developed and used for racing and light military work.

was a marvel to ride and loaded with four men, could take down any large horse. Another was a 142 cm chestnut; it was not in condition, but it was a wonderful animal that pulled his cart and followed any car from town to town and did a lot of heavy hauling work. He was a whole pony and was twenty years old when Mr. Deady met him in 1878. A mare purchased in Castlebar was the best he had ever met:

> *"I knew her to travel 32 km, 21 km of them carrying four men on a side car to the races, then to be stripped, saddled, mounted and run in a 3.2 km race, which she won from fresh horses and to travel 32 km back with the car and load the same day. I knew her to take four men 51 km against the wind and a Connemara storm and go back to Clifden still a fresh horse."*

Michael outlines ideas for introducing a limited amount of Arabian and English Thoroughbreds in a carefully controlled program. He argues that the old type of pony is now only found in the Rosmuc, Roundstone, Ballinahinch, and Maam Cross areas. He mentions that Mr. Beckett had successfully used an Arabian stallion in 1860. The correspondence ends with a letter from William O'Malley, M.P., written from the House of Commons in February 1913, in which he wishes Michael good luck in his efforts to revive the Connemara pony. He had brought the problem to the attention of the Minister of Agriculture, without success. Here is how he concludes his letter:

> *"My first trip to the City of Tribes was made from Ballyconneely, 90 or 92 km, and the pony that my Father drove on that occasion was a black mare called Bessie, a pure Connemara breed. Leaving home early in the morning, we reached Galway in the early afternoon of the same day and we started for the return journey the next morning. Except for feeding, there was no delay. At the end of the one 183 km Bessie was as fresh almost when as she set out. In those days the Connemara pony could do journeys of that length "without turning a hair", and if we are to see that admirable breed revived, the thanks will be due to you for the interest you have awakened in the subject by your interesting letters in the Press and by your individual efforts to preserve and improve the breed."*

This is how this collection of letters ends.

Figure 48. Ballinafad, Photo Daniel Chupin.

The Irishman does not begin by thinking, but by feeling and observing. He does this usefully, without ever being hindered by injunctions or regulations. He keeps his free will. This state of mind is reflected in his way of conceiving breeding.

THE CONNEMARA PONY ASSOCIATION

A period of twelve years elapsed between November 11, 1911, when a local committee of pony breeders met, and December 15, 1923, when the Connemara Pony Association was officially founded. Father White, Roundstone's parish priest, fought for justice and the betterment of life for his poor people. He did much more than attend to their spiritual needs. Father White was elected President at the first meeting in 1923. He took the chair and opened the meeting by saying:

> *"The Connemara has specific defining characteristics; the men are gritty and the women are charming and beautiful. As for the ponies, they could go anywhere, live anywhere, did not need luxurious food, had remarkable stamina, and were far more profitable than a larger horse. On mountainsides, in valleys, or on hard rocky surfaces, they were just as effective."*

He insisted that in the efforts to revive them failure was not an option. An open discussion showed a disagreement among the pony breeders present, on the use of Welsh Cob stallions. Mr. Lyons had had success with this blood being used on native mares. Christy Kerin believed that it had not done the breed any good.

The introduction of the Arabian by the Martin family was commented on favorably, but the Hackney blood was dismissed as a failure. It was felt that there were still many old strains to be found in central Connemara. Christy Kerin was sure that the breed could be reinvigorated again if they went back to the original strain. It is up to each of us, as far as possible, to develop our herd with this typical pattern and to put our characteristic nationality on it when they leave our country. It was decided to draw up a list of existing pony stallions and to ask the Ministry to inspect them. In this way, the Association would be able to determine if the improvement should be based on the existing stallions or if it should import new stallions, mentioning the Arabian strain from which the Connemara was derived. It was decided to organize mare shows in Oughterard, Carna and Clifden and to ask the Ministry of Agriculture for a grant. The first meeting ended with another, set for January 22, 1924, at which a full Council was elected.

Inspections were essential to the formation and development of the studbook; the stability of the team of inspectors was the most effective way to consistently establish the registered pony type. The four men chosen for this task were all from outside Connemara and had no vested interest. They were men of reputation and integrity who volunteered their services over a long period of time.

THE STUDBOOK

The introduction to Volume I of the C.P.S. Stallion Book, published in 1926 and sold for £1, clearly states the Society's objectives:

> " The publication of a Connemara Pony stud book is an attempt to foster and develop, on systematic lines, a native breed which has existed for centuries, the merits of which are recognized not only in Ireland but outside it. In Connemara, unlike many other pony breeding localities, breeding mares work throughout the year; consequently, a form of natural selection for utility purposes is continually at work. Awkward, ill-tempered, or badly constituted animals are of little or no value to the Connemara farmer owing to the nature of the work which has to be done and the conditions under which it has to be carried out. It will be understood, therefore, that only the very best can be retained for breeding which accounts for the fact that although unsuitable foreign blood has been introduced from time to time its influence on the permanent breeding stock has been slight ..

Ponies vary slightly in size and character, according to the district in which they are bred, but it is generally admitted that a compact, short-legged pony, about 13 hands 2 inches high with good shoulders and true and easy movement, is the most suitable type to develop. This class of animal, while eminently suitable for the work in Connemara, is also the type which is likely to meet with more demand from outside. The Society aims to secure by continued selection and careful fostering a breed of ponies uniform in size and shape, suitable for general utility purposes and which, when bred from under favorable conditions, would be capable of producing high class riding animals."

THE INSPECTIONS

The first inspections took place over five days, April 15-19, 1924. Ten different centers were used and covered a wide area extending from Galway to Clonbur. Advance notice was published in the Connaught Tribune giving details of the location and date of the inspections.

Two hundred and forty-nine mares and thirty-five stallions were presented at the first inspections. The largest number was seen at Cashel and Maam. Sixty mares and five stallions were accepted. Another inspection took place at the first show at Roundstone in September, where ninety mares and fifteen stallions were inspected. Of these, fifteen mares and one stallion were accepted. This was not an encouraging start for the pony owners, but it does highlight the high standard of the inspectors and the poor quality of the ponies shown.

At first, it was not easy to convince farmers that it was worthwhile to bring their ponies down from the mountains to an inspection center. The value of a registration certificate was difficult to explain and the free appointment of an Association stallion was not, in practical terms, of much value. There were many stallions available in the hills and their lack of quality was of little consequence to the breeders if they provided the annual foal. The high number of rejected ponies in 1924 could hardly encourage owners to present their ponies the following year and this is reflected in the number of ponies present in 1925.

In 1925, a newspaper headline on January 24 read: HUNGERED POPULATION IN CONNEMARA - "Not more than one family in ten had a fire. In Letterfrack, starvation was imminent because of the floods."

On February 24 of that year, Father White wrote to the newspaper to say:

"Not a sod of turf has been sold because of incessant rains – I have seen children burning bunches of old heather to boil a kettle."

It is in this context that the Committee was trying to impove the breed of their ponies.

THE MARES

From the very first inspections, the mares received favorable comments. The earliest report states:

> " In making our selections we endeavor to adhere to the type of pony which made the breed famous in the past, that is, a compact, deep-bodied animal, short backed and well ribbed up, standing on short legs, having good bone, sloping shoulders with well-balanced neck and head. The ideal height we regard as ranging from 13 hands to 14 hands; the average height of the selected ponies is about 13 hands 2 inches. We paid particular attention to the action and selected ponies of free, easy, and true movement. In this connection, it may be well to mention that a number of ponies which might have been regarded as otherwise suitable were rejected owing to action which was seriously faulty.
>
> We are pleased to be able to report that the selected mares conformed to the ideal standard and that a large proportion of them were excellent in type and quality. It was very noticeable,

however, that the best mares were for the most part over ten years and that, taken as a whole, the younger mares were somewhat disappointing. We are of the opinion that the majority of selected mares are as true to type and fully as good as the best which have been bred in Connemara in the past. After careful consideration we have come to the conclusion that these will form an excellent foundation stock ... It is clear the good old native type has been disappearing in recent years from many districts and it is essential that an earnest and sustained effort should now be made to foster and develop the breed. Insofar as the mares are concerned, at all events, we are quite satisfied that there is still sufficient good material available."

Even today, females are the great strength of the Connemara breed.

Figure 50. Mares on the moor near Glinsk. Photo Daniel Chupin.

THE STALLIONS

Initial inspections showed that the majority of stallions available in Connemara in 1924 were of very poor quality. Thirty-five stallions were presented and only five were accepted. In breeding competitions in the same year, fifteen more were inspected and only one was accepted. The inspection committee soon realized that unless the stallion population was completely controlled, it was unlikely that its goal would be achieved. Not only did they have to own and be responsible for the parking of approved stallions, but it was also important that rejected stallions be castrated or removed from the mountains and that a stallion replacement plan be established. In addition, the people themselves needed to be assured that the revolution in Connemara breeding was for the good of them and their ponies.

The inspectors' first report on stallions reads as follows:

> "With regard to the stallions, however, we regret that we are not in a position to report so favorably... The majority of stallions presented for inspection were of nondescript type and wholly unsuitable for the purposes of the Scheme. It appears to us that breeders have not exercised the same care and judgement in the selection of their stallions as they did in the case of broodmares. While we are satisfied that the stallions now recommended are of fair average quality and may, with advantage, be used for mating with the selected mares, we feel that an effort must be made to find for use in future years better class sires. We believe it may be possible to find such stallions in Connemara, or at least to breed a number of really high-class sires by mating the best selected mares with the stallions we now recommend for approval. From the detailed lists which accompany this report the present location of both the selected mares and stallions can be ascertained, and we desire to submit for the consideration of the Council the necessity for making a more equitable distribution of the available stallions so that a registered stallion may be within reasonable distance of all selected mares."

By 1943, twenty years after its inception, the Connemara Pony Association had truly reached a turning point in its male gene bank. Despite all their efforts, only three male lines had survived the test of time. Inbreeding could only lead to stagnation. It was at this point that the association took its first hesitant steps to introduce outside blood.

Three stallions were chosen, the Thoroughbred Winter, the Irish Draught Skibbereen, and an oversized cob Dynamite that was out of a registered Connemara stallion. They were listed as approved stallions and a limited number of their offspring were registered at the inspection. The Thoroughbred Winter was only on the stallion list for two seasons and the Irish draft stallions were reportedly disappointing.

By 1947, little progress had been made with the outside blood used. It was at this time that the Association decided to purchase another Thoroughbred, Little Heaven. In 1954, it purchased a foal out of a famous Arabian horse, Naseel.

There is no doubt that the inspectors maintained a high standard in their selection of stallions. Despite this, many of their choices have not met expectations as breeders. An unsuccessful stallion is quickly removed from the approved list. Those not considered good enough to remain stallions were castrated ; others of better quality were sold outside Connemara. Those with poor fertility were castrated; those with any kind of health abnormality, however slight, were castrated. No animal was registered with a pedigree unless it was one hundred percent verified.

Figure 51. Murphy Rebel in a meadow in the heart of Clifden in 1984. Two photos by Daniel Chupin.

STALLION HANDLING IN CONNEMARA

In 1928, the association decided to buy the best foals at weaning. It continued until the 50s. These males were sent to Innishagoil, were they were raised in freedom. Innishagoil, with nearly 120 hectares, is the largest of the islands of Lake Corrib. It can be reached from the port of Oughterard. This island is in the heart of Corrib Lake, halfway between Cong and Oughterard. At the age of 2 or 3 years old, after inspection, the best ones were put to breeding. For this purpose, they were entrusted to stallion keepers who trained them and used them for farm work.

During the breeding season, the stallions provided service (for a fee) to the breeders. In most cases, the stallion would "travel". The stallion would travel with his stallion keeper on horseback, harness, or bicycle to each breeder to cover the mares. At that time, there was no trailer, everything was done on foot.

Pat Lyne reports on Dun Lorenzo's activity:

> *"Josie gave me a colorful picture of this pony for whom he had great admiration. He described him as butty[40] with endless endurance and courage. His stallion course on Saturday was 93 km next to a bike. Josie assures me that he was as fresh at mile 80 as he was at mile 1. He was the sturdiest of all the ponies in his care and, according to Josie, he never raised a bad one. They may not have all been beautiful, but they all had a purpose."*

In 1984, I met Joseph Conroy at his home in Bunowen, and during our conversation, I was very surprised by this expression he often used to describe a pony. Useful, for him, a pony had to be useful. It had to work, it had to serve.

If this stallion system continued until the seventies, it must be admitted that for breeders outside Connemara, this stallion solution was complicated, because the stallion owners could not keep the mares in livery.

Mrs. Petch told me about the difficulties she encountered (she lived in the Cork area). She had to transport two mares in a trailer with a journey requiring a day of transport to go to the heart of Connemara. Once there, she had to find accommodation for herself and her two mares. She had to go to the stallion every day. She had faith.

---

[40] In the sense of a leader, a fighter.

Three stallion men in Connemara:

Figure 52. Michael King, Cushatrough, Claddaghduff with Thunder Storm.
Photo by Daniel Chupin

Figure 53. Bartley O'Malley, Derrathabeg,
Carraroe, presenting Maam Hill.
Photo by Daniel Chupin.

Figure 54. Joseph Conroy, Bunowen,
Ballyconneely with Somkey Duncan, Clifden
show 1997. Photo Daniel Chupin.

STUDY ON STALLIONS

Why do a study on stallion lines?

If a mare can produce from 1 to 19 foals for the most prolific, a stallion can produce up to 1150 foals (thanks to artificial insemination).

The impact of a stallion on the development and variety of genetics of an equine breed can be decisive. Since the creation of the studbook, only three male lines have survived. These three male lines are considered the most authentic.

I prefer to use the term authentic because as you are beginning to understand, it seems to me quite inappropriate to use the term "pure" breed to talk about the Connemara pony.

The Irish have given them color.

- The Blue Line: Cannon Ball
- The Red Line: Connemara Boy
- The Green Line: Mountain Lad
- The Violet line: the English Thoroughbred Little Heaven
- The Orange line: the Arabian Thoroughbred Naseel

For each lineage, I have synthesized the information contained in the book by Pat Lyne and Mrs. Petch.

As we will see in the next chapter, the Irish Association had to use outside blood by selecting English Thoroughbreds, an Irish Draught, and an Arabian Thoroughbred. In the chapter dedicated to inbreeding, I explain the advantages and disadvantages of inbreeding and the reasons for inbreeding.

For each of the lines, I have attached a table listing the stallions in France that I have selected from the information contained in the Harasire database. To make this selection, I have retained only the stallions having at least 10 products with at least 1 product indexed at 120 or more tested in the following disciplines: Show Jumping, Eventing, and Dressage.

Out of the 1281 inactive and active stallions, 334 stallions produced in France met these criteria, i.e., 26% of the stallions.

I made a general classification and a classification by lineage by calculating the percentage of indexed products compared to the number of foals born. Considering the number of stallions in the Cannon Ball and Little Heaven lines, I only retained the first 40. For the three other lines, given the number of stallions, I retained all the stallions. I added a ranking of the first 100 stallions born in France.

THE BLUE LINE: CANNON BALL

Bartley's article on the Connemara pony tells us that Cannon Ball is out of Dynamite and a native mare. Dynamite was by the Welsh Cob Prince Llewellyn. Born in 1904, Cannon Ball was twenty years old when the first inspections took place in Oughterard. Of the four stallions shown that day, Cannon Ball was the only one registered. He was entered in the first Connemara pony show at Roundstone the same year, 1924, and placed second to the young pony Charlie.

Figure 55. Cannon Ball with Henri at the 1924 Roundstone show. Source Shrouded in Mist.

Cannon Ball, in his lifetime, was a legend; for many years, he was the favorite and regular winner of the farmers' prize at Oughterard races, and his fame extended to winning races at Claddagh[41] and Roundstone Beach. He was a pony of great character and intelligence, with exceptional stamina. Cannon Ball lived with Harry Toole ("Henry" to his friends) at Learn, near Oughterard. Henry was completely devoted to him. His life was busy, a weekly trip to Athenry market on Saturday involved a 51km journey each way. It was common knowledge that Henry and Cannon Ball traveled this route, and at irregular intervals, a mare would be waiting by the roadside, her owner wanting Cannon Ball's services. Henry would unhitch him from his cart, remove his harness and let him cover the mare.

---

[41] The Claddagh races were located near Galway.

A more regular stop was called for, in both directions, so that Henry could quench his thirst. While he did so, Cannon Ball waited with his special mixture of six eggs in a quart of beer, which he promptly mopped up. By nightfall, after a few too many pints, Henry was lying at the bottom of the wagon, asleep. The old pony knew the way back so well that his master's reins were of no use. When he arrived home, he waited patiently between the shafts for Henry to wake up. Occasionally, when he was on horseback rather than in a carriage, Henry, in a similar state, would fall to the ground. Cannon Ball's response was to lift Henry to his feet by grabbing his jacket with his teeth. Henry would then struggle to get back on the horse and leave it to Cannon Ball to take him home. The understanding between master and pony was unique and when, on rare occasions, Henry left the house without Cannon Ball, he was always greeted with a joyful neigh.

But it was his exploits on the racetrack that made Cannon Ball so popular. His work between races kept him in top form. He was seen pulling a ton of rocks over a rough, stony surface, a task few ponies would have attempted.

Racing was the only occasion when Henry and Cannon Ball were not partners. John Costello, a butcher from Galway, was his most regular jockey. When he was not available, Mark or Jack were more than willing to take his place. Mark describes him as a difficult horse to ride. "He would run with his head down, like a rabbit." Nonetheless, he carried Mark's 72 kg to many victories. Henry would give his jockey £1.5 if he won the race and no one told me about the day Cannon Ball didn't win. When Cannon Ball saw the starter with his flag, he would shake his head in anticipation and be ready for the start. Oughterard's course was hilly and required courage and stamina, while others might pass him on the flat, he always passed them on the climbs. No whip was used or needed, but an encouraging "Ho. (Preferably said in Gaelic, Henry's language) got the response the jockey was looking for.

Cannon Ball died naturally of old age in March 1926. He is certainly the only pony to have been watched over and so honored. He was laid on the floor of it stable and after the formalities were completed, he was carried by ten strong men. He was buried on the hillside in a hay-covered grave facing the Oughterard racetrack, the site of his many triumphs.

His epitaph in the Connaught Tribune read:

> *"No more with earthly kin you mingle*
> *Dream of race course tracks you've won,*
> *Of noble steeds and epic deeds*
> *And bookies left without a jingle."*

Cannon Ball was known to win more than one race a day. On one occasion, it was bet that he could not beat the train from Learn to Oughterard, a distance of 6.4 km. But he did win!

REBEL his son, was born in 1922 and was bought at weaning by Jack Bolger at the Spiddal fair. The next day he was sold to Gil Ryan of Oranmore. Having been inspected and registered to Mr. Ryan in 1924, he was purchased by the Association in 1927. By this time Cannon Ball was dead. The Association retained one of his sons to ensure the continuation of this good line. For his first season of riding, he was placed with Mark Geoghegan who trained him to be both ridden and harnessed. He ran in local races.

Figure 56. Rebel and Val Keaney. Source Shrouded in Mist.

The following year, in 1928, he was transferred to Val Keaney of Gowla where he remained until 1937. It was unusual for an Association stallion to stay in the same area for more than three years. Val had another stallion working for the Association for many years, but he is best known for being the stallion keeper of Rebel. The Hynes family of Canal Stage in Ballinafad hosted Val and Rebel one day a week. He was stabled and the mares were introduced to him throughout the day. Later in the week, Val would take him in the opposite direction, to Carna.

Rebel was described as an endearing and cheerful pony with the same character and personality as his sire Cannon Ball. Jack noted that he stood on his hind legs with his wavy mane and wind-whipped tail; he was very white and photogenic. He won the stallion class of the Association show in 1927, 1928, and 1929 and again in 1936 at the age of fourteen. In 1938, he was sixteen years old and his lungs and heart were in bad shape. Mr. Kelly was sent to see him and advised to have him put down, which was done.

INNISHGOILL LADDIE was born in 1934 in Dooyher East, Carna. He is out of Dooyher Lass. The three Innishgoill stallions were the first foals bred by the Association, purchased as foals, and placed in a small herd to grow and mature in the most natural conditions.

Figure 57. Innishgoill Laddie at age 3. Source Shrouded in Mist.

He was on the stallion list for a long time, seventeen years, from 1937 to 1954, and during that time he was stationed with different stallion owners. By all accounts, he was kind and easy to work with, both in his stallion duties and on the farm. He started his life with Jack Bolger. He was "great at galloping and won many races." He was with Jack from 1937 to 1942 and won the stallion class for him in 1938 and 1940. In 1943 he was transferred to the Diamonds at Letterfrack and in 1947 to Peter Connolly at Bealadangen[42], on the coast, an exposed and bleak rocky area quite different from the greenery of Oughterard. This was no longer the cheerful racing life with Jack Bolger, but the hard, laborious life of serving the man to work his poor land. Peter rode his stallion three days a week, Monday, Thursday, and Saturday. His route took him many miles, his furthest point being Lettermullen (14 km away), and he often covered up to eighty mares in a week.

---

[42] Bealadangan is 3 to 4 km from Costelloe.

LAVALLEY REBEL was born at Pat Flaherty's in Derrada West. He is out of a mare named Derrada Fanny. He was born in 1935 and was part of the second generation of foals bred by the Association. They carried the prefix Lavalley which described a small village. He was bred beyond Tuam[43] , a milder climate than that offered on Innishgoill. At the age of two, he was sent to the home of John Costello of Spiddal for a year before moving to Val Keaney in Gowla. Val must have been very happy to receive the son of his favorite old stallion Rebel. He kept him for two years before he went back to Costello to a new stallion keeper who turned out to be very rough.

Figure 58. Lavalley Rebel at a show in England. Source Shrouded in Mist.

Between 1940 and 1942, many immigrants arrived from the Aran Islands. It was Lavalley Rebel's job to pull the barrel, heavily laden with these people and their goods, along the road between Costello and Moycullen. It was a rough, unmade road, and while the income for his master was great, it was at the expense of the stallion. He bore the scars of the wounds caused by the stick for the rest of his life. The Association retired him and he was sent to Peter Connolly who quickly restored him to good health. He won the stallion class at the Association's annual breeding show in 1944 and 1946. He spent 1945 with Jack Bolger and 1946 with Ed Conneely. In 1950 he was sold to Mr. and Mrs. John Meade and went to England.

---

[43] Tuam is located 35 km north of Galway.

CALLA REBEL was bred in 1938 by Val Keaney and is out of his mare by Charlie, Calla Roan. He was registered as Calla Rebel and spent the first six years of his life plowing the land and covering any mare willing to ride over the boureen[44]. In 1950 he spent a season with Jack Bolger before spending four years, 1951-1955, with Michael Conroy at Bunowen. Calla Rebel was very fertile and had an attractive type. He was appreciated by breeders in Connemara. Forty-seven mares and two stallions were registered by him between 1944 and 1959.

Figure 59. Templebready Fear Bui, one of Calla Rebel's great-grandsons, has sired numerous sport horses throughout Europe. Photo Sophie Soulez Larivière.

GIL was bred at Letterkeehaune by 1938 to Dudley McDonagh. It seems that Gil, although a very successful and prolific stallion, may not have had the personality of his ancestors. Gil spent his first four years as a stallion at Kilkerrin before spending one year at Bealadangan and another at Bunowen. In 1947 he was transferred to Anthony Faherty's home in Moyard where he remained until the end of 1951. In 1952, he was sold in County Kerry. He had twelve sons and fifty-nine daughters registered.

TOOREEN LADDIE was born in Letterfrack in 1947. He is out of Grey Swan. The Association bought him from his breeder Luke at the age of two and he was sent to Ed Conneely the same year. Ed's son John described him as a clumsy pony who would kick his hooves on the road[45]. Association records show that he was picked up in the winter of 1950 and returned to Killola's land[46]. It was probably

---

[44] A boreen or bohereen is a narrow and often unpaved country road in Ireland.

[45] The term stumbled could be used.

[46] Killola is located between Oughterard and Moycullen

decided that he needed time to mature and grow, which he was given. In the spring of 1952, eighteen months later, he was sent to Patrick Joyce of Knockilaree. Patrick Joyce considered him to be from a very old stock, which never carried much flesh but had strong bones and a good head and shoulders. In 1955 he was sold to the Dublin Dudgeons who exported him to the United States. He has two sons and eighteen daughters registered in the C.P.S. studbook.

CARNA BOBBY was born in 1946, bred at Callowfeenish by Patrick Mulkerrin Tom, and out of Carna Dolly. Like many others, he was purchased at the Maam Fair by the Association as one of their annual foal quotas. In 1948 he was placed with Jack Bolger where he spent three seasons. In 1954, he was sent to Festus King at Claddaghduff, where he stayed until the end of 1958. Finally, he spent three seasons at Kilkerrin with John Walsh. At the end of 1961, he was taken off the Association's list and sold to Paddy Lally living in Gort[47] . He remained with Paddy until his death at the age of twenty-seven in 1973. The most important sons are Killyreagh Kim and the famous Leam brothers Bobby Finn and Coosheen Finn. Paddy Lally had a constant flow of mares until the end of Carna Bobby's life. He won the stallion class in 1949, 1951, 1953, 1955, and 1957.

Figure 60. Carna Bobby No. 79 on the square at Clifden after having placed 3rd in the stallion class in his 20th year, 1966. Paddy Lally is in charge (in the inset at top right) His sire Gil No. 43 with Anthony Faherty. Source Shrouded in Mist.

---

47 Gort is located 35 km south of Galway.

Figure 61. Killyreagh Kim, in 1984. Photo Daniel Chupin.

Figure 62. Leam Bobby Finn in England in 1987. Photo Daniel Chupin.

TOOREEN ROSS was born at Rosscahill in 1954 out of the mare Wayfarer. He was on the stallion list for five years and during that time was with Mikey King at Claddaghduff and James Grealish at Oranmore. His son Tulira Mairtin proved to be a very successful sire for Lord and Lady Hemphill. Tooreen Ross was sold to Mrs. Duff in England in 1965.

Figure 63. Tulira Martin in 1982. Photo by Daniel Chupin.

INVER REBEL WAS born to the Mulkerrin family in Callowfeenish in 1950, out of Inver Bridge. He was purchased by the Association as a foal. He was not very tall and many of his offspring were also small. He was on the Association's list for ten years, staying for a while with Joseph Little in Bunowen. At the end of the 1963 season, he was sold in Kinvara. He was a prolific stallion who, with his most authentic Connemara characteristics, left his mark on his offspring.

Figure 64. Inver Rebel. Source Shrouded in Mist.

BRIDGE BOY will be remembered for his numerous championship victories in breeding competitions organized by the Association in the 1960s. It always took two men to lead him, one on each side. It must have been an impressive sight to see this pony displaying such strength and virility. He was bred by the Geoghegans in Oughterard from their favorite mare Irene.

Figure 65. Pady Mélody d'Auxence reserve supreme champion of the national Poitiers 2009.

Figure 66. Currachmore Cashel Supreme Champion 2012, presented by Joe Burke.

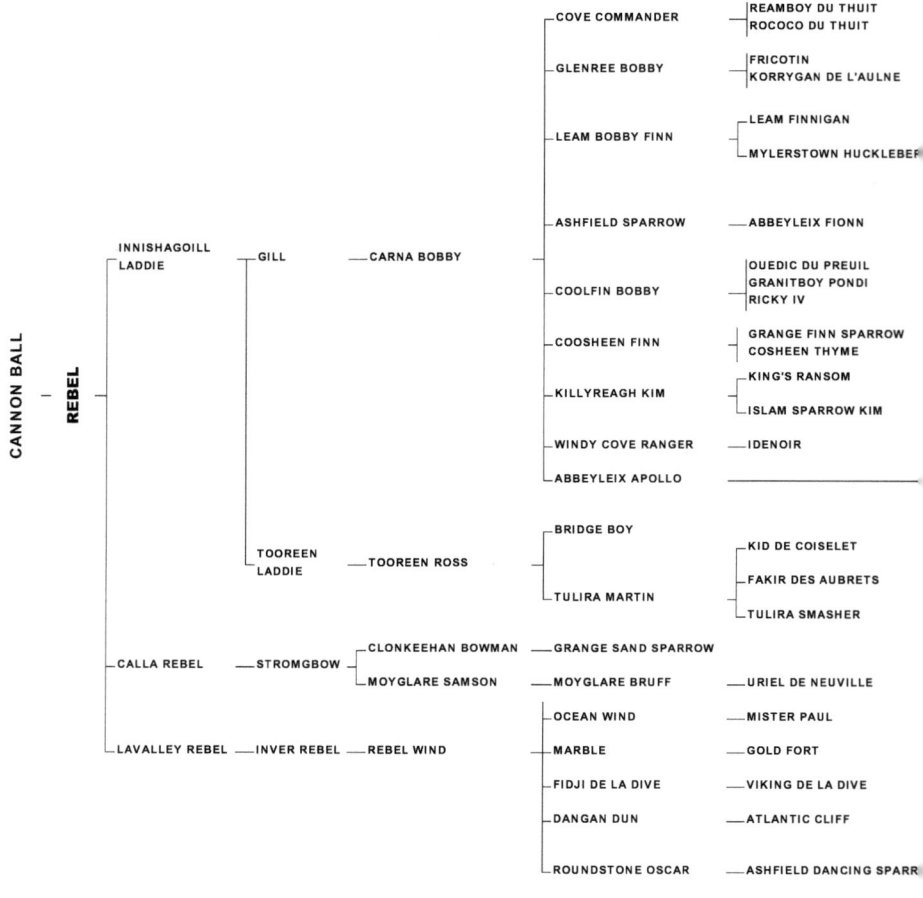

Figure 67. Cannon Ball lineage of French stallions. Daniel Chupin.

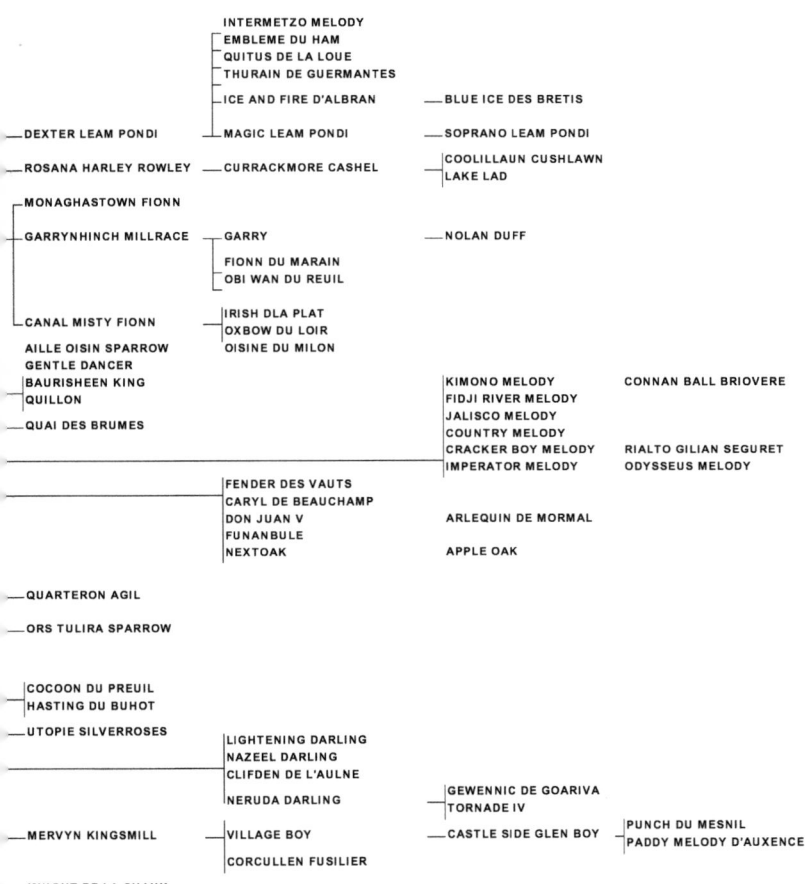

INTERMETZO MELODY
EMBLEME DU HAM
QUITUS DE LA LOUE
THURAIN DE GUERMANTES

ICE AND FIRE D'ALBRAN — BLUE ICE DES BRETIS

DEXTER LEAM PONDI — MAGIC LEAM PONDI — SOPRANO LEAM PONDI

ROSANA HARLEY ROWLEY — CURRACKMORE CASHEL
COOLILLAUN CUSHLAWN
LAKE LAD

MONAGHASTOWN FIONN

GARRYNHINCH MILLRACE — GARRY — NOLAN DUFF
FIONN DU MARAIN
OBI WAN DU REUIL

IRISH DLA PLAT
CANAL MISTY FIONN — OXBOW DU LOIR
OISINE DU MILON
AILLE OISIN SPARROW
GENTLE DANCER
BAURISHEEN KING
QUILLON
QUAI DES BRUMES

KIMONO MELODY   CONNAN BALL BRIOVERE
FIDJI RIVER MELODY
JALISCO MELODY
COUNTRY MELODY
CRACKER BOY MELODY   RIALTO GILIAN SEGURET
IMPERATOR MELODY   ODYSSEUS MELODY

FENDER DES VAUTS
CARYL DE BEAUCHAMP
DON JUAN V   ARLEQUIN DE MORMAL
FUNANBULE
NEXTOAK   APPLE OAK

QUARTERON AGIL

ORS TULIRA SPARROW

COCOON DU PREUIL
HASTING DU BUHOT

UTOPIE SILVERROSES
LIGHTENING DARLING
NAZEEL DARLING
CLIFDEN DE L'AULNE
NERUDA DARLING

GEWENNIC DE GOARIVA
TORNADE IV

PUNCH DU MESNIL
MERVYN KINGSMILL — VILLAGE BOY — CASTLE SIDE GLEN BOY
PADDY MELODY D'AUXENCE

CORCULLEN FUSILIER

KNIGHT DE LA CHAUX

% PI 120 and +: corresponds to the percentage of products indexed at 120 and more / Nb of births.

Ranking	Stallions	Father	Paternal grandmother	Dame	% PI 120 and +
1	CURRACHMORE CASHEL	ROSENA HARLEY ROWLEY	ROSENAHARLEY RONAMARA	TOLKA BRIDGE	42,3%
2	OBI WAN DU REUIL	GARRYHINCH MILLRACE	KILBRACKEN QUEEN	DRAGEE DE COISELET	33,3%
3	CANAL MISTY FIONN	ABBEYLEIX FIONN	FIONNUALA	GLOVES MISTY	32,5%
4	COOLILLAUN CUSHLAWN	CURRACHMORE CASHEL	TOLKA BRIDGE	GLENCARRIG AISHLING	31,8%
5	QUILLON	KING'S RANSOM	ERRISBEG ROSE	ROCKMOUNT RUBY	31,7%
6	FUNAMBULE II	ABBEYLEIX APOLLO	BLUE MOON	QUINTETTE III	31,3%
7	NEXTOAK	ABBEYLEIX APOLLO	BLUE MOON	ASTER	30,6%
8	BANAGHER MAGEE	DUNMORE KING	DANGAN GUAIRE	SPRINGLAWN STAR	30,3%
9	MAGIC LEAM PONDI	DEXTER LEAM PONDI	WHITE GRANIT	VOYEL DE BEAUCHAMP	30,2%
10	VIKING DE LA DIVE	FIDJI DE LA DIVE	EASTER ATLANTIC	EASTER CREG	30,0%
11	QUIOCO OF SCARPE	COSHLA BOBBY	ARANMORE VOCTORY	LARRAGOB LINDA	28,8%
12	JALISCO MELODY	IDENOIR	LITTLE CASHEL HILL	CARRABAUN CRACKER	28,1%
13	LEAM FINNIGAN	LEAM BOBBY FIN	FINOLA OF LEAM	CLOONISLE JUDY	28,0%
14	COUNTRY MELODY	IDENOIR	LITTLE CASHEL HILL	INISH CU	25,7%
15	FRICOTIN	GLENREE BOBBY	INISH BIGGLE	ULLA DE LA NIEVRE	24,3%
16	NAZEEL DARLING	GOLD FORT	FORT SILVER	CURRAGH DAISY	23,7%
17	PUNCH DU MESNIL	CASTLE SIDE GLEN BOY	GLENCROFT AMY	CALYPSO MELODY	23,5%
18	BAURISHEEN KING	KING'S RANSOM	ERRISBEG ROSE	PERLETTE III	23,2%
18	FIDJI RIVER MELODY	IDENOIR	LITTLE CASHEL HILL	ROUNDSTONE RIVER	23,2%
19	OXBOW DU LOIR	CANAL MISTY FIONN	GLOVES MISTY	BELLE DE NEUVILLE	22,7%
20	DEXTER LEAM PONDI	LEAM BOBBY FIN	CLOONISLE JUDY	WHITE GRANITE	22,0%
21	ASHFIELD DANCING SPARROW	ROUNSTONE OSCAR	DANCING SPANNER	WISE SPARROW	21,8%
22	ROCOCO DU THUIT	COVE COMMANDER	WINDY COVE	ROSBEG ROSIE	21,1%
23	HURRICANE OF LAPS	GARRYHINCH MILLRACE	KILBRACKEN QUEEN	WESTSIDE LITTLE MADAM	20,6%
24	KINGSTOWN RORY	MONAGHANSTOWN FIONN	APRIL STAR	KINGSTOWN SILVER	20,4%
25	GLENREE BOBBY	CARNA BOBBY	CARNA DOLLY	INISH BIGGLE	20,0%
26	REAM BOY DU THUIT	COVE COMMANDER	WINDY COVE	LEAM LENA	19,5%
27	NOAH DE LA SCARPE	COSHLA BOBBY	ARANMORE VICTORY	STORY OF SLIEVE NA MBAN	19,4%
27	COCOON DU PREUIL	URIEL DE NEUVILLE	SHIPTON MAURTEEN	ABBEYLEIX PEARL NECKLACE	19,4%
28	GARRYHINCH MILLRACE	ABBEYLEIX FIONN	FIONNUALA	KILBRACKEN QUEEN	18,5%
28	OUEDIC DU PREUIL	COOLFIN BOBBY	MOY HARVEST TIME	ABBEYLEIX PEARL NECKLACE	18,5%
29	ICE AND FIRE D'ALBRAN	DEXTER LEAM PONDI	WHITE GRANIT	UNDERLINE OF LAPS	18,3%
30	SAIAN DE KEZEG	MAGIC LEAM PONDI	VOYEL DE BEAUCHAMP	FARANDOLE MELODY	18,2%
31	COOLFIN BOBBY	CARNA BOBBY	CARNA DOLLY	MOY HARVEST TIME	18,1%
32	BRINDAMOUR MELODY	IDENOIR	LITTLE CASHEL HILL	CARRABAUN CRACKER	18,0%
33	DON JUAN V	ABBEYLEIX APOLLO	BLUE MOON	VINCA II	17,9%
34	GRANITBOY PONDI	COOLFIN BOBBY	MOY HARVEST TIME	WHITE GRANITE	17,9%
35	MISTER PAUL	OCEAN WIND	OCEAN MELODY	EASTER THEODORA	17,9%
36	LEO PONDI	DEXTER LEAM PONDI	WHITE GRANIT	HAZURE PONDI	17,6%
37	FENDER DES VAUTS	ABBEYLEIX APOLLO	BLUE MOON	ARIANE	17,4%
38	RICKY IV	COOLFIN BOBBY	MOY HARVEST TIME	MOLLY	16,8%
39	BRUCKLESS HERO	LINSFORT BOY	INISHOWEN ROSIE	ROBIN'S GIFT	16,7%
39	THOR DE SEGURET	ODYSSEUS MELODY	EQUINOX MELODY	QUENZA DE SEGURET	16,7%
39	CLIFDEN DE L'AULNE	GOLD FORT	FORT SILVER	PAYSE DE L'AULNE	16,7%
40	QUARTERON AGILE	FAKIR DES AUBRETS	TULIRA ANNIE	MORSTIRENN	16,5%

Figure 68. Results of the production of Cannon Ball stallions. Daniel Chupin.

114 stallions, from the Cannon Ball lineage, met my selection criteria. The analysis of the results shows the presence of 4 Irish stallions in the first 10 places. For Currachmore Cashel and his son Coolillaun Cushlawn, their presence in the Top 10 is all the more remarkable as their results are based on the birth of only 20 to 26 foals over only two breeding seasons at the Séguret stud. The presence of 50 stallions born in France for the Blue line is very satisfying for the French breeding.

Figure 69. Garryhinch Millrace. Photo LM Philibert.

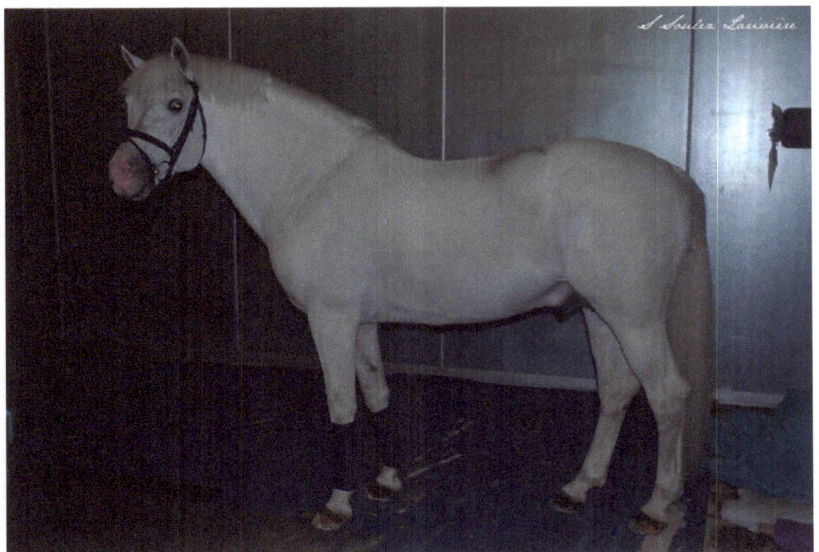

Figure 70. Dexter Leam Pondi. Photo Sophie Soulez Larivière.

Figure 71. Quillon. Photo Louis Marie Philibert.

Figure 72. Idénoir presented by Hubert Laurent in Tours. Photo Daniel Chupin.

Figure 73. Funambule II. Photo Sophie Soulez Larivière.

Figure 74. Punch du Mesnil presented by Olivier Vérove. Photo Pascal Wandon.

THE RED LINE: CONNEMARA BOY

Michael O'Neil was a large livestock dealer who lived in Clifden. At the time the Association was formed, he owned a good herd of Connemara ponies and some of them were registered. The first was Connemara Boy, a gray pony born in 1922. He was inspected at the Recess show in 1925 and was purchased by the Association. He was sent to Thomas de Courcey in 1926 where he stayed for a while before moving to John Walsh in Kilkerrin. Martin Lydon describes him as a strong-boned, well-built pony with a tough character and a willingness to do anything. He has certainly established a line of very tough, hardy males through his son Heather Bell and great-grandson Dun Lorenzo. Connemara Boy won the stallion class three times in 1926, 1930, and 1931 and was on the stallion list for ten years. He died of tetanus two years after leaving the Association.

Figure 75. Connemara Boy. Source Shrouded in Mist.

HEATHER BELL was a foal subsidized by the Association who was born in 1929 near Toombeola. He was later purchased by the Association. Heather Bell worked in Clifden, Claddaghduff, and Glentrasna between 1933 and 1942. While in Glentrasna, he helped Ed Gonneely with his work building roads in the Maam Valley. It was hard work. He was sold in late 1942 in Leitrim County. Many of his descendants were dun. His greatest gift was his son Dun Heath.

DUN HEATH is out of the small mare Winnie Nee located at Shinanagh, near Clifden. He was purchased by the Association as a yearling in 1947. Martin Lydon always made mental notes of the stallions that roamed his district, never missed a show, and cherished the stud books and show catalogs he owned. Dun Heath had more quality than most of the early stallions and his foals were always well placed in shows. Through his son Dun Lorenzo and grandson Carna Dun, he probably played as important a role as any other stallion.

DUN LORENZO The Currans of Ardmore in Carna, owned good mares. Dun Lorenzo's dam, Draighneann Donn, was born in 1930. She was bay brown[48] and stood 139 cm tall. Dun Lorenzo was stationed at six different centers for a long time. Josie Conroy had a great admiration for him. Dun Lorenzo won the stallion class in 1945. He was sold to Mrs. Westaway of Ballina, Mayo County. He spent a short happy retirement there before being euthanized due to colic.

MAC DARA was born in the dunes in Dolan out of the mare Dolan Rose who was by Lavalley Star. She was registered as blue-gray, but her son by Dun Lorenzo inherited his sire's coat and was dun. Born in 1949, he was purchased by the Association. He won the stallion class of the Association's show three times, in 1954, 1956, and 1958. He surpassed all previous records by remaining on the stallion list from 1952 to 1972, a full twenty years. After leaving Connemara, he spent two years in semi-retirement with Jimmy Jones in Carlow.

Figure 76. Ormond Oliver a son of Mac Dara, J. Jones, Daniel and Pierre Chupin. Photo Élevage de Briacé.

DUN AENGUS his Dame Rose of Killola was sired by the Thoroughbred, Winter. Dun Aengus was bred by P. K. Joyce of Clifden and was a rather insignificant little pony, pale cream. Dun Aengus is the sire of Atlantic Curragh, Mac Duff, and Kimble, all three founding stallions of the Red line in France. He was therefore a determining stallion for French breeding.

---

[48] Brown is used by some breed studbooks to describe dark bay. There is no distinct allele that darkens a bay's coat to dark brown, but it is not the cause of all forms of dark bay. Informally, the term 'brown' is applied to many distinct coats. Most often, horses described by casual observers as 'brown' are actually bay or chestnut. In the absence of DNA testing, chestnut and bay can be distinguished from each other by examining the mane, tail and limbs for the presence of black spots.

Figure 77. Abbeyleix Owen at Thomas O'Brien, Canal Stage, Ballinafad. Photo Daniel Chupin.

Figure 78. Mac Duff.
Photo Louis Marie Philibert.

Ranking	Stallions	Father	Paternal grandmother	Dame	% PI 120 and +
1	KINVARA JINGLE	MURRISK	GREY GIRL	KINVARA LILY	50,0%
2	NAUGHTY V. G. JANSHOF	ATLANTIC CURRAGH	ATLANTIC SURF	FABIANS PHILOMENA	39,8%
3	JINGLE-LILY	MURRISK	GREY GIRL	KINVARA LILY	35,3%
4	LEADERSHIP	NAUGHTY V. G. JANSHOF	FABIANS PHILOMENA	VINCA II	34,0%
5	QUIMPER III	MAC DUFF	CALLOWFEENISH PRIDE	HOLY	33,6%
6	ASHFIELD AENGUS	DUN AENGUS	ROSE OF KILLOLA	ATLANTIC SURF	29,2%
7	GRICHET ADEL	ATLATIC CURRAGH	ATLANTIC SURF	POLL'S STORY	28,8%
8	GILL DE BRIACE	TYNAGH DE BRIACE	NANCY KATE	COOSHEEN MUFFIN	23,1%
9	BUNOWEN PADDY	SILVER SHADOW	POETIC MOONLIGHT	IRISHTOWN BEAUTY	22,6%
10	ABBEYLEIX MOON	DUN AENGUS	ROSE OF KILLOLA	BLUE MOON	22,2%
11	TYNAGH DE BRIACE	NIPON II	HOLY	NANCY KATE	21,5%
12	BULLIT DE COISELET	KHAN DE COISELET	CARRAGH BAY	MERVYN FIRE FLY	20,3%
13	GINVARA DU PREUIL	KINVARA JINGLE	KINVARA LILY	NOVA II	20,0%
14	BLACKTHORN STAR	ABBEYLEIX OWEN	QUEEN OF DIAMONDS	STAR OF BLACKTOWN	19,5%
15	CLOON EILE CASHEL	CLOONISLE CASHEL	CLOONISLE LADY	TOLKA BRIDGE	19,0%
16	MISTRAL DE BRIACE	NAUGHTY V. G. JANSHOF	FABIANS PHILOMENA	COOSHEEN MUFFIN	18,9%
17	JUARISTE DU MOULIN	ROCKY GRICHET	DUNAMOON	CRYSTAL DU MOULIN	18,8%
18	NIMBUS IV	MAC DUFF	CALLOWFEENISH PRIDE	PEGEEN	18,5%
19	KHAN DE COISELET	CARRAGH KINSMAN	STORY OF TYNAGH LND	CARRAGH BAY	16,7%
20	ROCKY GRICHET	GRICHET ADEL	POLL'S STORY	DUNAMOON	16,3%
21	LOUP YES TU TARTIFUME	NAUGHTY V. G. JANSHOF	FABIANS PHILOMENA	VIOLINE II	14,8%
22	VADOR SHADOW DU GITE	SILVER SHADOW	POETIC MOONLIGHT	NINA DE GARENNE	14,3%
23	MEXICO	QUIMPER III	HOLY	FINOLA OF LAPS	14,3%
24	SILVER SHADOW	CLOONISLE CASHEL	CLOONISLE LADY	POETIC MOONLIGHT	13,0%
25	SIRUS TOUL AR C'HOAT	ERVELOUGH OISIN	CREGDUFF HEATHER	ALIDA DE ST THOMAS	13,0%
26	O IA SONN	IF YOU PLEASE LADY	CHECKPOINT MUFFET	JOIE DE RAVARY	12,7%
27	STENTOR PONDI	LEHID CANAL PRINCE	LEHID COLLEEN	VOYEL DE BEAUCHAMP	12,5%
28	NIPON II	MAC DUFF	CALLOWFEENISH PRIDE	HOLY	11,9%
29	STORMY WEATHER	ATLANTIC STORM	FLASH GRIL	ATLANTIC SURF	11,9%
30	MOR VEN STORM	ATLANTIC STORM	FLASH GRIL	GARAFIN	11,2%
31	LEHID CANAL PRINCE	OISIN	SILVER FORT	LEHID COLLEEN	11,0%
32	AREM DE BEAUREIL	LEGREY	LOVELY MAREE	SAFIR DE BEAUCHAMP	10,6%
33	FLANAGAN DUFF	QUIMPER III	HOLY	ULTIMA LINEA	9,8%
34	PILATUS DE VINCA	NAUGHTY V. G. JANSHOF	FABIANS PHILOMENA	VINCA II	9,1%
35	HURLEVAN DU PREUIL	KINVARA JINGLE	KINVARA LILY	NORMA	8,8%
36	ERVELOUGH OISIN	SLISNEOIR	MILFORD WREN	CREGDUFF HEATHER	8,5%
37	ALTO DE FERRALS	GRICHET ADEL	POLL'S STORY	GLENLO CUSTARD	8,3%
38	QUIZAQUO DU BRANA	KANGOO D'HARRIETEN	JAVA DU COURANT	AGATHA	7,7%
39	LUSTY	AURORA	SANDY	KILTOOMER ROSIE	7,3%
40	LEGREY	AURORA	SANDY	LOVELY MAREE	7,1%

Figure 79. Results of the Connemara Boy line stallions. Daniel Chupin.

Of the 48 stallions representing the Connemara Boy line, 31 were born in France. If Mac Duff has strongly marked this lineage, Murrisk, and the mare Kinvara Lily have produced two exceptional stallions, Kinvara Jingle and Jingle Lily. Kinvara Jingle leads the way with 50% of her production indexed at 120 and above, and nearly 10% of her production indexed at 140 and above! The import of Naughty V. G. Janshof by the Syndicat Linaro was a success and brought a lot to the Red line, the Connemara Boy line.

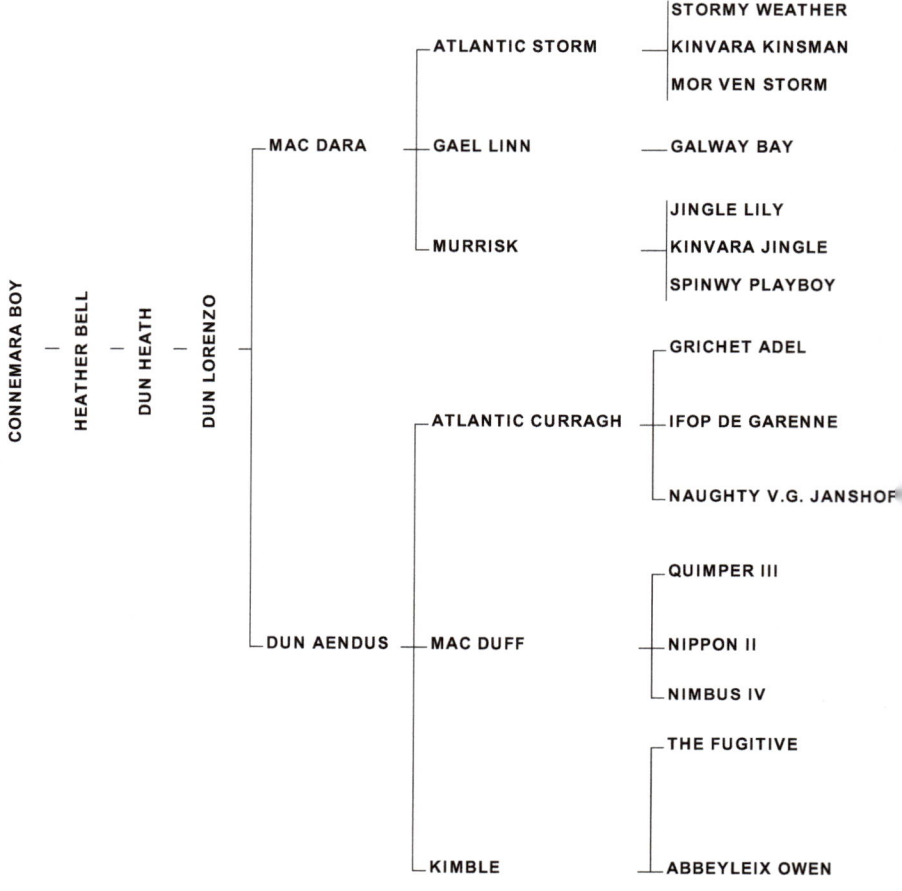

Figure 80. Connemara Boy lineage of French stallions. Daniel Chupin.

CARRAGH KINSMAN —————KHAN DE COISELET ——BULLIT DE COISELET

LUSTY

AURORA ————LEGREY ——AREM DE BEAUREIL

JARS

HURLEVAN DU PREUIL
GINVARA DU PREUIL

ROCKY GRICHET ——JUARISTE DU MOULIN
ALTO DU FERRALS

LEADERSHIP
MISTRAL DE BRIACE
LOUP YES TU TARTIFUME
FLANAGAN DUFF   PILATUS DE VINCA
GRIMM DUFF
MEXICO

GILL DE BRIACE
TYNAGH DE BRIACE   TORNADO DE BRIACE

ORINCE DU VAL

IF YOU PLEASE LADY ——O IA SONN

SLISNEOIR ——ERVELOUGH OISIN
CUCHULAINN
OISIN ——LEHID CANAL PRINCE

CLOONISLE CASHEL   SILVER SHADOW ——BONOWEN PADDY

CLOON EILE CASHEL
GLENCARRIG PRINCE   COOSHEEN FINBARR

Figure 81. Quimper III. Photo Louis Marie Philibert.

Figure 82. Kinvara Jingle. Photo Hiago-Coupier.

Figure 83. Silver Shadow. Photo Élevage d'Albran.

Figure 84. Gill de Briacé was ridden by Maeva Normand in the CCE Amazone event at Le Lion d'Angers. Photo Daniel Chupin.

Figure 85. Mistral de Briacé. Photo Daniel Chupin.

Figure 86. Mistral de Briacé. Photo Sophie Soulez Larivière.

Figure 87. Best Shadow Mélody, Supreme Champion 2014. Photo by Mélody Breeding.

Figure 88. Grichet Adel, photo private collection Willem Goedhart.

THE GREEN LINE: MOUNTAIN LAD

MOUNTAIN LAD In 1938, the Association had to give up hope of finding a new, quality native stallion. Many had been presented for inspection, but few had been retained. A drastic operation to cull unsuitable stallions had to take place while the registrations were being made. Jack Bolger went to the Galway Fair on the day that Malcolm Wallace brought in a wild ten-year-old stallion to sell. The stallion had never seen a halter and Jack described him as "as wild as a deer." Malcolm owned a mountain range extending over 810 acres in the back of Inverin[49] and on which he raised a large herd of Connemara ponies, as his sire had done before him. After buying it, Jack let it go, by mistake, on his return from Galway. It took three men a day's work to catch him. Finally, a trap made with rope was set in the corner of a field and the stallion was driven into it. Tempers flared, patience ran out, and once caught, he was tied to a tree for several hours. In the following days, the stallion was bought back by the Association and changed his name to Mountain Lad. He was immediately put on the list of approved stallions, but he was not registered until 1939. Born in 1928, his characteristics indicate that he was gray, although Jack called him chestnut.

Since then, this line has often worn a chestnut coat in the early years of its life; the gray seems to intrude and take over with age. This is almost unheard of in the horse world where once a chestnut, always a chestnut. It's strange how often the Connemara breed has been described as being primarily chestnut in the past. Association records show that Mountain Lad died in 1939.

He left behind a line of incredibly resilient and valuable males. This is a small strain that has always been on the verge of extinction. The strength of this line has always been its males who are known to produce ponies with great jumping abilities.

TULLY LAD was born in 1938 to Tully Beauty and grew up in a free-ranging herd like his father. He was registered to Malcolm Wallace in 1943 but remained in the mountains until Jack bought him in 1949. He was a little less wild than his sire when he arrived in Oughterard. It wasn't long before Jack sold him to the Association. They left him in Jack's care for one season. He was then put out to pasture for a year with no reason given.

In 1952 he was sent to James Grealish at Oranmore for two years before being transferred to John de Courcey in 1954 for two more years, and to Martin Walsh at Snabo for one year in 1955. In 1956, he was sold to P. Treacy near Gort who shortly thereafter sold him to Paddy Lally. Stallion records show that he was put down in 1961 at the age of twenty-three. He spent only six of those twenty-three years on the Association's list, two of which were beyond the reach of most breeders in Connemara.

---

[49] Inverin is located between Spiddle and Rossaveel.

Tully Lad lost an eye at one point in his career, which became his trademark. He was always referred to as the "one-eyed black stallion". Those who knew him remarked that he was a Connemara pony of "tough stock[50] " and it seems that those bred on Wallace's mountain were indeed tough and that this valuable characteristic was passed down from generation to generation. Tully Lad had forty-four registered offspring, including five stallions.

TULLY GREY was born in Carna in 1957, his Dame was Cait ni Dhnibhit, a mare by Dun Lorenzo. Tully Grey spent all his life with the Harrold family of Mullingar. Thomas Harrold had nine daughters, each of whom learned to ride and jump with this amazing pony. In the 1960's he was placed three years in a row in the Ballsbridge show jumping competition. He could follow the Foxhounds[51] from Longford or Westmeath all day. He could also win a pony race at the end of a long day of competition or shine in all types of gymkhana events. Since he spent his entire life in Longford County, he was used very little.

THUNDER was never an Association's stallion and was bought at weaning from Michael Walsh by Jim Lee, who then sold him to John Brennan. John Brennan had good mares at his home in Fort Lorenzo on Taylor Hill in Galway. John Brennan was aware of her genetic value. Irene Grey, one of his mares, produced Thunderbolt in 1963. He became spotted grey. He was registered chestnut, which John said was his coat as a two-year-old.

Figure 89. Thunderbolt in England at the home of Mr. and Mrs. Williams, Cocum Farm, 1987. Photo Daniel Chupin.

---

[50] Strong, resistant, and tough could also be used.

[51] The English Foxhound is a breed of dog originating from the United Kingdom. It is a large, powerful and well-proportioned hound, created for fox hunting.

Figure 90. Dale Haze in 1984, age 1. Photo by Daniel Chupin.

Figure 91. Padraic Hynes presenting Canal Cormac. Photo by Daniel Chupin.

Figure 92. Hazy Dawn at 1-year-old at the Clifden show. Photo Daniel Chupin.

Ranking	Stallions	Father	Paternal grandmother	Dame	% PI 120 and +
1	ESPOIR KERHAMONIC	GALWAY DE LA DIVE	EASTER THORN	RATZKI GUERNADRAN	33,0%
2	COCUM THUNDER BOY	THUNDERBOLT	IRENE GREY	COCUM BELLA DONNA	21,0%
3	LUSTY DU BAILLY	HARRIS DE LA DIVE	EASTER BALL	GRACEFUL GUIDE	18,6%
4	GALWAY DE LA DIVE	BAMBU	SLIGO ROSE	EASTER THORN	18,6%
5	OURAGAN DU RULGOAT	CYRANO PONDI	WHITE GRANITE	JEANNIE AR CRANO	16,7%
6	CYRANO PONDI	GALWAY DE LA DIVE	EASTER THORN	WHITE GRANITE	16,6%
7	ICE'N'BLUE TIME	COCUM THUNDER BOY	COCUM BELLA DONNA	O'MAMMY BLUE	15,8%
8	KEFIR DE L'ETANG	COCUM THUNDER BOY	COCUM BELLA DONNA	COLOMBINE	15,8%
9	POMPON DE JAX	GALWAY DE LA DIVE	EASTER THORN	JAVA	15,5%
10	SPINWAY PIRATE	SPINWAY COMET	SPINWAY CAILIN	SPINWAY BOUNTY	14,3%
11	PHARAWAY DES TOUCHES	GALWAY DE LA DIVE	EASTER THORN	IN LOVE DE L'AULNE	13,3%
12	THEOREME DE JAX	POMPOM DE JAX	JAVA	MILTON BREEZE	12,5%
13	SIMBA DE KERDUFF	GALWAY DE LA DIVE	EASTER THORN	NECTARINE	11,1%
14	URIANO DE L'AMBRE	CYRANO PONDI	WHITE GRANITE	ARIANE DE LA DIVE	10,0%
14	HARRIS DE LA DIVE	BAMBU	SLIGO ROSE	EASTER BALL	10,0%
14	JAMAI DE L'AUBIER	COCUM THUNDER BOY	COCUM BELLA DONNA	MILADY DE RAVARY	10,0%
15	BAIKAL DES EVIERES	HARRIS DE LA DIVE	EASTER BALL	LAVANDE DU PEUX	9,1%
16	CINDY DE LA DIVE	SILVER STORM	WINDY EVENING STAR	IRISH PEARL	8,2%
17	JOLI GOOD DE KERLAN	CYRANO PONDI	WHITE GRANITE	FASCINATION MELODY	7,7%
18	INNELLAN THUNDERBIRD	THUNDERBOLT	IRENE GREY	INNELLAN LARK	6,8%
19	DREAM DE LA DIVE	SILVER STORM	WINDY EVENIG STAR	IRISH PEARL	6,3%
20	PAPS LATE	COCUM THUNDER BOY	COCUM BELLA DONNA	IOLICK LATE	5,6%
21	QERWAN DE L'AUBIER	COCUM THUNDER BOY	COCUM BELLA DONNA	MILADY DE RAVARY	5,0%
22	CAORANBEG CHAMP	MOORLAND SNOWY RIVER	EASTER TRIXIE	GALLOWSTOWN BIBI	3,4%
23	GORKY DE LA DIVE	BAMBU	SLIGO ROSE	STREAMSTOWN DREAM	3,2%
24	BUNOWEN CASTLE MICK	LAERKENS CASCADE DAWN	LEARKENS CAMILLE	DOOHULLA LUCKY STAR	3,2%
25	TOTEM DU MARTRAY	SPINWAY PIRATE	SPINWAY BOUNT	MELDIE DU MARTRAY	2,9%
26	BAMBU	TULLY GREY	CAIT NI DHUIBHIR	SLIGO ROSE	

Figure 93. Results of the production of the Mountain Lad line stallions. Daniel Chupin.

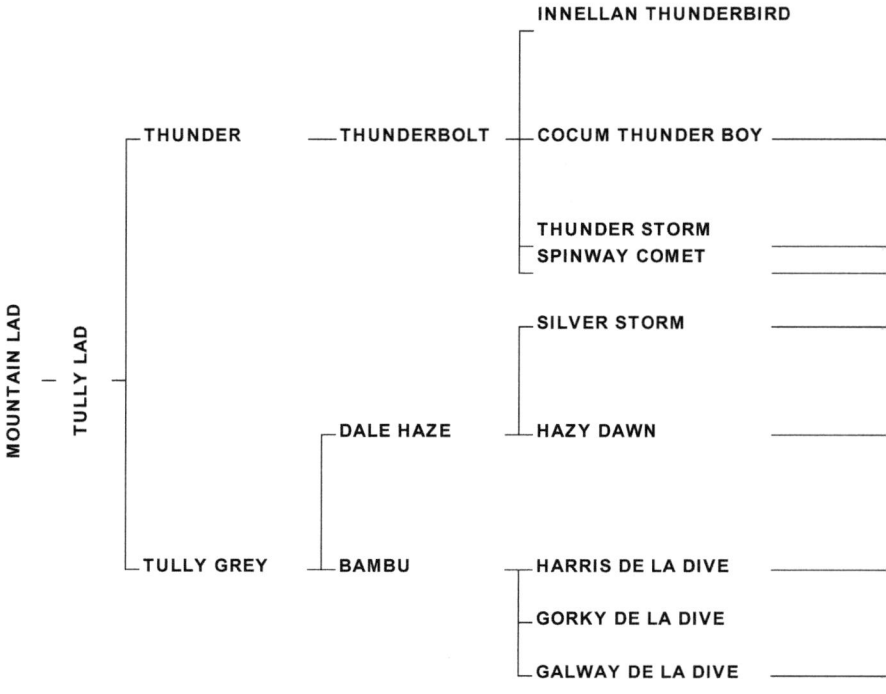

Figure 94. Mountain Lad line of French stallions. Daniel Chupin.

KEFIR DE L'ETANG
ICE'N'BLUE TIME
CARUSO MELODY
PAPS LATE
QERWAN DE L'AUBIER
JAMAI DE L'AUBIER

SLANEY
SPINWAY PIRAT　　　　　　　　TOTEM DU MARTRAY

DREAM DE LA DIVE
CINDY DE LA DIVE

FREDERICKMINDE HAZY MERL　　KIPPURE ALKATRAZ

MOY HAZY COVE　　　　　　　　KILLYON KING

LAERKENS CASCADE DAWN　　　　MOORLAND SNOWY RIVER　　CAORANBEG CHAMP

　　　　　　　　　　　　　　　　BUNOWEN CASTLE MICK
BAIKAL DES EVIERES　　　　　　D'ARCY TOBY
LUSTY DU BAILLY

POMPON DE JAX　　　　　　　　THEOREME DE JAX

　　　　　　　　　　　　　　　　URIANO DE L'AMBRE
CYRANO PONDI　　　　　　　　　OURAGAN DU RULGOAT

ESPOIR KERHAMONIC　　　　　　JOLI GOOD DE KERLAN
PHARAWAY DES TOUCHES
SIMBA DE KERDUFF

This lineage is like the Connemara Boy lineage, very precious. It is only represented in France by 28 stallions, two of which are English and three Irish. Bambu has strongly marked this lineage. The importation of Cocum Thunder Boy was a success if we take into account the results of his production. I regret the return of the stallion Caoranbeg Champ to Ireland because I am convinced that he could have brought a lot to the French gene pool.

Figure 95. Cocum Thunder Boy, photo by Melody Breeding.

Figure 96. Caoranbeg Champ. Photo by Jeannine Marolleau.

INBREEDING AND OUTCROSSING

In 1940, the Association was faced with the harsh reality of how few male lines it had available. What was the alternative to outcrossing and if this direction was chosen, what bloodline should be used?

In volume V, it is written:

> *"There were sixteen stallions eligible for breeding to mares registered as Connemara ponies for the 1942 season. Thirteen of them are registered in the Connemara pony studbook. Of the three remaining stallions, one is a privately owned, strong-boned cob[52] Dynamite (II), the other is an Irish Draught, Skibbereen, owned by the Association. The Association also owns the English Thoroughbred Winter, a stallion registered as a grey horse measuring 160 cm. It has proposed to keep the offspring of a strictly limited number of pony mares covered by the Irish Thoroughbred and Draught stallions for observation. Given previous experience with foreign blood, it is not expected that many of the foals from these crosses will be retained for breeding, but the experiment should provide useful information."*

To alleviate the problem of inbreeding, the Irish Association engaged in outcrossing.

Before developing the measures used to introduce outside blood, I will explain as simply as possible these notions of inbreeding, and outcrossing.

ADVANTAGES AND DISADVANTAGES OF INBREEDING

Inbreeding is the mating of closely related ponies, such as dame/son, sire/daughter, sibling mating, and half-sibling mating. It is the crossing of animals that are more closely related than the average population. For breeders, it is a useful way to establish the characteristics of a breed. The pedigrees of some Connemara ponies show that many of their ancestors are closely related. To produce ponies that meet the breed type, breeders usually mate related animals that share desirable characteristics. Over time, sometimes only one or two generations, these traits will become homozygous (genetically consistent) and all of the inbred animal's offspring will inherit the genes for these traits.

---

[52] A cob is a small, stocky horse, intermediate between a pony, a saddle horse and a draught horse, used for farm work, driving and riding.

Line breeding is not a term used by geneticists, but comes from livestock breeding. It refers to lighter forms of inbreeding. Line breeding is still a form of inbreeding, that is, breeding within a family line, and includes cousin/cousin, aunt/nephew, niece/uncle, and grandparent/grandchild relationships. The difference between inbreeding and outbreeding may be defined differently for different species of animals and even for different breeds within the same species. It is complicated by the fact that an animal's half-brother can also be its sire!

Inbreeding presents potential problems. The limited gene pool caused by continuous inbreeding means that deleterious genes spread and the breed loses vigor. A controlled amount of inbreeding can be used to set desirable traits in livestock, such as milk yield, lean/fat ratio, growth rate, etc. In human terms, inbreeding is considered incest; ponies do not have incest taboos.

Here are some of the terms used by breeders.

Homozygous means that one has inherited the same gene for a particular characteristic from both parents. Barring random mutation, 100% of the offspring of a homozygous individual will inherit that gene. Inbreeding increases homozygosity by fixing a particular trait. Purebred animals have a high degree of homozygosity compared to crossbred animals. The idea of purebred animals is that they should breed true. When a purebred animal is mated with another of the same breed, the offspring will have uniform characteristics and resemble the parents.

Heterozygous means having inherited from each parent a different gene for a particular characteristic. 50% of the offspring of a heterozygous individual will inherit one form and 50% of the other. Carefully controlled outcrossing increases heterozygosity for selected traits by introducing new genes into the hybrid offspring.

Heterosis is the scientific term for the vigor of hybrids. There may be bad genes that produce less vigorous individuals in the homozygous state because the good genes were eliminated along with the undesirable traits; in theory, the "bad" genes could be eliminated by selection, but in practice, this does not seem to happen. The other theory is that it is enough to have a mixture of two different genes to get the desired effect because they complement each other in some way; highly inbred animals lack this diversity and have a less efficient immune system.

INBREEDING IN FREE-RANGING HERDS

In some cases, inbreeding occurs naturally. An isolated wild colony (this was certainly the case in some areas of Connemara), can become very inbred, especially if a dominant male mate with his sisters, then with his daughters and granddaughters. When he is ousted, it will most likely be by his son or grandson, thus continuing the inbreeding. The effect of any deleterious gene is felt in subsequent generations, as the majority of the offspring inherit these genes. Therefore, it can be assumed that all purebred animals will eventually become non-viable due to inbreeding and breeders must strive to maintain type while slowing the deleterious effects of selective breeding.

MEASURING INBREEDING

Inbreeding is measured and expressed by the coefficient of inbreeding (COI) on a scale of 0 to 1. It is widely used in the breeding of domestic animals, both pets and farm animals. A COI of 0 = no inbreeding; a COI of 0.25 = 25% inbreeding (usually brother-sister) and a COI of 0.01 = 1% inbreeding. In livestock breeding, the term "inbred" refers to highly inbred animals with a high COI.

OUTCROSSING

Outcrossing is the mating of unrelated animals within the same breed. It brings new qualities or reintroduces lost qualities. Outcrossing brings vigor. The ponies remain "pure", even if there is less consistency and predictability in the offspring. Outcrossing is when the two parents are completely unrelated. In pedigree animals, this often means that there is no common ancestor behind either parent in a four or five-generation pedigree. In the Connemara pony, whose basic gene pool is small, this condition became impossible to fulfill, so the Irish used English Thoroughbreds, an Arabian, Hunter, and Irish Draught stallions.

PREPOTENCY

This is the ability of a parent to pass on traits to their offspring so that the likelihood of their offspring resembling the parent is higher than usual, so a horse is said to "brand" its offspring. Inbred offspring generally show more prepotency than outbred offspring because they have a greater number of homozygous gene pairs. This term is sometimes used to express the strength of a breed, lineage, or stallion. This term is also used by some breeders to hide their laziness about exploiting their animals outside the show ring. They consider that their ponies have "it in the genes", in the blood. But this is not true. To succeed, all Connemara ponies must work.

The debate on inbreeding is often the same: should a breed be based on genotype (the genes it has inherited) or on phenotype (the type, despite more than four generations of outcrossing)? The Irish have worked on genotype and phenotype by ruthlessly selecting a few male products of outcrossing.

Inbreeding is a double-edged sword. On the one hand, a certain amount of inbreeding can fix and improve the type to produce excellent animals. On the other hand, too much inbreeding can limit the gene pool so that the breed loses its vigor. Breeds in the early stages of development are the most vulnerable, as numbers are small and ponies may be closely related to each other. It will always be up to the responsible breeder to balance inbreeding and crossbreeding with unrelated ponies to maintain the overall health of the Connemara breed. Another element to consider is DNA typing which no longer allows some Irish breeders to "tinker" as they did in the past. Thanks to outcrossing, the inbreeding coefficient of the French herd is currently 2.54%.

In the report "Characterisation of the Connemara Pony Population in Ireland" by Deirdre Feely, Patrick Brophy, and Katherine Quinn, the authors present their findings on the racial composition of the Connemara pony:

> " The breed composition of the reference population a small number of Thoroughbred, Arab and Irish Draught stallions sired registered Connemara Ponies in the 1940s and 1950s. There were also two stallions in the pedigree file that were known to have Welsh Cob genes. The proportion of genes that the animals in the reference populations possessed, originating from these stallions, was estimated to obtain the influence that the Thoroughbred, Arab, and Irish Draught had on the reference populations:

> The Thoroughbred was the most influential of the foreign breeds, accounting for approximately 6% of the genes of the reference populations. The Arab, Irish Draught and Welsh Cob accounted for approximately 3.7%, 1.2%, and 0.9% of the genes of the reference populations respectively. Approximately 88% of the genes in the animals in the reference population are assumed to be Connemara Pony.

> The majority of the animals in the reference populations possessed at least some Welsh Cob, Thoroughbred and Arab genes. Approximately 50% of the animals in the reference populations had Irish Draught in their ancestry."

Below, I have attached two graphs summarizing the situation of French breeding. The first one represents the average inbreeding coefficient per lineage on the selected stallions.

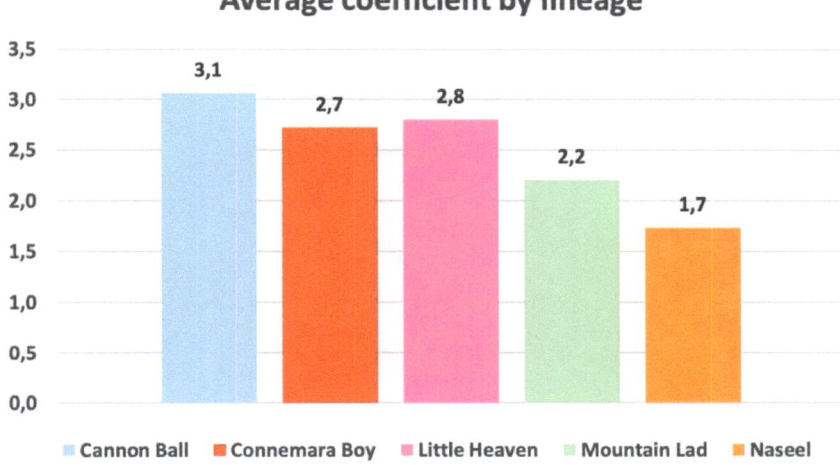

Figure 97. Diagram representing the average inbreeding coefficient by lineage for the 196 selected stallions. Daniel Chupin.

The second graph shows the evolution of the inbreeding coefficient by taking the average of the lines Cannon Ball. Connemara Boy and Little Heaven. I did not take into account the lines Mountain Lad and Naseel because of insufficient data. But this would not change the results very much due to the low number of stallions. This is a logical trend, as the Connemara studbook is closed. So we have to be careful with our breeding choices and take into account this inbreeding coefficient.

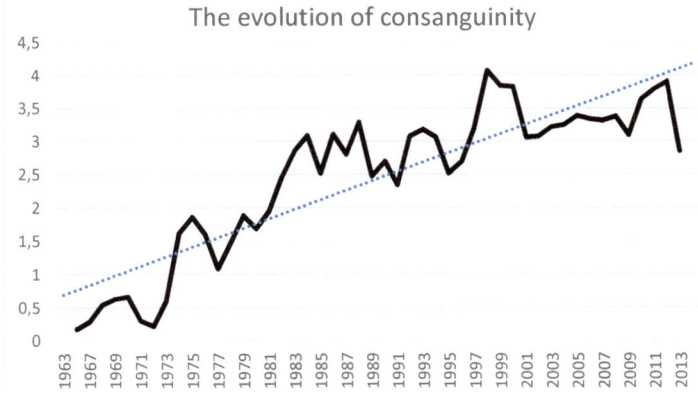

Figure 98. Graph showing the evolution of inbreeding for the 196 selected stallions. Daniel Chupin.

- Poetic Justice whose inbreeding coefficient is 9.28%, is a linebreeding on Camlin Cicada (Carna Dun) lineage Little Heaven and Carna Bobby lineage Cannon Ball.
- His sire line is the Little Heaven line, but his major ancestor is Carna Bobby (Cannon Ball line).
- He has 18.75% Carna Bobby blood and 9.37% Camlin Cicada blood (including 7.8% Carna Dun blood).

ANOTHER INTERESTING EXAMPLE: FLEUR DU MOULIN D'EAU

- Fleur is a linebreeder on Coosheen Muffin. Coosheen Muffin is her paternal granddame and also her maternal great-granddame.
- Her inbreeding coefficient is 11.14 %. Her major ancestors are Carna Bobby 20% (Blue lineage); Dun Lorenzo 14% (Red lineage) and Carna Dun 13.7 % (Violet lineage).
- She has 3.5 PACE[53] points which is very good.

The first impression is to think that she will not be easy to cross! Her size, 139.5 cm is her main asset. Fleur du Moulin d'Eau, IPO 134 (0.83) in 2021, is one of the C ponies that runs on the D circuit. In 2021 she competed in show jumping on the classic circuit for six-year-old D ponies. Her size opens up many more crossing possibilities than most mares and above all it allows her to be crossed with stallions of 148 cm and more. By crossing her, for example, with the following stallions Impérial du Blin, Quartil des Foltiers, Caruso Melody, or Borsalino Family, the foal will have an inbreeding coefficient between 3 and 5%.

With these two examples, I wanted to show you that you have to take into account all the branches of the family tree.

The calculator available on Harasire is an interesting help, but not sufficient. It is up to the breeder to analyze the possibilities of crossing, and to make choices! And it is often difficult.

THE USE OF THE ENGLISH THOROUGHBRED

The use of English Thoroughbreds was decisive in regenerating the Connemara pony. Thoroughbred refers to all horses whose ancestors are from the first English studbook.

All the Thoroughbreds in the world belong to a single breed founded in England. The variations of Thoroughbreds: French, German, American, or Irish correspond more to different choices of selection within the same breed.

---

[53] PACE points allow a mare to benefit from PACE premiums. The calculation of the number of PACE points depends on the sport performance of the brood mares and their offspring.

The American Thoroughbred, more massive and robust, is suitable for short distances on the flat, as Americans prefer fast and spectacular races. The French Thoroughbred, more nervous, is more suitable for long-distance races (2800 m and more).

The Irish Thoroughbred is most at home on Steeple-Chases certainly because of their vigor, power, and jumping ability. They are often considered true jumpers, Steeple chasers, and Hurdlers. At the age of two, the horses intended for endurance races were less demanding. It was not until they were three years old that they had to show what they could do. Lower training costs allowed the endurance and stamina of four and even five-year-olds to be tested. Only the horses with the best physical and mental abilities succeeded. Through this system, Ireland produced a large number of flawless, well-proportioned horses that were free of nervousness and imbalance.

The breeding of flat racehorses is nowadays international, erasing the distinctions between countries.

WINTER (Manna X Snow Maiden) came from a very classical background. He ran on the flat as a two- and three-year-old and was placed seven times before winning the Killiney Plate over 1000 meters at Phoenix Park. He then ran unsuccessfully over hurdles. He was presented to the Association in 1941 at the age of six. The Association was not very lucky with WINTER. After a season and a half with Jack Bolger, he died in 1943 of a ruptured liver, leaving only five registered descendants. Three of his daughters are known at the Connemara racetracks: Nancy Winter 1003, Rangoon, and Rose of Killola. He had one registered son.

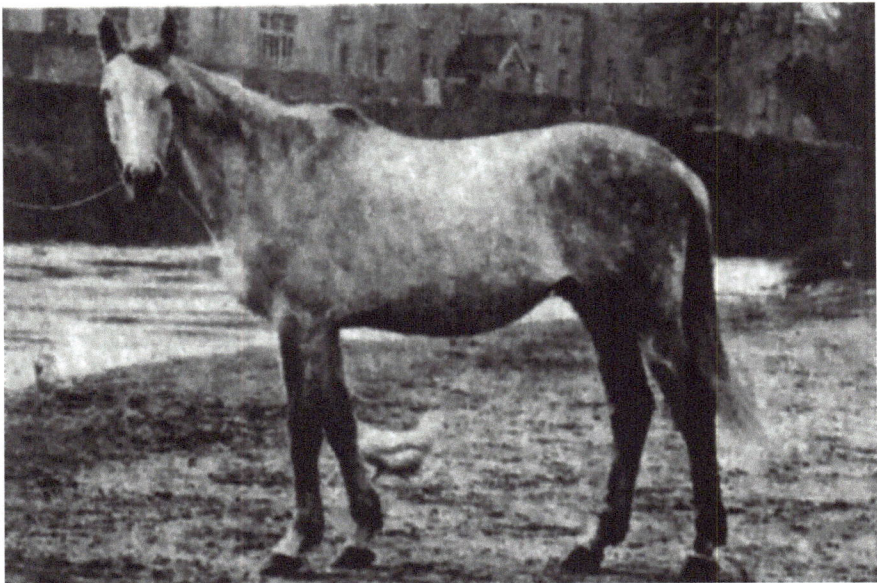

Figure 99. Winter. Source Shrouded in Mist.

CREGANNA WINTER Oranmore is a good distance from Oughterard, but Creganna Peggy born in 1936, a small chestnut mare who lived at Oranmore, was covered by Winter. In 1943, she produced a bay colt that was purchased by the Association the following year. He was not registered until 1946 and spent eleven years on their roster before being put down due to a broken hind leg in 1957. He had nearly fifty registered offspring, including six stallions. Mare owners have had every opportunity to use this stallion. He spent one season at Carna, one at Oughterard and one at Bunowen; then three at Bealadangen, one at Snabo, one at Oughterard, and two in his dame's hometown of Oranmore. Creganna Winter was not well known and used. His four best-known daughters were: Winter Heather, Winter Mollie, Winter Roche, and Honey Belle.

THE VIOLET LINEAGE: LITTLE HEAVEN

The Association had to decide to persevere with the use of Thoroughbreds and in December 1946, it purchased **Little Heaven** from Orchardstown Stud, in Clonmel[54] . He was only 152.5 cm tall.

Figure 100. Little Heaven. Source Shrouded in Mist.

---

[54] Clonmel is a town located in County Tipperary.

The Association presents Little Heaven:

> *"The small T.B. Little Heaven was recently purchased by the Society and he looks ideal for crossing with the Connemara pony . . . when carefully chosen stallions of a correct type are crossed with pony mares of good substance and quality it is likely to produce beneficial results."*

He was born in 1942, in a bay colour. He is out of Bala Hissar and Outport. He ran on the flat twice as a two-year-old and was not placed.

In the spring of 1947, he was sent to Jack Bolger and listed as "approved for Connemara mare service." In 1949, he was stationed at Clifden. In 1950, he went by trailer to Cashel and Carna on Saturdays. This allowed more breeders to use him. He was on the Association's list from 1947 to the end of 1951. In Vol. VII, this blunt statement was made: the small Thoroughbred stallion Little Heaven mentioned in Volume VI is eliminated. He was entitled to a strictly limited number of pony mares each season. By a recent decision of the Association's Board of Directors, his offspring can no longer be entered in the stud book. In 1952, the Association discovered that he had a cataract and castrated him. He was then sold on the Athenry market.

The Association's policy on stallions has always been uncompromising. As soon as a stallion was considered doubtful or unsuitable, it was removed from the from the list. The number of registered offspring is small, ten mares and his son Carna Dun.

CARNA DUN

Little Heaven's great legacy to the studbook was undoubtedly Carna Dun. Carna Dun had grown up on Birr Island, just off the coast of Ardmore. He was brought from the island to be shown as a two-year-old and with little preparation, he performed as if he had drunk a glass of potcheen[55]. He won his class and was sold to the Association. In 1952, Carna Dun won the stallion class at Clifden and was seconded by Carna Bobby and Mac Dara in 1953 and 1956.

He was not very handsome and perhaps a little too big and looked more like a small horse than a pony. But he was nevertheless robust despite his Thoroughbred origin. He lived the same hard life as all the stallions of the Association. In 1951 he was placed at Claddaghduff ; in 1952 he was sent to Errisbeg, where he spent two seasons before going to Carna for three seasons.

---

[55] Ancestor of the Irish whiskey, the potcheen is to Ireland what the absinthe is to France (degree of alcohol: between 60 % and 95 %).

In 1958 he went to Oughterard where he spent five seasons and then three final seasons in Connemara at Bunowen. In 1966 he was sold to James Palmer of Glenlo Abbey, near Galway, where he stayed until 1973 when he was twenty-five years old. He was sent to Paddy Foy in Westport before being shot.

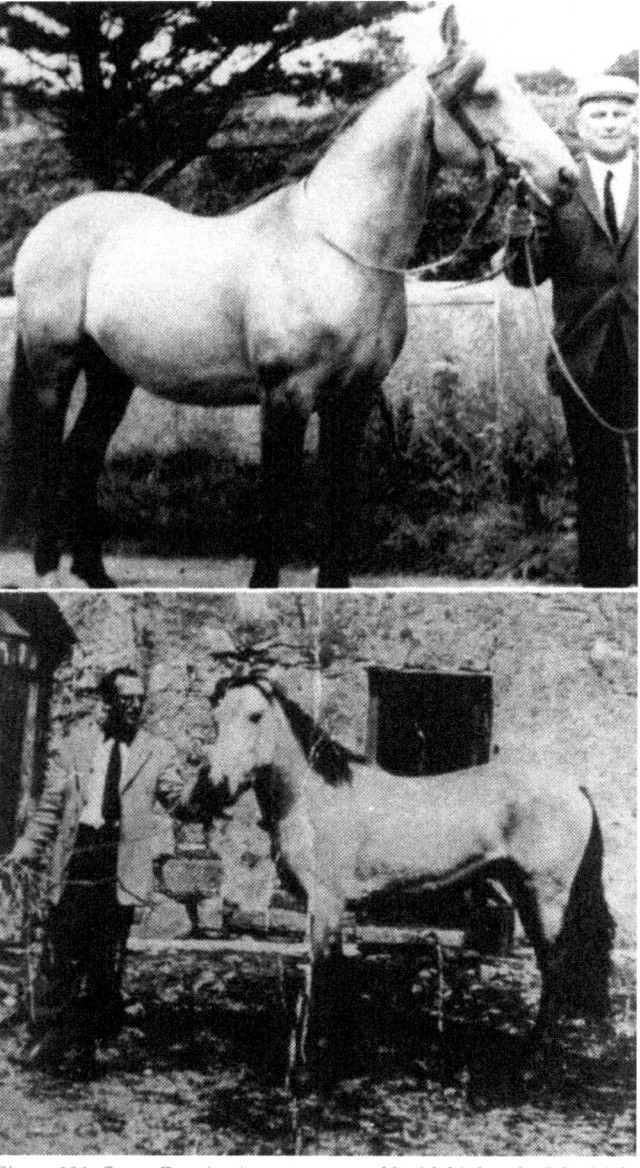

Figure 101. Carna Dun (top) as a two-year-old with his breeder John Mylote and (bottom) in 1965 at the age of seventeen. Source Shrouded in Mist.

Figure 102. 4-year-old chestnut Imperial du Blin 146cm at the National de Poitiers.
Photo Private collection Françoise Clémenceau.

Figure 103. Fort Doolin, presented by Louis Marie Philibert. Photo LM Philibert. Fort Doolin is a
great-grandson of Carna Dun by sire and dame.

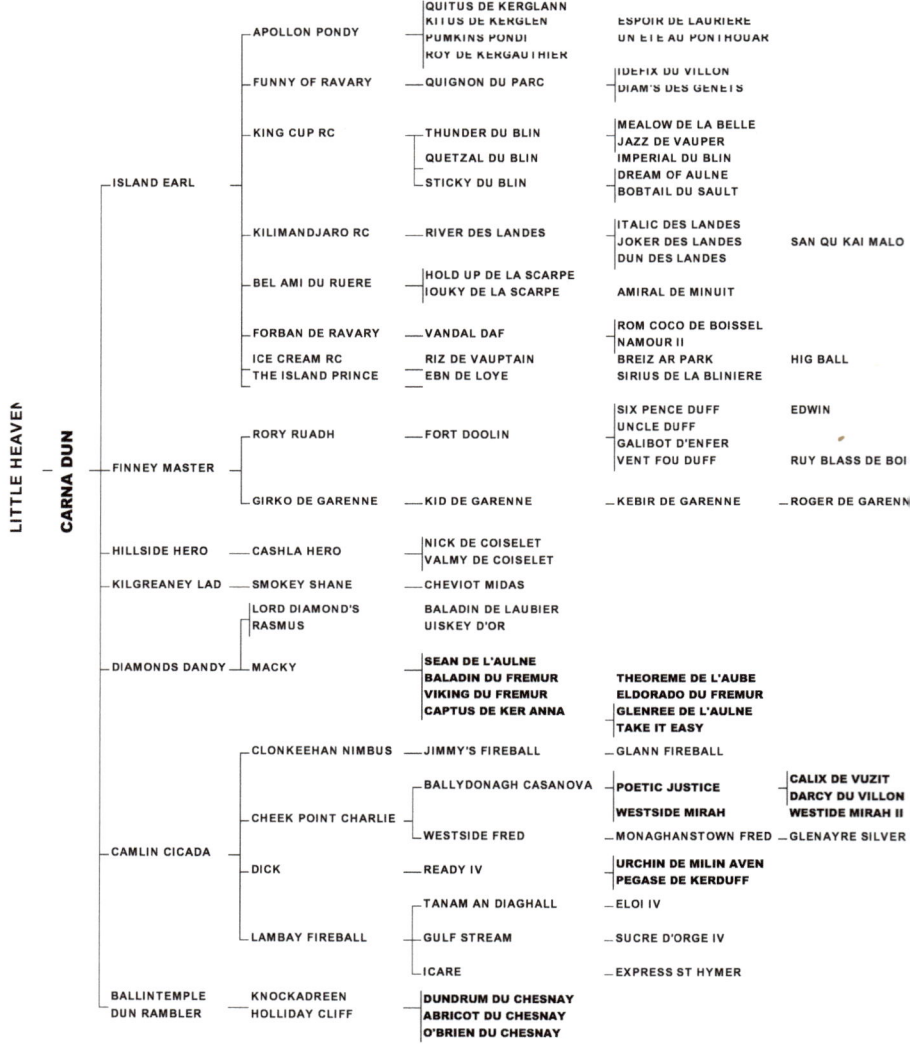

Figure 104. Little Heaven lineage of French stallions. Daniel Chupin.

Figure 105 (next page). Results of the production of stallions of the Little Heaven line. Daniel Chupin.

Ranking	Stallions	Father	Paternal grandmother	Dame	% PI 120 and +
1	PUMKINS PONDI	APOLLON PONDY	WHITE GRANITE	DAKOTA MELODY	41,4%
2	KID DE GARENNE	GIRKO DE GARENNE	VILLAGE DUN	CLONROSS COOL STAR	40,0%
3	MEALOW DE LA BELLE	THUNDER DU BLIN	FORT HELEN	ASTUCE DE LA BELLE	39,2%
4	QUARTZ DU BLIN	KING-CUP R.C	EASTER TROY	SHEEAUN STORM	37,5%
5	VERTGALAN DU RUERE	ISLAND EARL	HELPMATE	GANTY DELLA	37,0%
6	HABLEUR DE RAVARY	ISLAND EARL	HELPMATE	RAFORD LADYBIRD	36,9%
7	ROY DE KERGAUTHIER	APOLLON PONDY	WHITE GRANITE	DOUCHKA III	35,7%
8	VANDALE DAF	FORBAN DE RAVARY	GARRISTOWN STARLING	JOY OF VICTORY	35,2%
9	HELP DE LA SCARPE	BEL AMI DU RUERE	CAROLINE'S PET	MADELIA OF SCARPE	33,3%
10	KILKADY DARLING	RORY RUADH	FORT IRENE	BALLYNEW KATE	31,9%
11	AS DU BEGUE	GO DU PLANTAUREL	CASCADE OF ARROW	NUSTY MAUREMONT	30,9%
13	HIG BALL	BREIZ AR PARK	TINA AR PARK	JASMINE	30,0%
13	FRED DES RIOLES	LORD RAVARY	WHITE WINE	RIKA DE CHANTELOUP	30,0%
14	APOLLON PONDY	ISLAND EARL	HELPMATE	WHITE GRANITE	29,8%
15	READY IV	DICK	COISMEIGHMORE	LEHID SWEETHEART	29,3%
16	TAIWAN II	DICK	COISMEIGHMORE	SHIPTON MARA-WARRA	29,2%
16	KNOCKADREEN HOLIDAY CLIFF	BALLINTEMPLE DUN RAMBLI	MOONLIGHT RAMBLER	BOBBY'GIRL	29,2%
17	THUNDER DU BLIN	KING-CUP R.C	EASTER TROY	FORT HELEN	28,8%
18	UNCLE DUFF	FORT DOOLIN	FORT LADY	HONEY MOON	28,3%
19	VOLTEFACE DU RUERE	ISLAND EARL	HELPMATE	NEXT TO ME RAVARY	26,3%
20	SUCRE D'ORGE IV	GULF STREAM	PASSPORT	TULIRA HONEY	26,2%
21	KEBIR DE GARENNE	KID DE GARENNE	CLONROSS COOL STAR	KIM DE GARENNE	25,7%
22	JAZZ DE VAUPER	THUNDER DU BLIN	FORT HELEN	DAPHNE DE LA DIVE	25,0%
22	IMPERIAL DU BLIN	QUETZL DU BLIN	FORT HELEN	RIZINE	25,0%
23	STICKY DU BLIN	KING-CUP R.C	EASTER TROY	SHELA'S PAL	24,7%
24	BREIZ AR PARK	RIZ DE VAUPTAIN	CORA	TINA AR PARK	24,6%
25	EXPRESS ST HYMER	ICARE	PASSPORT	OPALE DE COISELET	24,4%
26	RIVER DES LANDES	KILIMANDJARO RC	ERRISLANNON HATTIE	LICORNE DE RAVARY	24,3%
27	FAKIR DE RAVARY	ISLAND EARL	HELPMATE	URRACHREE STAR	24,2%
28	FLASH DE CONQUET	GO DU PLANTUREL	CASCADE OF ARROW	NUSTY MAUREMONT	23,3%
29	FORBAN DE RAVARY	ISLAND EARL	HELPMATE	GARRISTOWN STARLING	22,6%
30	VLAVENT DU RUERE	ISLAND EARL	HELPMATE	IRA DE GARENNE	22,2%
31	O'BRIEN DU CHESNAY	KNOCKADREEN HOLIDAY CL	BOBBY'S GIRL	EARLY SUN RISE	22,1%
32	HE MAN DU BRANA	VOLTEFACE DU RUERE	NEXT TO ME RAVARY	BILONGO DU CHESNAY	21,7%
33	POWER BOY DU PARC	FUNNY OF RAVARY	SCREEN LADY	BOOGIE WOOGIE	21,6%
34	GALIBOT D'ENFER	FORT DOOLIN	FORT LADY	SON DU BOIS JULIEN	21,4%
35	ITALIC DES LANDES	RIVER DES LANDES	LICORNE DE RAVARY	DEESSE DES LANDES	20,6%
36	TANAM AN DIAGHALL	LAMBAY FIREBALL	CLONKEEHAN EASTER LI	LEM LILLY	20,5%
37	RASMUS	DIAMONDS DANDY	GLENLO BIDDY	OXENHOLM TENDERLY	20,4%
38	DIAM'S DES GENETS	QUIGNON DU PARC	BOOGIE WOOGIE	LIBELULLE	20,0%
38	ICARE	LAMBAY FIREBALL	CLONKEEHAN EASTER LI	PASSPORT	20,0%
38	ROM COCO DE BOISSEL	VANDALE DAF	JOY OF VICTORY	VENUS DU PETCH	20,0%
39	AMIRAL DE MINUIT	IOUKY DE LA SCARPE	NOUGATINE RAVARY	BRENDA DE MINUIT	18,8%
39	ELOI IV	TANAM AN DIAGHALL	LEAM LILLY	VINCA II	18,8%
40	MACKY	DIAMONDS DANDY	GLENLO BIDDY	LEHID SWEETHEART	18,6%
40	GLANN FIREBALL	JIMMY'S FIREBALL	BOBBY'S GIRL	CHARM BRACELET	18,6%
41	ISLAND EARL	CARNA DUN	DOUBLE DUN	HELPMATE	18,4%
42	QUIGNON DU PARC	FUNNY OF RAVARY	SCREEN LADY	BOOGIE WOOGIE	18,2%
42	NAMOUR II	JASMIN DE VILFIN	GIPSY DE LA DIVE	DOWAGH CINDERELLA	18,1%
43	LOOK AT ME	FINNEY MASTER	WINTER ROCHE	BRIGHT SUNBEAM	18,1%
44	QUETZAL DU BLIN	KING-CUP R.C	EASTER TROY	FORT HELEN	17,9%
45	VIKING DU FREMUR	MACKY	LEHID SWEETHEART	DOIREANN	17,6%
45	BEL AMI DU RUERE	ISLAND EARL	HELPMATE	CAROLINE'S PET	17,6%
45	ITKTAR DU MARTRAY	LOOK AT ME	BRIGHT SUNBEAM	PERLA DU MARTRAY	17,6%
46	FORT DOOLIN	RORY RUADH	FORT IRENE	FORT LADY	17,4%
47	SPARROW ALUINN	KNOCKADREEN HOLIDAY CL	BOBBY'S GRIL	POGEEN ALUINN	16,8%
48	MIDNIGHT DU BRANA	VOLTEFACE DE RUERE	NEXT TO ME RAVARY	VIKY DE LA DIVE	16,7%
49	UN PRINCE DU RUERE	ISLAND EARL	HELPMATE	WHITE GRANITE	16,6%
50	VALERA DU CHESNAY	KNOCKADREEN HOLIDAY CL	BOBBY'S GRIL	SHEPHARD'S BEAUTY	16,3%
50	GULF STREAM	LAMBAY FIREBALL	CLONKEEHAN EASTER LI	PASSPORT	16,3%

145

Figure 106. Meallow de la Belle. Photo Valérie Wilmot.

Figure 107. Pumkins Pondi. Photo of Pondi Breeding.

146

Figure 108. Apollon Pondy. Photo of Pondi Breeding.

Figure 109. Apollo Pondy. Photo Daniel Chupin.

Figure 110. Vent Fou Duff a son of Fort Doolin. Photo by Élevage d'Albran.

Little Heaven, an English Thoroughbred, has firmly established this line in France, thanks to his son Carna Dun. 134 stallions were selected, of which 122 were born in France. This line is the most represented in France. Island Earl, Finney Master, and Fort Doolin have strongly influenced the Violet line. Pumkins Pondi with only 59 births and 41.4 % of his production indexed at 120 or more of which 10 % indexed at more than 140 takes the lead. He is closely followed by Kid de Garenne a grandson of Finney Master with 40 % of his production indexed at 120+ and 17.6 % indexed at 140+ on only 85 births!

Figure 111. Knockadreen Holiday Cliff. Photo by Daniel Chupin.

The Irish Association also used a Purebred Arabian.

The Arabian Thoroughbred is a breed of saddle horse originating from the Middle East. The evolution of this breed can be traced over more than 2,000 years due to iconographic documents and archaeological findings. The Arabian Thoroughbred accompanied the expansion of Islam and reached other regions of Arab or European culture during wars or commercial exchanges. This horse has traditionally lived in a harsh desert climate and has developed exceptional resistance to the prolonged effort through its use as a war horse. Described as a small square horse with a concave profile, the Arabian shows great morphological and genetic variability depending on its origins. This breed is used in crossbreeding with many other horses, its improving effect having been established as a dogma. Due to relative inbreeding, the Purebred Arabian is affected by six diseases of genetic origin (I will let you pursue your research if you want to know more, but this subject is very vast...), two of which are fatal. The Arabian Thoroughbred is now known to be one of the best mounts in endurance competition.

Many breeders in Connemara found the Association's decision to reintroduce Arabian blood unacceptable. These genetics were viewed with disfavour and with some distrust. Nevertheless, there has always been a strong presence of Oriental blood in Connemara, whether it be Barb or Arabian. The Council had to decide that the blood introduced in the 1940s by the Irish Thoroughbred and Draft stallions was insufficient for the growth of the studbook. An Arabian stallion was chosen. This choice is sometimes questioned by some breeders. Rightly or wrongly, he provided the "outcross" that the Connemara pony needed.

THE ORANGE LINEAGE: NASEEL

NASEEL was a high-class Arabian stallion and for a long time, his offspring dominated the breeding shows in Ireland and England. He produced ponies for riding that had both quality and substance. He was born in 1936 by Raftan and Naxina. He was 145 cm tall and grey-white. Frances Lee Norman used him on her registered mare Western Lily 1522 in 1953. The Association asked Tim Cotter to visit Clonkeehan and inspect this colt. A letter containing his report, dated October 22, 1954, is on file with the Society. It reads as follows:

> *"He is well balanced, full of quality with good bone, good mover, nice head with pony character; he is darker (more golden cream) than Carna Dun but not so dark as Mac Dara; he has no trace of white or cream in the skin or about the eyes. The only faults I could see are, that he is a little short of bone above and below his hocks and that his neck is a little short but he holds his head very well. I could not fault his colour. I think he is a very good foal. He is well done though not looking his best yesterday as he had been dosed for worms."*

On this recommendation, he was purchased by the Association. The introduction of Arabian blood was implemented through the use of an Arabian thoroughbred son from a native mare, rather than allowing the use of an approved Arabian sire as had been done in the case of the Thoroughbred and the Irish Draught. This was a more conservative approach and, for a time at least, the use of this son himself was limited.

Figure 112. Naseel. Source Shrouded in Mist.

CLONKEEHAN AURATUM in 1956, as a two-year-old, Auratum was sent to Joseph Hoade in Barna and was limited to twenty mares. In 1957, he was transferred to Anthony Faherty's home in Moyard. He was still limited to twenty mares. He remained with Anthony until the end of 1959. Auratum spent 1961 and 1962 with Josie Conroy at Bunowen before being transferred to Peter Kyne at Knockranny, where he spent two more years. He was then loaned indefinitely to Thomas Whelan in Ardrahan where he remained until he was put down at the age of twenty-two in 1976. To this day, he is known as "the Arabian" and mare owners were tempted to use this new stallion. Josie remembers that he was more feisty and harder to handle than the stallions he had had in the past. He was taken off the Association's list when he was sent to Ardrahan. During his last years with Tom Whelan, he worked on the farm and more than earned his keep.

Like his sire Clonkeehan Auratum, Ashfield Alex had a strong character, more difficult to use for everyday work. This is certainly one of the reasons that led the breeders in Connemara to little use this stallion.

Figure 113. Joseph Conroy presented Ashfield Alex (Clonkeehan Auratum x Lambay Starry Eyes by Carna Dun) at the Clifden show in 1984. Photo Daniel Chupin.

Louis Marie Philibert also goes in this direction:

> *"If the Irish are enthusiastic about the benefits of the English Thoroughbred, the Naseel line is the line they would rather ignore.*

Not everyone shares this opinion. Willem Godhart considered that the contribution of the Arabian Thoroughbred has been beneficial for the Connemara breed.

My father had purchased a Robber Boy girl. Like many of Robber Boy's products, she was very emotional, too emotional, and complicated in her daily life. Maybe we were unlucky!

Orange line NASEEL

Ranking	Stallions	Father	Paternal grandmother	Dame	% PI 120 and +
1	BAMBI DE BAZIRE	PALLIKARE D'ANJOU	LISA DE BROSSAY	ILIADE H	50,0%
2	DADY BOOM	QUARTZ DE RAVARY	CLONDYLE PRINCESS	QUI VIVE V	34,8%
3	SIMOUN DE RAVARY	ROBBER BOY	RINSO	WHITE GRANITE	26,1%
4	NICHOLAS	ROBBER BOY	RINSO	SHEILA'S PAL	22,2%
5	QUICKLY OF RAVARY	ROBBER BOY	RINSO	GAIETY GIRL	21,6%
6	NOUGAT DU RAVARY	ROBBER BOY	RINSO	WHITE WINE	20,0%
7	TULIRA CRACKER JACK	CREGMORE COLM	OUR SMOKEY	TULIRA CHARM	13,8%
8	OIL KING RAVARY	ROBBER BOY	RINSO	MYCULLEN ANN	12,5%
9	OLIVER DE RAVARY	ROBBER BOY	RINSO	FORT HELEN	11,7%
10	QUARTIL DES FOLTIERS	OLIVER DE RAVARY	FORT HELEN	ALESIA	10,0%
11	ADMIRAL DU BLIN	NICHOLAS	SHEILA'S PAL	FORT HELEN	9,3%
12	PALLIKARE D'ANJOU	ROBBER BOY	RINSO	LISA DE BROSSAY	8,6%
13	ROBBER BOY	CLONJOY	JOYCE GREY	RINSO	4,6%

Figure 114. Results of the production of French stallions of the Naseel line. Daniel Chupin.

In France, it is Robber Boy who marked this lineage. Bambi de Bazire, one of his grandsons, is at the top of the ranking of the best sires. Only the stallion Quartil des Foltiers is left to represent it. This stallion is one of the Connemara stallions with the best index in Pony Eventing with an index of 173 (0.72) and an index in Horse Eventing of 144 (0.71). In 2021, he is 17 years old and still no male descendant. Wouldn't it be wise to use this stallion before it is too late and the Orange line is no longer represented in France!

Figure 115. Robber Boy. Photo Daniel Chupin.

Figure 116. Quartil des Foltiers (Oliver de Ravary x Alesia by Fort Doolin) IPC 173 (0.72).

MISSED OPPORTUNITIES

THE YELLOW LINE: NOBLE STAR Noble Star's dam was sold when he was no more than four months old. She was put on the train at Clifden and the colt was sent back with the rest of Michael O'Neil's herd to roam the mountains and valleys and fend for himself at that tender age. He was born in 1928 but was not registered until 1932 at the age of four. He was certainly a late foal in his early weaning. It is not surprising that he needed two more years to grow and mature. After his registration, he was purchased by the Association and placed with Jack Bolger where he remained until 1938 when he was transferred to Tommy McDonagh.

Figure 117. Noble Star. Source Shrouded in Mist.

In 1942, he was transferred to John Costello's home in Spiddal where he remained until December 1944. He won the Association's stallion class for four consecutive years from 1932 to 1935. He was very popular with mare owners and had eleven sons and eighty-five registered mares. It is difficult to understand why this line did not survive. But for Jack Bolger "he produced them flat with too much white on the front." Michael Diskin of Cornamona went further and said, "No good product came from this line, they had bad limbs."

LAVALLEY STAR is the only son of Noble Star who seemed to be able to provide sufficiently deserving offspring to continue the line. The fact that he did not is perhaps not his fault. His dame was Village Bell. He was on the Association's list from 1938 to 1942 and during that time forty mares and four stallions were registered by him. At least six of these mares made useful contributions: Loughconeera Star ; Bunreacht ; Heather Black ; La Vesta ; White Spot ; Dolan Rose. He sired the foal class winner in 1940 and 1941 and other of his offspring were highly placed in those same shows. Lavalley Star was sold in Offaly County in 1943.

THE PINK LINE: SILVER PEARL was born at Keelkyle near Letterfrack to Stephen Walsh. He is out of his roan mare Bess in 1931. Stephen's son Patrick confirmed that Bess was the dam of Silver Pearl. He was always privately owned but was on the Association's approved stallion list. Stephen Walsh was a hardworking and progressive farmer who "reclaimed" many poor bogs, working with his stallion and with his stallion's dame at his side with a two-horse plow.

Figure 118. Silver Pearl and Stephen Walsh. Source Shrouded in Mist.

Pat Lyne states:

> " I can understand this man resisting the temptation to sell his
> stallion to the Society. His ponies were cared for in a very special
> way. The sweet tops of furze were clipped to mix in with the corn
> feed and the ponies were taken to the water's edge for a swim in
> a low tide at the end of the day. Stephen believed it was sweet
> relief for the weary limbs which had pulled the plough through
> deep land for many hours. It was a sad day for his family when
> Stephen died at a young age and too bad that Silver Pearl should
> be erroneously held responsible for his death. The true story is
> that in 1940 at Carna Show, Stephen was showing Silver Pearl
> in an overcrowded small ring full of stallions. It was all too easy
> to catch the flying heels of another stallion. This is what
> happened, and Stephen died two days later as a result of his
> injuries. "

When Stephen Walsh died, Silver Pearl had to be sold. It was purchased by
Jack Bolger in the spring of 1941. He won the stallion class in 1941 and 1943 and
it was a great loss to the breed that he was sold in Wexford County in 1949
without leaving behind enough sons to ensure the continuity of this line.
His sixty daughters registered between 1937 and 1945 made up for this to some
extent.

THE IRISH DRAUGHT

The Irish Draught is not easy to define. This draft horse had to meet many
requirements. The Irish Draught is not a heavy horse like the French draught
horses. This horse has a powerful and somewhat heavy stature necessary for farm
work, but it must also be used under saddle, for hunting, and even for district
racing. Because of their history, the Irish have often been poor and could only
afford one horse. A single horse, sociable and calm, 155 to 165 cm hight, had to
meet all these requirements. This is the essence of the Irish Draught. Once a farm
horse, it is now destined for equestrian sports, after having played a great role in
the creation of the Irish Sport Horse studbook. The current studbook was
opened in 1972. Irish draught horses are often crossed with Thoroughbred
stallions to produce the Irish Hunter which competes in show jumping.

In his article on the Connemara Pony (1939), Bartley O'Sullivan includes
the following paragraph:

> " A small Irish Draught type stallion, Lough Ennel, foaled 1905
> by Prince Henry, located at Leenane about 1909, stood in that
> district until 1932 and got some very useful stock. If a short-
> legged, strong boned Irish Draught stallion, not more than

15 hands were available and crossed with suitable pony mares, the progeny would be likely, I believe, to command a ready sale to meet home requirements as well as the demand from buyers attending local fairs."

Figure 119. Prince Henry, an Irish Draught born in 1890. Source Shrouded in Mist.

SKIBBEREEN WAS born in 1939 (Clonmult X Lisacarig). He was bought by the Association at the age of two on the advice of Mr. Cotter. The following report is preserved in the archives of the Association: "This colt presents beautiful characteristics for breeding; beautiful hard head, which is not likely to affect the character of his production when crossed with pony mares." Skibbereen was on the Association's roster from 1941 to 1946 before being castrated in 1947 and resold.

HILLSIDE ROVER was a bay horse born in Westport in 1942 (Owenbeg X Locan na Gleanna). He was purchased by the Association when he was two years old. By all accounts, he was a heavier and simpler pony than Skibbereen. He spent four years with Michael Conroy, but only three of his offspring were registered. He must have sired many more. His output was not considered worthy of recording. Hillside Rover was sold in 1950.

MAY BOY was a grey horse bred in County Longford in 1929. He is said to be out of Irish Mail and his dam is out of Lord Shannon. May Boy's progeny numbered twenty, registered between 1944 and 1952. One son, Farravane Boy, was kept by the Association for some time. Two good mares by May Boy are out of Retreat, Ruby and May Retreat.

RANKING OF CONNEMARA STALLIONS BORN IN FRANCE

Of the 1281 inactive and active stallions, 196 stallions born in France met the initial criteria. For reasons of readability, I have retained only the first 100.

Ranking	Stallions	Year of birth	Father	Paternal grandmother	% PI120 and +
1	BAMBI DE BAZIRE	1989	PALLIKARE D'ANJOU	LISA DE BROSSAY	50,0%
1	KINVARA JINGLE	1976	MURRISK	GREY GIRL	50,0%
2	PUMKINS PONDI	2003	APOLLON PONDY	WHITE GRANITE	41,4%
3	KID DE GARENNE	1976	GIRKO DE GARENNE	VILLAGE DUN	40,0%
4	MEALOW DE LA BELLE	2000	THUNDER DU BLIN	FORT HELEN	39,2%
5	QUARTZ DU BLIN	1982	KING-CUP R.C	EASTER TROY	37,5%
6	VERTGALAN DU RUERE	1987	ISLAND EARL	HELPMATE	37,0%
7	HABLEUR DE RAVARY	1973	ISLAND EARL	HELPMATE	36,9%
8	ROY DE KERGAUTHIER	2005	APOLLON PONDY	WHITE GRANITE	35,7%
9	JINGLE-LILY	1975	MURRISK	GREY GIRL	35,3%
10	VANDALE DAF	1987	FORBAN DE RAVARY	GARRISTOWN STARLING	35,2%
11	DADY BOOM	1991	QUARTZ DE RAVARY	CLONDYLE PRINCESS	34,8%
12	LEADERSHIP	1999	NAUGHTY V. G. JANSHOF	FABIANS PHILOMENA	34,0%
13	QUIMPER III	1982	MAC DUFF	CALLOWFEENISH PRIDE	33,6%
14	OBI WAN DU REUIL	2002	GARRYHINCH MILLRACE	KILBRACKEN QUEEN	33,3%
14	HELP DE LA SCARPE	1995	BEL AMI DU RUERE	CAROLINE'S PET	33,3%
15	ESPOIR KERHAMONIC	1992	GALWAY DE LA DIVE	EASTER THORN	33,0%
16	KILKADY DARLING	1976	RORY RUADH	FORT IRENE	31,9%
17	QUILLON	1982	KING'S RANSOM	ERRISBEG ROSE	31,7%
18	FUNAMBULE II	1993	ABBEYLEIX APOLLO	BLUE MOON	31,3%
19	AS DU BEGUE	1988	GO DU PLANTUREL	CASCADE OF ARROW	30,9%
20	NEXTOAK	1979	ABBEYLEIX APOLLO	BLUE MOON	30,6%
21	MAGIC LEAM PONDI	2000	DEXTER LEAM PONDI	WHITE GRANIT	30,2%
22	FRED DES RIOLES	1993	LORD RAVARY	WHITE WINE	30,0%
22	HIG BALL	1995	BREIZ AR PARK	TINA AR PARK	30,0%
22	VIKING DE LA DIVE	1987	FIDJI DE LA DIVE	EASTER ATLANTIC	30,0%
23	APPOLLON PONDI	1988	ISLAND EARL	HELPMATE	29,8%
24	READY IV	1983	DICK	COISMEIGHMORE	29,3%
25	TAIWAN II	1985	DICK	COISMEIGHMORE	29,2%
26	THUNDER DU BLIN	1985	KING-CUP R.C	EASTER TROY	28,8%
26	QUIOCO OF SCARPE	1982	COSHLA BOBBY	ARANMORE VICTORY	28,8%
27	UNCLE DUFF	1986	FORT DOOLIN	FORT LADY	28,3%
28	JALISCO MELODY	1997	IDENOIR	LITTLE CASHEL HILL	28,1%
29	VOLTEFACE DU RUERE	1987	ISLAND EARL	HELPMATE	26,3%
30	SUCRE D'ORGE IV	1984	GULF STREAM	PASSPORT	26,2%

Figure 120. Classification of Connemara stallions born in France. Daniel Chupin.

Ranking	Stallions	Year of birth	Father	Paternal grandmother	% PI 120 and +
31	SIMOUN DE RAVARY	1984	ROBBER BOY	RINSO	26,1%
32	KEBIR DE GARENNE	1998	KID DE GARENNE	CLONROSS COOL STAR	25,7%
33	COUNTRY MELODY	1990	IDENOIR	LITTLE CASHEL HILL	25,7%
34	JAZZ DE VAUPER	1997	THUNDER DU BLIN	FORT HELEN	25,0%
34	IMPERIAL DU BLIN	1996	QUETZL DU BLIN	FORT HELEN	25,0%
35	STICKY DU BLIN	1984	KING-CUP R.C	EASTER TROY	24,7%
36	BREIZ AR PARK	1989	RIZ DE VAUPTAIN	CORA	24,6%
37	EXPRESS ST HYMER	1992	ICARE	PASSPORT	24,4%
38	RIVER DES LANDES	1983	KILIMANDJARO RC	ERRISLANNON HATTIE	24,3%
38	FRICOTIN	1993	GLENREE BOBBY	INISH BIGGLE	24,3%
39	FAKIR DE RAVARY	1971	ISLAND EARL	HELPMATE	24,2%
40	NAZEEL DARLING	1979	GOLD FORT	FORT SILVER	23,7%
41	PUNCH DU MESNIL	2003	CASTLE SIDE GLEN BOY	GLENCROFT AMY	23,5%
42	FLASH DE CONQUET	1993	GO DU PLANTUREL	CASCADE OF ARROW	23,3%
43	BAURISHEEN KING	1989	KING'S RANSOM	ERRISBEG ROSE	23,2%
44	FIDJI RIVER MELODY	1993	IDENOIR	LITTLE CASHEL HILL	23,2%
45	GILL DE BRIACE	1994	TYNAGH DE BRIACE	NANCY KATE	23,1%
46	OXBOW DU LOIR	2002	CANAL MISTY FIONN	GLOVES MISTY	22,7%
47	FORBAN DE RAVARY	1971	ISLAND EARL	HELPMATE	22,6%
48	NICHOLAS	1979	ROBBER BOY	RINSO	22,2%
48	VLAVENT DU RUERE	1987	ISLAND EARL	HELPMATE	22,2%
49	O'BRIEN DU CHESNAY	1980	KNOCKADREEN HOLIDAY CLIFF	BOBBY'S GIRL	22,1%
50	DEXTER LEAM PONDI	2013	LEAM BOBBY FIN	CLOONISLE JUDY	22,0%
51	HE MAN DU BRANA	1995	VOLTEFACE DU RUERE	NEXT TO ME RAVARY	21,7%
52	QUICKLY OF RAVARY	1982	ROBBER BOY	RINSO	21,6%
52	POWER BOY DU PARC	1981	FUNNY OF RAVARY	SCREEN LADY	21,6%
53	TYNAGH DE BRIACE	1985	NIPON II	HOLY	21,5%
54	GALIBOT D'ENFER	1994	FORT DOOLIN	FORT LADY	21,4%
55	ROCOCO DU THUIT	1983	COVE COMMANDER	WINDY COVE	21,1%
56	HURRICANE OF LAPS	1995	GARRYHINCH MILLRACE	KILBRACKEN QUEEN	20,6%
57	ITALIC DES LANDES	1996	RIVER DES LANDES	LICORNE DE RAVARY	20,6%
58	TANAM AN DIAGHALL	1969	LAMBAY FIREBALL	CLONKEEHAN EASTER LILY	20,5%
59	KINGSTOWN RORY	2003	MONAGHANSTOWN FIONN	APRIL STAR	20,4%
60	BULLIT DE COISELET	1989	KHAN DE COISELET	CARRAGH BAY	20,3%
61	ICARE	1974	LAMBAY FIREBALL	CLONKEEHAN EASTER LILY	20,0%
61	NOUGAT DU RAVARY	1979	ROBBER BOY	RINSO	20,0%
61	ROM COCO DE BOISSEL	2005	VANDALE DAF	JOY OF VICTORY	20,0%
61	DIAM'S DES GENETS	1991	QUIGNON DU PARC	BOOGIE WOOGIE	20,0%
61	GINVARA DU PREUIL	1994	KINVARA JINGLE	KINVARA LILY	20,0%
61	GLENREE BOBBY	1970	CARNA BOBBY	CARNA DOLLY	20,0%
62	REAM BOY DU THUIT	1983	COVE COMMANDER	WINDY COVE	19,5%
63	COCOON DU PREUIL	1990	URIEL DE NEUVILLE	SHIPTON MAURTEEN	19,4%
63	NOAH DE LA SCARPE	1979	COSHLA BOBBY	ARANMORE VICTORY	19,4%
64	MISTRAL DE BRIACE	2000	NAUGHTY V. G. JANSHOF	FABIANS PHILOMENA	18,9%
65	JUARISTE DU MOULIN	1997	ROCKY GRICHET	DUNAMOON	18,8%
65	ELOI IV	1992	TANAM AN DIAGHALL	LEAM LILLY	18,8%
66	AMIRAL DE MINUIT	2010	IOUKY DE LA SCARPE	NOUGATINE RAVARY	18,8%
67	LUSTY DU BAILLY	1977	HARRIS DE LA DIVE	EASTER BALL	18,6%
67	MACKY	1978	DIAMONDS DANDY	GLENLO BIDDY	18,6%
67	GALWAY DE LA DIVE	1972	BAMBU	SLIGO ROSE	18,6%
68	OUEDIC DU PREUIL	1980	COOLFIN BOBBY	MOY HARVEST TIME	18,5%
68	NIMBUS IV	1979	MAC DUFF	CALLOWFEENISH PRIDE	18,5%
69	ICE AND FIRE D'ALBRAN	1996	DEXTER LEAM PONDI	WHITE GRANIT	18,3%
70	QUIGNON DU PARC	1982	FUNNY OF RAVARY	SCREEN LADY	18,2%
70	SAIAN DE KEZEG	2006	MAGIC LEAM PONDI	VOYEL DE BEAUCHAMP	18,2%

159

Ranking	Stallions	Year of birth	Father	Paternal grandmother	% PI 120 and +
71	LOOK AT ME	1977	FINNEY MASTER	WINTER ROCHE	18,1%
71	NAMOUR II	1979	JASMIN DE VILFIN	GIPSY DE LA DIVE	18,1%
72	BRINDAMOUR MELODY	1989	IDENOIR	LITTLE CASHEL HILL	18,0%
73	GRANITBOY PONDI	1994	COOLFIN BOBBY	MOY HARVEST TIME	17,9%
73	DON JUAN V	1991	ABBEYLEIX APOLLO	BLUE MOON	17,9%
73	QUETZAL DU BLIN	1982	KING-CUP R.C	EASTER TROY	17,9%
74	VIKING DU FREMUR	1987	MACKY	LEHID SWEETHEART	17,6%
74	ITKTAR DU MARTRAY	1996	LOOK AT ME	BRIGHT SUNBEAM	17,6%
74	BEL AMI DU RUERE	1989	ISLAND EARL	HELPMATE	17,6%
74	LEO PONDI	1999	DEXTER LEAM PONDI	WHITE GRANIT	17,6%
75	FENDER DES VAUTS	1993	ABBEYLEIX APOLLO	BLUE MOON	17,4%
76	RICKY IV	1983	COOLFIN BOBBY	MOY HARVEST TIME	16,8%
76	SPARROW ALUINN	1984	KNOCKADREEN HOLIDAY CLIFF	BOBBY'S GRIL	16,8%
77	MIDNIGHT DU BRANA	2000	VOLTEFACE DE RUERE	NEXT TO ME RAVARY	16,7%
77	CLIFDEN DE L'AULNE	1990	GOLD FORT	FORT SILVER	16,7%
77	THOR DE SEGURET	2007	ODYSSEUS MELODY	EQUINOX MELODY	16,7%
77	OURAGAN DU RULGOAT	2002	CYRANO PONDI	WHITE GRANITE	16,7%
77	KHAN DE COISELET	1976	CARRAGH KINSMAN	STORY OF TYNAGH LND	16,7%
78	CYRANO PONDI	1990	GALWAY DE LA DIVE	EASTER THORN	16,6%
78	UN PRINCE DU RUERE	1986	ISLAND EARL	HELPMATE	16,6%
79	QUARTERON AGILE	1982	FAKIR DES AUBRETS	TULIRA ANNIE	16,5%
80	GULF STREAM	1972	LAMBAY FIREBALL	CLONKEEHAN EASTER LILY	16,3%
80	ORIGAN MELODY	1980	IDENOIR	LITTLE CASHEL HILL	16,3%
80	ROCKY GRICHET	1983	GRICHET ADEL	POLL'S STORY	16,3%
80	VALERA DU CHESNAY	1987	KNOCKADREEN HOLIDAY CLIFF	BOBBY'S GRIL	16,3%
81	CLAFOUTIS DES CRAS	1990	RIVER DES LANDES	LICORNE DE RAVARY	16,1%
82	LICKEN PERFECT	1999	CLIFF OF LAPS	WESTSIDE LITTLE MADAM	16,0%
83	KEFIR DE L'ETANG	1998	COCUM THUNDER BOY	COCUM BELLA DONNA	15,8%
83	ICE'N'BLUE TIME	1996	COCUM THUNDER BOY	COCUM BELLA DONNA	15,8%
83	THURAIN DE GUERMANTES	2007	DEXTER LEAM PONDI	WHITE GRANITE	15,8%
84	KIMONO MELODY	1998	IDENOIR	LITTLE CASHEL HILL	15,6%
84	EVER OAK	1992	JUMBO	BLUE BELL	15,6%
85	POMPON DE JAX	1981	GALWAY DE LA DIVE	EASTER THORN	15,5%
85	CARYL DE BEAUCHAMP	1990	ABBEYLEIX APOLLO	BLUE MOON	15,5%
86	IMPERATOR MELODY	1996	IDENOIR	LITTLE CASHEL HILL	15,4%
86	GWENNIC DE GOARIVA	1994	NERUDA DARLING	GANTY CORAL	15,4%
86	THE ISLAND PRINCE	1985	ISLAND EARL	HELPMATE	15,4%
86	ALLADIN DU PARK	1988	MAYLORD SPARROW	BODEN PARK MINX	15,4%
87	LORD RAVARY	1977	HABLEUR DE RAVARY	RAFORD LADYBIRD	15,0%
87	INTERMETZO MELODY	1996	ABBEYLEIX FIONN	FIONNUALA	15,0%
88	LOUP YES TU TARTIFUME	1999	NAUGHTY V. G. JANSHOF	FABIANS PHILOMENA	14,8%
89	VA TOUT DU RUERE	1987	ISLAND EARL	HELPMATE	14,7%
89	I DES CARTES	1974	ISLAND EARL	HELPMATE	14,7%
90	ARLEQUIN DE MESCAM	1988	GULF STREAM	PASSPORT	14,6%
91	IDENOIR	1974	WINDY COVER RANGER	WINDICOVE	14,5%
91	URIEL DE NEUVILLE	1986	MOYGLARE BRUFF	RAMBLING LINDON	14,5%
92	MEXICO	2000	QUIMPER III	HOLY	14,3%
92	QUARTZ DE VAUPTIN	1982	FUNNY OF RAVARY	SCREEN LADY	14,3%
92	JIVARO III	1997	APOLLON PONDY	WHITE GRANITE	14,3%
92	FORBAN PONDY	1993	APOLLON PONDY	WHITE GRANITE	14,3%
92	KORRIGAN D'AULNE	1976	GLENREE BOBBY	INISH BIGGLE	14,3%
92	VADOR SHADOW DU GITE	2009	SILVER SHADOW	POETIC MOONLIGHT	14,3%
93	VIZIR DU RUERE	1987	ISLAND EARL	HELPMATE	13,9%
94	LICOL	1977	FRIPON DE LA DIVE	STREALSTOWN DREAM	13,8%
95	SULTAN OF SCARPE	1984	COSHLA BOBBY	ARANMORE VICTORY	13,6%
96	JOUEUR DE RAVARY	1977	ISLAND EARL	HELPMATE	13,5%
96	GO DU PLANTUREL	1972	ISLAND EARL	HELPMATE	13,5%
97	TORNADE IV	1985	NERUDA DARLING	GANTY CORAL	13,4%
98	PHARAWAY DES TOUCHES	2003	GALWAY DE LA DIVE	EASTER THORN	13,3%
98	VENT FOU DUFF	1987	FORT DOOLIN	FORT LADY	13,3%
98	PRISME	1981	CALMORE SWAGMAN	SCARTEEN OF CALMORE	13,3%
99	ABRICOT DU CHESNAY	1988	KNOCKADREEN HOLIDAY CLIFF	BOBBY'S GRIL	13,1%
100	SIRUS TOUL AR C'HOAT	2006	ERVELOUGH OISIN	CREGDUFF HEATHER	13,0%
109	URCHIN DE MILIN AVEL	2008	READY IV	LEHID SWEETHEART	12,9%

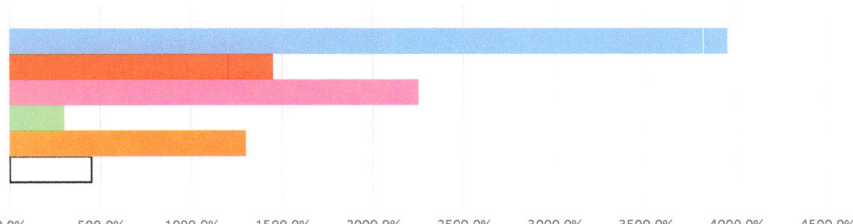

0,0%   500,0%   1000,0%   1500,0%   2000,0%   2500,0%   3000,0%   3500,0%   4000,0%   4500,0%

Figure 121. Diagram showing the % of male lines in the paternal granddames of the 196 selected French stallions. Daniel Chupin.

The two graphs are self-explanatory. However, you will notice a significant decrease in the number of dams with the Naseel bloodline. The white line corresponds to paternal granddames and dams with no known ancestors or sires not belonging to the five male lines.

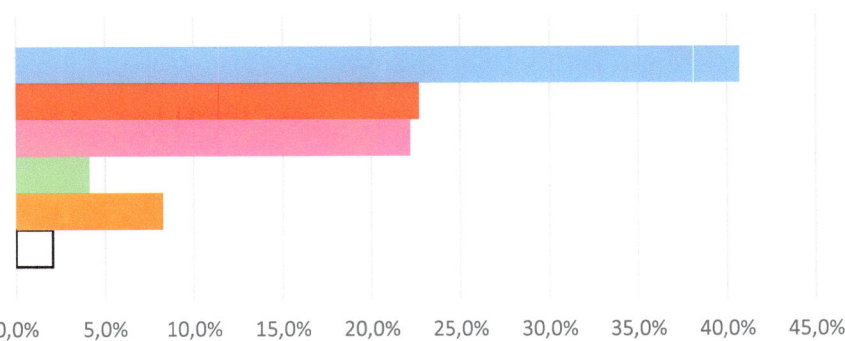

0,0%   5,0%   10,0%   15,0%   20,0%   25,0%   30,0%   35,0%   40,0%   45,0%

Figure 122. Diagram showing the % of male lines in the dams of the 196 selected French stallions. Daniel Chupin.

161

RANKING OF THE BEST FEMALES BORN IN FRANCE

The strength of the Connemara breed has always been its mares. The Connemara heritage is strong enough to compensate for the impoverishment of the show type-based breeding. But we must remain rigorous in the selection of breeding stock to maintain the characteristics that have made the qualities of this pony.

Here is a ranking of the best females by discipline. Considering the number, 10185 females were born in France of which 1039 indexed at 120 and more in show jumping, eventing, and dressage. I will process all these data soon, but not in this book.

I have retained only the 17 best-indexed females in Show Jumping Pony, the 13 best-indexed females in eventing Pony, and the 5 best-indexed females in Dressage.

I don't have enough data to take into account the results in breeding and in particular the results in the French National. So I made a special line for Poésie Mélody who can be qualified as the best French pony in breeding competition with Reserve champion of the international show of Fontainebleau and the French national show in 2012,2013,2014 and Supreme Champion in Clifden in 2017.

Figure 123. Vanille de Briacé ridden by Alix VILEYN French Champion Eventing AS Poney 1, in 2017. At its head, Daniel Chupin. Photo Jeannine Marolleau.

The best performing females in jumping

Female	Birth	Size	JPI	Father	Paternal grandmother	Dame	Maternal grandmother
NIEL AR CRANO	2001	148	171	READY IV	LEHID SWEETHEART	VAK PLACH AR CRANO	NOS STERENNUS
BEAUTY ROCQ	2011	148	161	DEXTER LEAM PONDI	WHITE GRANITE	TESS ROCQ	LEA DE MONTMAIN
TIGA DU MARAIS	2007	146	160	FRICOTIN	ULLA DE LA NIEVRE	MELODIE DE LA PLAT	CALINE DES OUCHES
COUNTRY GIRL DU MILON	2012	146	160	IDEFIX DU VILLON	HILDA DES LUDES	IRELAND GIRL	QUERIE DE GARENNE
RUMBA DU VERRON	2005	148	158	RASMUS	OXENHOLM TENDERLY	JAVA DU VERRON	PERLE DE COISELET
TAMARA DU MOULIN	2007	145	155	JUARISTE DU MOULIN	CRYSTALE DU MOULIN	GWENDOLINE AUBIER	MILADY DE RAVARY
VIXEN TRUST CLADDAGH	2009	147	155	DEXTER LEAM PONDI	WHITE GRANITE	O'HARA DES GRAVES	COURBETTE DE GERE
PSYLLA DU CHAPELAN	2003	148	154	QUILLON	ROCKMOUNT RUBY	KALIE DE LA HOCQ	VENUS DE LA SCARPE
QUAY QUICK	2004	144	153	QUIMPER III	HOLY	VIOU DUFF	PERLETTE III
ANGELA DU BOC	2010	148	153	FRICOTIN	ULLA DE LA NIEVRE	VANESSE II	ISABELLE
DIVINE ICE DE SEIZENN	2013	148	153	ICE AND FIRE D'ALBRA	UNDERLINE OF LAPS	ITIKET AR CRANO	VOTER AR CRANO
NOUCHKA TIME	2001	145	152	COCUM THUNDER BOY	COCUM BELLA DONNA	VANILLE DE RUERE	MOYCULLEN ANN
ORCHIDEE DE LOIRE	2002	148	152	BALADIN DE FREMUR	DOIREANN	ROXANNE DE RAVARY	CLOUGH DUN
NIOUI NINON TARTIFUME	2001	144	151	NAUGHTY VAN GRAAF	FABIANS PHILOMENA	VIOLINE II	OSOLEMIO
PAROLIA DE GUERMANTES	2003	146	151	NAUGHTY VAN GRAAF	FABIANS PHILOMENA	DIVA DE BRIACE	CALLOWFENNISH WAVE
MADEIRA	2000	140	150	CANAL MISTY FIONN	GLOVES MISTY	FANNY DE BRIACE	COOSHEEN MUFFIN
NAIADE PEGUIGNON	2001	144	150	VANDAL DAF	JOY OF VICTORY	JINGLE DU PREUIL	NOVA II

JPI: Jumping Performance Index

The best performing females in eventing

Female	Birth	Size	EPI	Father	Paternal grandmother	Dame	Maternal grandmother
QUANDY DE BOISSY	2004	146	155	TORNADE IV	LADY DU VERGER	KABRIOLE DE LA BELLE	ASTUCE DE LA BELLE
ODREENAGH ALUINN	2002	147	153	SPARROW ALUINN	POGEEN ALUINN	DRIMCONG CAROLINE	BALLINAKILL CAROLINE
PROVIDENCE DU BAMA	2003	143	151	INTERMETZO MELODY	QUEEN RIVER MELODY	MERYL DE GUERMANTES	HOTESSE DU BLIN
RIVER DANSE MELODY	2005	147	147	EBN DE LOYE	HELEN'S LYRE	GERRY RIVER MELODY	ROUNDSTONE RIVER
VANILLE DE BRIACE	2009	145	146	GARRY	NELLY DUFF	KATE DE BRIACE	COOSHEEN MUFFIN
PATIENCE MELODY	2003	147	146	CASTLE SIDE GLEN BOY	GLENCROFT AMY	KYRIELLE MELODY	SILVER SPARROW
RAGTIME D'AZY	2005	145	146	CRACKER BOY MELODY	CARRABAUN CRACKER	JACKSON III	REINE DES PRES
TEEPEE D'AMOUR	2007	148	145	BRINDAMOUR MELODY	CARRABAUN CRACKER	VANITY II	MAY OF HERINE
RAFALE D'OUTRE MER	2005	147	145	DUN DES LANDES	JEWELS NICE	CHEVRENN AR CRANO	NEUS VAT
ARGAZEG PONTHOUAR	2010	146	144	PUMKINS PONDI	DAKOTA MELODY	VOULOUZ AR CRANO	NEUS VAT
ODENDSEE MODESTY	2002	145	144	DREAM OF AULNE	PAYSE DE L'AULNE	JOY SCHUERACHER	JUDY V SCHUERACHER
TANIA DE CISAI	2007	140	142	CORCULLEN FUSILIER	GAELTACHT DREAM GIRL	LASKA DE L'AULNE	BLASKA DE BASIRE
PEGEEN DE BOISSIS	2003	147	140	GARRYHINCH MILLRACE	KILBRACKEN QUEEN	JAINA DE BOISSIS	VEDA DE LACHAUX

EPI: Eventing Performance Index

The best performing females in dressage

Female	Birth	Size	DPI	Father	Paternal grandmother	Dame	Maternal grandmother
KALINKA DE ROUVY	1998	145	154	QUETZAL DU BLIN	FORT HELEN	QUENELLE DE RAVARY	CLOUGH DUN
JOLLY FILLY DUMARTRAY	1997	147	146	STORMY WEATHER	ATLANTIC SURF	ASHFIELD BLUE RIBBON	ASHFILD BLUE MOLLY
GLAKENNE DE ROCHA	1994	145	144	QUARTZ DE VAUPTIN	VINCA	COKENN DE ROCHALON	TEKENN AR CRANO
FALINE III	1993	145	143	STEEL HEAVEN	WISE SPARROW	PAIRLE	LASSIE II
UPPERCLASS DE FLORENT	2008	140	141	LEHID CANAL PRINCE	LEHID COLLEEN	CLEMENCE II	SAGA DE TROMEUR

DPI: Dressage Performance Index

Figure 124. Three tables summarize the performance of mares in C.S.O., C.C.E., and Dressage. Daniel Chupin.

Figure 125. Poésie Melody. Photo P. Wandon.

PERFORMING STALLIONS BORN IN FRANCE AFTER 2000

On this list, I have retained only the best-indicated active stallions or those with significant results in breeding. These stallions, because of their sporting career, have in certain cases a production still too young to be analyzed. We have a very good representation of the Cannon Ball, Connemara Boy, and Little Heaven lines. A stallion like Lake Lad is as successful in breeding as in sport. However, I am concerned about one fact: there are only two C stallions left. The others are almost all maxi sizes!

Figure 126. Ungaro Deux Seguret IPC 140 (0.81) in 2018. Third at the French Eventing Championship CCE AS Pony 1. Photo Élevage de Séguret.

Figure 127. Caruso Melody, photo of Haras Melody.

Stallions	Size	Index	Father	Paternal grandmother	Dame
EMBLEME DU HAM	147	129	DEXTER LEAM PONDI	WHITE GRANIT	GREY ROCK TINA
DARCY DU VILLON	140	141	POETIC JUSTICE	GLOVES MISTY	HIRA DU VILLON
CALIX DE VUZIT	148	148	POETIC JUSTICE	GLOVES MISTY	UNASTELLA DE VUZIT
CANNON BALL BRIOVIERE	148	126	KIMONO MELODY	EQUINOXE MELODY	OCEANE BRIOVERE
CARUSO MELODY	148	131	COCUM THUNDER BOY	COCUM BELLA DONNA	IMAGINE MELODY PONDI
CELTIK DES MIOKO	148	137	LOUP YES TU TARTIFUME	VIOLINE II	VIXEN TRUST CLADDAGH
BORSALINO FAMILY	152	E1	BUNOWEN PADDY	IRISHTOWN BEAUTY	POESIE MELODY
BLUE ICE DES BRETIS	147	136	ICE AND FIRE D'ALBRAN	UNDERLINE OF LAPS	QEAM FINNIGANSILLES
BAD BOY DE LA COMOE	148	132	BUNOWEN PADDY	IRISHTOWN BEAUTY	KABRIOLE DE LA BELLE
AMIRAL DE MINUIT	148	129	IOUKY DE LA SCARPE	NOUGATINE RAVARY	BRENDA DE MINUIT
AZZARO DES BRETIS	148	131	BUNOWEN PADDY	IRISHTOWN BEAUTY	SEPIA DES BRETIS
LAKE LAD	148	130	CURRACHMORE CASHEL	ROSENAHARLEY RONAMARA	PORTDUFF JENNIE
VANDAL DU TYRIA	148	137	WESTIDE MIRAH II	GRANGE SANDY	HOELLA
VOL BLEU D'ARCALIE	148	137	RASMUS	OXENHOLM TENDERLY	HAPRIL BLUE TIME
KILLAUGHEY HAZY OLIVER	148	130	FREDERIKSMINDE HAZY MOVE	OXENHOLM MOVIE STAR	ASHFIELD HONEY SPARROW
UN ÉTÉ AU PONTHOUAR	145	135	PUMKINS PONDI	DAKOTA MELODY	JENNY DE BEUSEYER
UNGARO DEUX SEGURET	148	140	GANGE SURF SPARROW	KILKERRIN SURF	QUENZA SEGURET
URCHIN DE MILIN AVEL	148	149	READY IV	LEHID SWEETHEART	JADE DE KERGLENN
UBAYE PONDI	148	147	APOLLON PONDY	WHITE GRANITE	VOYEL DE BEAUCHAMP
UCELLOW DES GRAVES	148	144	MEALOW DE LA BELLE	ASTUCE DE LA BELLE	QUASSIA DES GRAVES
ULYSSE DES VALLOTS	148	131	VANDALE DAF	JOY OF VICTORY	DEESSE DES VALLOTS
USHUAIA ELIZA MODESTY	148	142	DREAM OF AULNE	PAYSE DE L'AULNE	ELIZA SCHUERACHER
UNANEEM CARRAGHEEN	148	138	DEXTER LEAM PONDI	WHITE GRANITE	KAIROUAN
TORNADO DE BRIACE	138	127	TYNAGH DE BRIACE	NANCY KATE	COOSHEEN MUFFIN
TOTEM DU MARTRAY	148	150	SPINWAY PIRATE	SPINWAY BOUNTY	MELDIE DU MARTRAY
TEXTO FOX	148	154	DEXTER LEAM PONDI	WHITE GRANITE	LORENA FOX
THEO DUFF	148	131	GARRY	NELLY DUFF	A BIG GAELLE DUFF
THURAIN DE GUERMANTES	148	141	DEXTER LEAM PONDI	WHITE GRANITE	HOTESSE DU BLIN
TOP DU VERRON	147	131	ROCOCO DU THUIT	ROSEBEG ROSIE	JAVA DU VERRON
SEAN DE L'AULNE	148	131	MACKY	LEHID SWEETHEART	JURANDE DE L'AULNE
SIXTEEN DU COLOMBIER	146	124	VANDALE DAF	JOY OF VICTORY	GUILTY DU PIGNAT
SAPHIR DE CORMEILLES	148	156	THUNDER DU BLIN	FORT HELEN	ANNINA DU THENNEY
ROGER DE GARENNE	146	141	KEBIR DE GARENNE	KIM DE GARENNE	ANTILOPE DE RUERE
ROM COCO DE BOISSEL	148	157	VANDALE DAF	JOY OF VICTORY	VENUS DU PETCH
REXTER MADELICE	146	152	DEXTER LEAM PONDI	WHITE GRANITE	NIKITA DES COUDRIE
RUBIS DES ROSEAUX	147	146	JUARISTE DU MOULIN	CRYSTALE DU MOULIN	HAZARA DES ROSEAUX
QUARTIL DES FOLTIERS	146	144	OLIVER DE RAVARY	FORT HELEN	ALESIA
PAPS LATE	146	146	COCUM THUNDER BOY	COCUM BELLA DONNA	IOLICK LATE
PEGASE DE KERDUFF	148	123	READY IV	LEHID SWEETHEART	VLADYS
PUNCH DU MESNIL	148	132	CASTLE SIDE GLEN BOY	GLENCROFT AMY	CALYPSO MELODY
OLYMPE MODESTY	148	129	DREAM OF AULNE	PAYSE DE L'AULNE	ELIZA SHRUERACHER
NOLAN DUFF	145	150	GARRY	NELLY DUFF	OONA DUFF

Figure 128. List of performing stallions born in France after 2000. Daniel Chupin.

166

Figure 129. Lake Lad Regional Supreme Champion 2018, 3rd French Championship CCE AS Pony 1, presented by Stéphane Jault. Photo Élevage de Séguret.

Figure 130. Borsalino Family Supreme Champion 2018 (Bunowen Pady and Poesie Melody). Photo by Pascal Wandon.

Figure 131. Nolan Duff. Photo LM Philibert.

Figure 132. Tornado de Briacé, a performing stallion measuring 138 cm. Photo Daniel Chupin.

CONCLUSION ON THE ANALYSIS OF THE MALE LINES

In France, all the lines are represented. This is one of the strengths of French Connemara breeding.

Two lines, the Blue "Cannon Ball" and the Violet "Little Heaven" represent 73% of the selected stallions.

The Red line "Connemara Boy" represents only 15% of the stallions analyzed. The Green line "Mountain Lad" represents only 8% and the Orange line "Naseel" only 4%.

If we have to remain vigilant about the number of stallions representing the Connemara Boy line, the situation remains worrying for the Mountain Lad line and is becoming alarming for the Naseel line which, if we do not do anything, could disappear from France. This situation is all the more worrying as the results in % of the number of products with an index equal or superior to 120 show little difference between the lines.

So there are no good or bad lines!

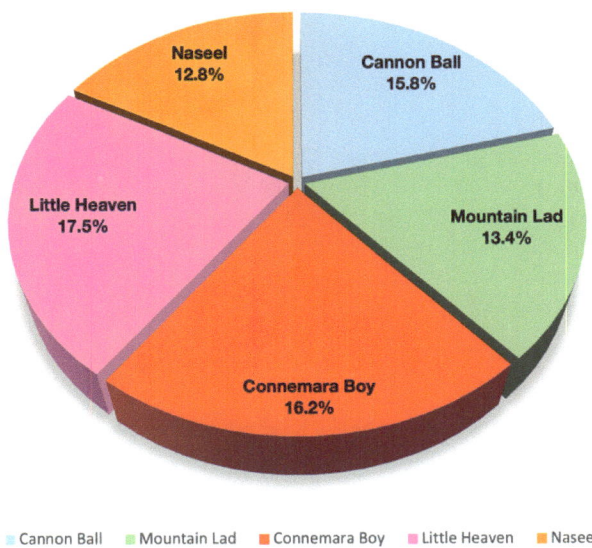

Figure 133. Summary table of the production indexed at more than 120 in Show Jumping, Eventing and Dressage for each of the lines. Daniel Chupin.

While the Cannon Ball and Little Heaven lines are represented in number, this is not evident in the quality of their production. Indeed, there are no important differences with the other lines.

For the Cannon Ball line, the descendants of Leam Finnigan through Dexter Leam Pondi seem to be anchored durably in the French breeding, the recent contributions of Currachmore Cashel, Canal Misty Fionn, Coolillaun Cushlawn, and Banagher Magee seem very promising.

The Little Heaven line is historically well represented by the descendants of Island Earl and Finney Master have brought in new blood. Fort Doolin since the 80s. More recently, Poetic Justice and Rasmus have come to play the spoilsport by bringing in new blood.

For the Connemara Boy line, it is the same. If Mac Duff initiated this line in France, Murrisk has produced very well and the arrival of Naughty V.G. Janshof and Bunowen Paddy have undoubtedly been a plus for French genetics.

Concerning the Mountain Lad line, the situation is quite different. Galway de la Dive is the only son of Bambu to have had offspring. The importation of Cocum Thunder Boy was a success. Given the low representation of this line, it is regrettable that Caoranbeg Champ was not used to his full potential and went back to Ireland (33 mares covered in 8 breeding seasons). The arrival of a few sons of Frederiksminde Hazy Move will perhaps stabilize the situation.

Finally, if we don't do something, we risk losing the Naseel lineage.

Several observations can be made:

- There is no correlation between the number of products and the quality of production. For example, Dexter Leam Pondi with 645 products is 20th; Don Juan with 893 products is 33rd in the ranking in the Blue lineage. Thunder du Blin with 1151 offspring is 17th of the ranking in the Violet line, considering the quality of the mares who used his services I consider that his production was not up to what could be expected.

- The ratio of the number of indexed products for the French National Studs and Private stallions is similar with less than a 1% difference.

- The disappearance of the HNs has not changed the results. If genetic "distributors" occupy an important part of the market, this is not reflected in the results of the production of their stallions.

- Stallions that have produced well have an average of 50 foals in their stallion career. But their production was valued in a very professional way. Some breeders coupled their breeding structure with their equestrian center using the production of their stallion. For Vergalan du Ruere, Jalisco Melody or Oxbow du Loir, this has been quite successful for them.

- If the development of the Connemara pony is mainly based on large breeding shids up the end of the 80s, it is now the result of small structures producing only 1 to 4 foals per year. This atomization of the farms has led to a drastic selection of the mares and a better valorization of the production.

- For some breeders, of which I am one, a system has been set up to enhance their production. According to Stéphane Jault (Séguret breeding farm): "the breeder's input only represents 30% of the success in producing a top performing pony. Success is 70% based on a system that the breeder must put in place in partnership with a trainer, a parent/child and grandparent team (who generally finances the operation), a good farrier, a dentist, and an osteopath... ". For Stéphane Jault, it is team work.

- The list of stallions born after 2000, in activity in France, is eloquent by the results of these stallions in sport. Here again, all lines are represented.

- Because of the quality, the variety and results of the stallions representing each of the lines, it is not reasonable to present certain sires as breed leaders.

This analysis has been made only on sport criteria. Until now, it has not been possible to qualify and quantify the results in breeding competitions. The breeding program currently being developed by the A.F.P.C. will allow for a more balanced analysis between sports results and results in breeding competitions.

The strength of French breeding compared to Irish breeding is largely based on the use of our ponies in sports events. I am convinced that the competition that exists with the French Riding Pony (PFS) has created a favorable dynamic for the emergence of a French Connemara pony with sporting abilities in all disciplines.

To produce successfully, we must maintain the level of performance of our ponies while remaining attentive to the conformation. We need to bring these two complementary factors together.

IRELAND WITHIN EUROPE

Since 1949, Ireland has been a parliamentary republic.

MODERNIZATION OF THE IRISH ASSOCIATION

A meeting of the Council was held at the Office of the Committee on Agriculture in Galway, on December 22, 1959, to ratify the transition to the new association. In his speech, Lord Killanin stated that this was the end of the first Connemara Pony Breeders' Association, founded at a public meeting in Oughterard on December 12, 1923. Mr. O'Sullivan and all those who have worked over the years to position the Association on the very strong footing it now occupies in the world were warmly thanked. This was the closing of a chapter in the history of the Connemara pony, and the transition from the old Association to the new Cumann Lucht Capaillini Chonamara[56] , marked the end of an era.

While Éire has built peaceful independence over the years, the question of the Catholic minority in Northern Ireland arose in the late 1960s. At the end of the 1960s, the brutal repression of a peaceful demonstration organized by NICRM (the Northern Ireland Civil Rights Movement) marked the beginning of 30 years of civil war in Ulster between unionists who favored reunification with Great Britain and republicans in favor of a reunification of the two Irelands.

FIRST INTERNATIONAL CONFERENCE

On March 12, 1970, the first international conference of Connemara Pony Associations was opened by the Minister of Agriculture, Mr. James Gibbons, at the University College in Galway. Delegates from all the Connemara Pony Associations of Great Britain, the United States of America, Sweden, Denmark, Holland, and France, as well as from the Connemara Pony Breeding Association (the Irish Association) were present. There were also representatives from countries where Connemara pony associations had not yet been established, Germany, Belgium, and Italy, and a total of 200 delegates attended the conference. In his opening address, the president of the Connemara Pony Breeders Association, Lord Killanin, welcomed all delegates and stated that since the founding of the association in 1923, ponies were used only in Connemara and their main purpose was as working ponies. Today, as ponies have become a major export product, conditions have changed considerably. The time was right to call a conference so that Connemara pony breeders from around the world could meet and the many points of mutual interest, and possibly disagreement, could be discussed freely. Several associations stated that blue-eyed cream ponies were not accepted in their studbooks and that there were problems with oversized ponies.

---

[56] Cumann Lucht Capaillini Chonamara is the name of the new association of Connemara pony breeders in Ireland.

Some associations also required two generations of pure Connemara blood in the pedigree of a pony registered in their studbook, which caused difficulties for ponies bred in Ireland from crossbred sires or from certain ponies registered at the creation of the studbook that had been registered without their production being known. These were the main points of divergence raised. There were some useful exchanges of views with the general feeling that the participants were optimistic and that there was a lot of goodwill between the different associations.

Figure 134. A batch of mares with the stallion Napoleon at Tulira Castle in 1982. Photo by Daniel Chupin.

At the end of the conference, delegates were invited to visit Tulira Castle and to watch a stallion parade. The stallions were paraded in order of seniority, with 24-year-old Carna Bobby leading the parade, followed by 22-year-old Carna Dun, 21-year-old Mac Dara, 16-year-old Clonkeehan Auratum, and 13-year-old Thunder. These five stallions represented the five stallion lines that are still active, with the Blue, Red, and Green lines going back to the original foundation sires, and the Purple and Orange lines representing the English and Arabian Thoroughbreds of the two outcross sires.

During this period, Ireland experienced violent episodes, notably Bloody Sunday in 1972. On Sunday 30th January, thirteen Catholics were killed by British paratroopers while demonstrating in the city of Derry against a law allowing the army to carry out arbitrary imprisonments. Following this tragic episode, the IRA (Irish Republican Army), some of whose members had close ties with Sinn-Fein (Northern Ireland Republican Party), increased its terrorist acts, denouncing the British government's policy towards Republican political prisoners.

Figure 135. 1982. Tulira Stud. Lady Hemphill presenting Tulira Martin to Daniel Chupin.
Photo of Briacé Breeding.

In 1973, on January 1, Ireland became a member of the European Union.

Margaret Thatcher's opposition to any compromise on the issue of Republican political prisoners led to an attack in Brighton in 1984, while she was on her way to the Conservative Party conference. The British Prime Minister narrowly escaped. And the dialogue resumed the same year between London and Dublin.

The first step towards peace was taken with the signing of the Hillsborough Agreement. It was followed by a series of new agreements leading to the IRA ceasefire in 1997. A few months later, hopes for a return to peace were confirmed with the signing of the Good Friday Agreement on April 10, 1998.

The Good Friday Agreement, signed by British Prime Minister Tony Blair and his Irish counterpart Bertie Ahern, as well as the leaders of the main unionist and nationalist parties on April 10, 1998, ended 30 years of conflict, which resulted in the deaths of nearly 3,500 people. The Good Friday Agreement provides for the disarmament of the IRA, the abolition of the Republic of Ireland's territorial claim to Northern Ireland, and the recognition of the right of everyone in Northern Ireland to identify and be accepted as Irish, British or both.

The U.K.'s exit from the European Union could therefore have jeopardized the Good Friday Agreement. The return to a physical border could also have hindered the movement of the 30,000 people who travel back and forth across the island every day, as well as trade, which amounts to 3.3 billion euros per year between the two parts of the island.

The exit agreements concluded with the EU by Theresa May in November 2018, then by her successor Boris Johnson on October 17, 2019, as well as the trade and cooperation agreement of December 24, 2020, governing the new relationship between London and Brussels, has been particularly concerned with avoiding the re-establishment of a hard border between the two Irelands, by granting a specific status to Northern Ireland.

Grace Neville[57] writes:

> "For me, the real day that marks Ireland's independence is not 1921, but 1er January 1973, the day we joined the Common Market. It was that day that marked the end of our identity as a former colony and allowed us to re-establish our relationship with the wider European family, without our always being defined with Britain.
>
> From the very first day, our European friends welcomed us, on an equal footing with all the others, a poor country, certainly, in economic terms, but rich in history, music, literature, poetry, imagination, and creativity. They have allowed us, finally, to play in the big league!

POLITICAL SYSTEM: Ireland is a parliamentary republic composed of 26 counties. The head of government, the Prime Minister, is appointed by the President after nomination by the lower house (Dáil) and exercises executive power. The head of state, the President, has mainly honorary powers. The parliament is composed of two chambers (an upper and a lower house).

THE CELTIC TIGER: nicknamed the "Celtic Tiger" for its record growth from 1995 to 2007, Ireland was the envy of the world with an average annual growth of 6%. In one decade, the unemployment rate was divided by three and its GDP had doubled.

During a trip in October 2007, I was amazed by the very arrogant attitude of young Irish people. This attitude contrasted with the attitude of their grandparents. But the dream turned into a nightmare.

Ireland's economy collapsed like a house of cards in the 2008 crisis, before recovering under the support of Europe and the IMF. As in other countries, the

---

[57] Grace Neville is Professor Emeritus of French at University College Cork, where she also served as Vice President for Teaching and Learning from 2008 to 2012. She received a double degree in French and Irish, a French government scholarship to the University of Caen (1972-73) and earned her doctorate at the University of Lille. She has published extensively on Franco-Irish relations (medieval-modern period), linguistic issues and women's writing. She has presented more than 250 research papers at such venues as the Sorbonne, the Collège de France, the French Senate, Harvard, and Berkeley.

crisis was precipitated by the bursting of a property bubble. From 1996 to 2006, property prices quadrupled. Then they collapsed by 40%. This country of 4.6 million people took more than three years to regain its economic and financial independence, before exiting the international aid plan in December 2013. Ireland was saved from bankruptcy. But the price was high for the population, hard hit by tax hikes and painful reforms imposed by the EU and IMF. The numbers have since turned decisively green again. In 2014, Ireland recorded growth of 4.8 percent, the strongest in the European Union. But the effects of austerity continue to be felt and the Irish, exhausted after the heavy sacrifices made, are slow to see the recovery materialize in their lives.

The history of Ireland is above all the history of an island open to the world.

THE RISE OF THE CONNEMARA PONY

Louis Marie Philibert confirms that in the 70s, the Connemara pony was at a dead end. Its expansion is directly linked to the development of pony competition in France and Europe. From the end of 1970 - the beginning of the '80s, pony competitions in France created a boom, a real need. French people started to buy Connemara ponies and recognized in them an easy pony that could jump!

For Stéphane Jault:

> *"The dynamic of the development of the breeding of the Connemara pony in Ireland was strongly increased by the influence of 2 factors in the years 1990/2000: Europe and the Internet. The creation of a free trade zone within the old continent has allowed creating around the Connemara pony an increase in production. A real frenzy seized the breeders who suddenly saw a strong frequentation of their farms by a foreign clientele and consequently their selling prices soared. At the beginning of the year 2000, the creation of the eurozone came to support the exchanges and facilitate transactions a little more. At the same time, the development of the internet created new relationships between breeders. The proximity and visibility allowed by this new tool very quickly triggered a new functioning in the Connemara universe. The visibility of each breeding stud as well as the creation of online sales rooms make Irish ponies accessible to the rest of the world.*

As for Hubert Laurent:

"At the moment the market in Ireland is very strong again with very high prices, the non-grey are more and more sought after, there are always many requests for coverings from the stallions having won at Clifden (too much as always in Ireland). As soon as a stallion is popular, he is overused resulting in inbreeding problems. On the other hand, and it's great for our breeding, more and more performer stallions in sports come from France because for some Irish breeders we have the best Connemara sport ponies in the world.

The lovers of a certain Ireland, of which I am a part, those of monks, poets, saints, nationalist fighters, of their way of life with their horses, of the music and the pubs bathed by this traditional atmosphere could not but succumb to its romanticism. I had the chance to discover Ireland and Connemara in the early 80s. Clifden was not so developed, it was not invaded by B&Bs which now look more like hotels. Today, in pubs, traditional songs are sung only to attract tourists.

The state of mind of the breeders has changed, and the relationship they had with their ponies too. At the end of the 90s, I saw the appearance of stables in Connemara with whole feed to fatten the foals.

I think that Connemara and Ireland have evolved under the effects of progress or because of a natural evolution of customs and ideas. This evolution is also an indirect consequence of the integration of Ireland into the European Union, which undermined the breeding of the Connemara pony. The breeders no longer raised useful ponies, but rapidly exportable consumer goods. At first, it was an economic boom for the Irish breeders who received European subsidies. But they did not perceive that the steamroller of the European technocracy was going to have an indirect impact on their autonomy of decision and their independence as the cradle of the breed. Among other things, this was the case for the approval of stallions. The European Union has slowly and skillfully implemented a policy of standardization by imposing its laws. Will the Irish breeders be able to take back the reins of their breeding ethics? Only the Irish can answer this question.

RULES FOR PREFIXES IN IRELAND

In Ireland, breeders use prefixes to name their ponies and represent their breeding stock. For example, Mrs. Petch uses the prefix Coosheen to identify her ponies: Coosheen Nutmeg, Coosheen Muffin. But this does not mean that the pony is from her breeding because she bought a foal at birth and named him Coosheen Finn.

The issue of prefixes had been raised several times in the past and was finally included in the registration rules on the March 11, 1970 GA. Before 1970, many breeders and dealers used a prefix on all ponies they owned at registration age, This created confusion for foreign buyers. As of 1970, a breeder had the right to register a prefix with the Society for life, and it could not be used by another person. It was also decided that a prefix could not be used as a suffix.

In France we use Affixes. For example, I use the affix "de Briacé" to represent my breeding: Mistral de Briacé, Lyre de Briacé, Vanille de Briacé...

Recently, I noticed that ponies imported from Ireland had a French affix. These ponies are often of low quality and harm the French breeders. I requested the SIRE to have some precisions about the respect of the regulation on the use of a French breeders affix by an Irish breeder.

Here is the response I received from SIRE:

> *"An affix registered at the IFCE is only valid for identification documents issued by the IFCE for foals born in France. For example, a foreign breeder can register an affix if he has his foal born in France and has his booklet published by the IFCE.*

> *On the other hand, a foreign equine or having obtained its identification document through a foreign studbook is not subject to the rules of nomination or deposit of cattery of the IFCE ".*

This is a problematic that should be looked into with the mother society, CPBS.

CONNEMARA PART-BRED

Little Heaven was also the sire of several crosses with Connemara mares. These crosses called Part-Bred produced famous half-bloods that did much for the promotion of the Connemara pony in the 1960s.

Little Model won international fame as a dressage horse, having been ridden in the 1960 Rome Olympics by Mrs. Brenda Williams, and placed third at the European Championships in 1963.

Figure 136. Dundrum. Archive Daniel Chupin.

The most famous son of all was the brilliant show jumping horse Dundrum, who was Tommy Wade's mount. This little horse of only 152 cm excited the international show jumping world with his amazing abilities. Dundrum's dam was a registered Connemara mare named Evergood by Gil and Queen Maeve by Lavalley Star. She was bred by Joe Joyce near Recess and sold to Patrick Crowe in County Tipperary. She was in foal to Little Heaven when she left Connemara. Her foal was then purchased by the Wade family who lived in the village of Dundrum, County Tipperary. The little bay horse was given the name Dundrum. His remarkable achievements on the international show jumping scene during the 1960s are legendary and include such famous victories as the King George V Cup, the RDS Power, and the Dublin Grand Prix. He was part of the Irish team that won the Aga Khan Cup.

His successes drew attention to his pony origins and the fact that his dame was a Connemara mare.

CONNEMARA PART-BRED IN FRANCE

At the end of December 2012, the A.F.P.C opened the Connemara Part-Bred register. The objective of this Connemara Part-Bred register was to answer the need of the breeders to valorize their production and to make visible the results of the crossings made with Connemara Ponies.

Indeed, the analysis of statistics on ponies not registered in a studbook, clearly revealed that Connemara genetics is very widely used. In particular, a study was made by the A.F.P.C. on Connemara stallion breeding. It showed that over 10 years Connemara stallions were the most used pony breed stallions, with an average of between 1,700 to 2,000 services per year.

Half of the Connemara stallions' coverings was producing into the Connemara studbook and the other half producing crossbreeds. The cross-bred coverings were divided as follows: one-third into the French Saddle Pony studbook and the other two-thirds represent ponies that were registered OC (a simple filial identification without incorporating a particular studbook).

So, regularly, 600 to 700 ponies from a Connemara sire were born each year and are registered in OC. The Connemara genetics was not being highlighted because it was drowned in the "catch-all" of the registered origins.

To be a Connemara Part-Bred, an animal must have both parents registered in a Bloodhorse or pony studbook, or a registry or Recorded Origin or Unrecorded Origin. It must have a Connemara sire or dam. In the case where neither the sire nor the dam is Connemara, the pony must be able to prove a minimum of 62.5% Connemara blood over three generations. Therefore, it is necessary to have at least 5 Connemara great-grandparents.

There are now 1101 horses registered as Connemara Part-Bred. The most famous ones being Shamrock du Gite and Vedouz de Nestin.

SHAMROCK DU GITE, IPO (show jumping index) 172 in 2015, under the saddle of Justine Maerte, is a team bronze medalist and individual gold medalist at the European Championships in Malmö, Sweden in 2015. Son of Welcome Sympatico and Nina de Garenne a Connemara mare. Nina de Garenne is the daughter of the very good stallion Kid de Garenne.

VEDOUZ DE NESTIN, IPO 208 in 2021! Under the saddle of Jeanne Hirel, was French Champion 2021 in As Pony Excellence, team gold medal, and an individual gold medal at the European Championships in Strzegom. Son of the international performance stallion Impérial du Blin and Leila du Nereau SFA mare by O Malley SFA (we find the Anglo-Arabian Iago C and the thoroughbred Monceaux in the maternal origins).

Figure 137. Impérial du Blin, the sire of Vedouz de Nestin, is a chestnut Connemara stallion, an international performer, who transmits his very good character, his aptitudes, and his competitive temperament to his progeny. Photo Private collection Françoise Clémenceau.

THE CREAM GENE, THE DUN GENE, AND THE HWSD

For these subjects which were for a long-time source of polemics, in particular the Cream ponies, I wished to explain the Irish position which has evolved after the last few years. To avoid any misunderstanding on the three subjects, I used the elements contained in the technical sheets established by Equipédia on reinvestigating the I.F.C.E. website.

CREAM PONIES WITH BLUE EYES

At the General Assembly held in Galway on March 21, 1966, there was a discussion on the problem of blue-eyed cream ponies. Dr. Peter Cullen suggested that in the interest of the breed steps should be taken to reduce the risk of breeding them with darker-colored stallions. Another breeder stated that it was difficult to find a market for Browns and Bays, as Duns, Greys, and Creams were considered more typical of the breed.

Blue-Eyed Cream ponies had ceased to be acceptable for registration in the Connemara Pony Breeders' Society Stud Book. This decision had been the cause of much controversy among Connemara pony breeders. It had been a regular point of discussion at international meetings.

Since then, the regulations have evolved and blue-eyed cream ponies from Connemara parents can access classification since 2018. This decision, which is far from unanimous in Ireland, was taken to meet the need for dun ponies. This decision was also taken to mitigate the predominance of grey coats. In 2021 a cream stallion with blue eyes was approved by the CPBS.

THE DUN GENE

The[58] Dun gene, noted "D", is also called the "wild" gene because of its presence in primitive horses like Przewalski[59] . It acts on the two pigments: pheomelanin (yellow/red) and eumelanin (black/dark brown). In addition to the dilution of the base color, it is responsible for the presence of primitive markings: Cap de Maure head, dark extremities, mullet stripe, scapular band[60] , and welts. Fjords,

---

[58] Genes are the basic unit of heredity. They are responsible for physical traits, cell function and also for certain diseases. In cells, genes are located on a specific part of a chromosome. Chromosomes are located in the heart of the cell, the nucleus. If the nucleus of the cell is the library that contains the genetic heritage of an individual, the chromosome is a book and the gene is a page in one of its books.

[59] Przewalski's horse, also called Prjevalski's horse or *takh* in Mongolian, is characterized by a massive aspect, a big head, a strong neck and a bay/dun coat, which reminds the representations of the prehistoric art. It measures 1.30 m on average at the withers. Przewalski's horse is the oldest population of horses living in the wild. They were discovered in Dzugaria in 1879 by the explorer Nikolai Mikhailovich Przhevalsky.

[60] Stripe going down to the shoulders.

for example, have the typical coat caused by the presence of the[61] dominant allele of the Dun gene[62]. Two alleles are known for this gene, the dominant allele DD (causing dilution of eumelanin and pheomelanin) and the recessive allele Dd (present in a homozygous state, it does not cause any coat modification). Unlike the CCR Cream allele, the Dun DD allele is full dominant. The phenotype will be the same whether the individual is heterozygous or homozygous.

The coat colour obtained depend on the basic coat. They are thus:

	Dd / Dd	Dd / DD ou DD /DD
Chestnut	Chestnut	Chestnut Dun
Bay	Bay	Bai Dun > Bai Fjord
Black	Black	Mouse Dun

Figure 138. Table of coats obtained from the basic coats. Daniel Chupin.

Its result or effect can sometimes be confused with that of the Cream gene. However,
these genes have a different action, and thus can be distinguished:

- The Dun DD allele affects the density of the pigments. It, therefore, creates a visually diluted effet while the CCR Cream allele appears to affect the pigments themselves by altering their chemical structure.
- The Dun DD allele acts on the pheomelanin by diluting it on the body, but not on the manes, while the Creame CCR allele dilutes the pheomelanin on the body and the manes. The Dun gene dilutes the black base coat to mouse gray, which the cream gene does not.
- The Dun allele causes primitive marks, which can help to discern its presence. Beware, however, that in rare cases it may be a dilution caused by the cream gene, associated with the presence of a mullet line, without the Dun DD allele being present.

---

[61] An allele (short for allelomorph) is a variable version of the same gene. There are usually a few alleles for each gene. The alleles of a pair of homologous chromosomes can be identical, that is homozygosity, or different, that is heterozygosity.

[62] Mouse Dun is a variant of dun family as grulla or grullo, also called blue dun, gray dun or mouse dun.

The crossbreeding table below allows, from a blood test, to predict the future foal will have a diluted coat because of the Dun gene, according to the coat of its parents:

	DD / DD dilution	DD / Dd dilution	Dd / Dd None Grey
DD / DD dilution	100% de dilution	100% de dilution	100% de dilution
DD / Dd dilution	100% de dilution	75% de dilution complete dilution 25% de non dilution	50% de dilution 50% de non dilution
Dd / Dd absence de dilution	100% de dilution	50% de dilution 50% de no dilution	100% de no dilution

Figure 139. Crossing table gene dun. Daniel Chupin.

HWSD - HOOF WALL SEPARATION DISEASE

HWSD (Hoof Wall Separation Disease) is a genetic disease affecting the pony's foot. It is transmitted exclusively through breeding stock. Good management can influence the evolution of this disease. Screening helps to avoid risky crossbreeding. There are many symptoms variably apparent in ponies affected by the disease. However, in all cases, the following elements are present:

- The disease appears before weaning
- All 4 feet are affected
- Separation of the dorsal wall of the hoof
- End of the hooves in "coconut fiber "
- Sole and white line healthy

As the disease appears in young animals, early detection is a major element in limiting symptoms. Thus, it allows early care and vigilance on the condition of the horn. The disease is not gender-specific. Horses that carry a single copy of the gene pass it on to their offspring. They are perfectly healthy, with no symptoms of the disease. This disease can also go through several generations before manifesting itself. The pony is considered:

- **Non-carrier** and cannot transmit the anomaly. It is **N/N**.
- **Healthy carrier**, not diseased, but likely to transmit the defect. It is **N/HWSD.**
- **Carrier expresses the disease rapidly** after birth. It is **HWSD / HWSD.**

The table below shows the different crossing possibilities with the risks of obtaining a non-carrier, healthy carrier, or rapidly expressing the disease foal.

	Mare N/N	Mare N/HWSD	Mare HWSD/HWSD
Stallion N/N	100% N/N	50% N/N 50% N/HWSD	100% N/HWSD
Stallion N/HWSD	50% N/N 50% N/HWSD	25% N/N 50% N/HWSD 25% HWSD/HWSD	50% N/HWSD 50% HWSD/HWSD
Stallion HWSD/HWSD	100% N/HWSD	50% N/HWSD 50% HWSD/HWSD	100% HWSD/HWSD

Figure 140. Crossing table to avoid the HWSD gene. Daniel Chupin.

This is not a new problem in Connemara, but the breeders I met in the 1980s knew their ponies' genetics. They used their ponies and knew their strains. The information was passed on orally, but the information was being passed on.

Mistakes were made a few years ago in Ireland, leading the Department of Agriculture to implement a systematic screening of foals under the dam. This was a good initiative that clarified the situation regarding this disease and favored the market. Tests were conducted in Ireland on 15177 foals born between 2016 and 2021.

- 80.15% of the foals were N/N.
- 18.85% of foals were N/HWSD (healthy carrier).
- 152 foals were HWSD/HWSD or 1%.

In summary, we could consider that the problem lies only in 1% of foals born between 2016 and 2021! In 2021 only 11 foals were concerned (0.47%).

However, we need to go further in our thinking.

In France, I fear that many breeders will take refuge behind a maximum of indicators to make their crosses. This situation will inevitably lead to an impoverishment of genetics. I too have been challenged by this problem of HWSD.

The knowledge of maternal and paternal genetics is fundamental. We are confronted with the arrival of new breeders who have very little knowledge of

Connemara breeding, who, through ignorance, take refuge in the results of tests, which ends up limiting their possible crosses.

To breed is to take a risk. It is because I evaluated the risks that I used Garryhinch Millrace. These choices allowed me to produce Ulza du Moulin D'Eau. Ulza has HWSD. But by crossing her with Mistral de Briacé who was N/N, she only produced animals with very good hooves. Her first two offspring (Fleur du Moulin d'eau IPO 134 and Eliand IPC 145) are performing at the highest level (Eliand being the best pony of his generation in eventing).

For Stéphane Jault:

> *"If you listen to people, people want only N/N ponies (Not carrying the HWSD gene). There are a hundred diseases that come directly from our genes. If we wanted to be certain to avoid all of them, we would never produce, and even prohibit the reproduction of the human species (Laughter). So, there would be theoretically perfect animals. But this does not exist. It is a delusion. Let's stop this headlong rush. Breeding is not that. It is not to hide behind indicators. Of course, if you have a carrier mare, you have to use an N/N stallion. But breeding is taking a risk!"*

Hubert Laurent considers that:

> *"The HWSD test will keep a lot of very good N/HWSD stallions away from breeding, it's a real shame, yet stallions like Currachmore Cashel bred a lot before this test was introduced, I'm not saying it's useless, but it mustn't harm the breed in the long run with even more inbreeding problems."*

> *Focusing only on N/N stallions and limiting or discarding N/HWSD stallions could be a mistake for Connemara breeding. We use an adage in the French horse world, to appease people who are too assertive about a sire or a breeding method: "There is always a horse to prove you wrong."*

CONCLUSION ON HWSD

The fact that a pony is N/HWSD (healthy carrier) is without consequence for leisure activities and any intensive sports activities.

Geneticists and veterinarians are not able to explain why an N/HWSD pony can have a better-quality hoof than an N/N (non-carrier) pony.

Breeding is, above all, analyzing and making crossbreeding choices. It is therefore the breeder's responsibility to make reasoned crosses. In the case of a mare having the HWSD disease, this disease is not redhibitory for reproduction, because the test is a chance for certain mares. It gives them access to breeding using stallions with N/N status. In France, the implementation of HWSD testing for males and females presented for classification is therefore desirable.

CONNEMARA HAS ITS POSTAGE STAMP

On Friday, October 23, 1981, the Irish Post Office issued the fourth set of stamps in its series illustrating the fauna and flora of Ireland.

This issue featured famous Irish horses, and the stamps were available in four denominations and five distinct designs.

The horses featured on the stamps were the Thoroughbreds Arkle and Ballymoss, representing the steeplechase and flat race horses, the show jumping horse Boomerang, the Irish draft stallion King of Diamonds, and the Connemara pony stallion Coosheen Finn. The stamp paintings were done by Wendy Walsh, who was the artist for all the flora and fauna series.

Coosheen Finn (who stood only 138 cm) was chosen by the Irish Post to represent the Connemara pony because he was the winning stallion at the Clifden show in 1978, the first sire in 1979 when his offspring won the two-, three- and four-year-old classes at the Dublin Horse Show and again at the Clifden show. He also sired the supreme champion Coosheen Nutmeg at the Clifden show in 1979 and 1980 and his sister Coosheen Muffin was 4th at 3 years old at the Clifden show in 1984. He was chosen for the 36 pence stamp, which was the airmail stamp to the United States and Australia because many people from the west of Ireland had emigrated to those countries and it was thought that they would appreciate receiving a letter from home with a Connemara pony on the stamp.

Figure 141. Coosheen Fin. Photo from the private collection of Elisabeth Petch.

FROM USEFUL PONIES TO LEISURE PONIES

The pony today leads a very different life from that of its ancestor, the small farmer's draft pony, which was used for all the pulling and transport work needed throughout the season.

The Irish tested the health and temperament of their broodmare by daily use. Together with the owner, the pony ploughed, cultivated, sowed, harvested, and gathered hay. Together they worked the small stony fields of Connemara, hauling seaweed to enrich the soil, where potatoes and other vegetables were grown. They hauled stone from the quarries to build roads and drew peat from the bog to keep the family warm in winter and to cook food.

Only the strongest and bravest ponies survived this arduous and exhausting work, as an animal that tired easily or had a "faulty" temperament was quickly discarded by the farmer. The Connemara pony carried goods and family everywhere, to town or to markets many miles away to sell the farm's products, and carried family members to mass, funerals, and weddings throughout the year.

The mare usually gave birth to a foal each year, the sale of which brought much-needed additional income to the household. Breeding was semi-wild. The conformation was not perfect, but the ponies were useful. These ponies were often just over 133 cm in height when they were entered in the studbook, and there were a greater number of blacks, chestnuts, bays, duns, and roans, whereas grey has become a predominant coat today.

CREGG LASSIE Pat Lyne paints a beautiful portrait of this mare:

"Between 1954 and 1973, Lassie bred fifteen foals, eight colts, and seven fillies. Six of them were by Carna Dun and provided her most successful progeny... Lassie's story could fill more than a page. Her pedigree was not established until well after registration and indeed she was not registered until the age of seven, having failed her first inspection at three years. Her parentage came to light when Oughterard's garda, Charles Friel, was able to verify that his father-in-law Matt Ridge of Derrycoyle, Costello, had bred her from his mare Lady Jane No. 455 who visited Tully Lad No. 48. Larry Duggan who bought her as a foal is shown as her breeder in the studbook. However, in the Society records her full pedigree is included and thus she provides the female we need to represent the Mountain Lad line... She is one of the few to die of old age in her stable at Cregg with the man she had served so well. She left a big gap in Jim's life, one which he has never really filled. There are no longer

ponies at Cregg and Lassie's cart and harness lie idle and her empty stable. Jim is still there in semi-retirement, enjoying his favorite hobby, fishing. She represents so completely all that is best in the mares of Connemara."

Figure 142. Cregg Lassie is still at work at age 22. Source Shrouded in Mist.

Figure 143. Lehid Rose, 37 in 1986, was the oldest mare in Connemara. Photo by Daniel Chupin.

Thanks to natural selection, then artificial selection, the Connemara pony has become a leisure animal that excels in many disciplines.

The Connemara is a versatile pony par excellence. Perfect for leisure, it is also a good competitor in high-level equestrian sports, such as CCE (eventing), CSO (show jumping), Dressage, Hunter, Amazon, Driving, Track riding competition, Endurance, Polo, and in Handisport.

He is considered the number one sport pony in the world.

For leisure, it is a perfect riding pony by its gentle nature and its assurance. The Connemara pony is suitable for children as well as for parents, it is the pony for the whole family. His strength, his balance, his amplitude, and his excellent temperament, allow him to adapt to all levels and to all disciplines of leisure and sport competitions.

Capable of carrying an adult and gentle enough for a young child, it is favored by children and parents alike for its ease of use over other breeds.

An example of a versatile and successful pony: **Jaguar de Briacé**.

The Marolleau family bought Jaguar in 2002 at the age of 5 years old for their daughter Jeanne who wanted to compete in eventing. Jeannine and Jeannick Marolleau made this choice because they were looking for security for their child. Jaguar's calm character and strength seduced the whole family. This pony competed in eventing up to D1 Ponam Elite GP (the couple ranked 2nd of the event in Jau Dignac). This level corresponds to the current CCE AS Poney Elite GP. This pony performed in Dressage and Show Jumping with the following results: IPD 122; IPC 120 and IPO 133.

As is often the case, customers become friends and, in the autumn of 2007, Jeannick told me how much he would enjoy driving Jaguar to fetch his bread in the neighboring town of Chemellier, a few kilometers from the Moulin d'Eau. No matter, I take care of bringing the harnesses and the trainer. Together we broken-in Jaguar. On Friday we start by getting the pony used to the harness, then we work on the long reins. Two hours later, Jaguar was on the trainer's stretchers and was quite willing to participate in this new activity. The next day we repeated the different exercises in the morning and afternoon. At the end of the afternoon, I validate the availability of the pony by evaluating the risks that Jeannick could incur. On Sunday morning, after the last test, I leave the guides to Jeannick.

For safety reasons, I accompany him riding bike. Jeannick and Jaguar set off at a slow trot through the beautiful Anjou countryside to park in front of the Chemellier bakery to do their shopping. The return trip was just as nice.

Through this anecdote, I just want to show you that a good Connemara pony is not only a high-level sport pony but also a versatile leisure pony for the whole family.

Figure 144. Jaguar of Briace and Jeannick Marolleau. Photo Daniel Chupin.

Hubert Laurent states:

> "At the club, Connemara ponies are very popular and we use them for teenagers and some adults, they are practical, friendly, and always ready to adapt. Unfortunately, my selection means that we often have the impression that we are wasting some ponies with lots of qualities when they are ridden by the smaller levels. All our ponies live in a herd, in the meadow during the good season where the riders go to get them. They are stabled loose in a barn in winter. The best ponies compete (up to 13 of them at the French championships, 3 years ago) up to P elite, but I don't have an instructor skilled enough to bring them further, on even if some of them are well capable.
>
> The Connemara is criticized for not having enough blood. But paradoxically, this is its strength, because it is more easily used by riders of all levels.

The Connemara is a hardy pony and a lot of young breeders raise them like horses, with a lot of vitamin-enriched food, and sometimes in stables. The result is precocious ponies, but often prone to joint problems. Ideally, they should be raised as naturally as possible in large hilly spaces so that they acquire strength, solidity, and stamina."

For Romeo Thilvert (Chimera Equestrian Center):

"The Connemara's versatility is essential. The work is sometimes longer. For them, life is beautiful, without stress. But they always end up giving you what you ask for. They're not all going to go to Grand Prix, but if you leave them within the framework of what they're capable of doing, you can't be disappointed. And then there's life outside of competition, kids who go off on their own to ride bareback, you can have them do pony games, horse ball. You can do everything with them. I can't see myself working with any other breed. For me, it is not a problem. The Connemara pony evolves when he meets problems. It's when the problem happens that the pony progresses. If you show him the problem too early, you destroy him. If you show him the problem little by little, the pony never says no." Regarding blood: "If you take your time, you build it, it's a pony that gives you. The "blood" will improve with work. "

And he concludes:

"What I like about the Connemara pony is the mental aspect, the rusticity. For me, the Connemara pony is perfect!"

The Connemara pony is also a pony for disabled people.

Lætitia Bernard has been blind since birth, suffering from complete and irreversible congenital blindness. Journalist at Radio France, she presents the sports news on France Inter. She covered for Radio France the Paralympic Games of London in 2012, then Sochi in 2014, Rio in 2016, and Pyeongchang in 2018. In May 2021, she published the book "My life is a team sport". Lætitia Bernard started horseback riding competitions at the age of 13. She is a five-time French champion in show jumping, winning in 1997, 1998, 2000, 2002, and 2005. She was also French champion in dressage in 1997 and 2000. She has been guided by renowned riders such as Michel Robert at the Bordeaux International Jumping in 2004 and the Geneva International Show Jumping Competition in 2005. She was also guided by John Whitaker in Bordeaux in 2006. She qualified for the French Equestrian Championships with able-bodied riders on two occasions, including the Generali Open de France in Lamotte-Beuvron in 2009.

I later sold Oscar de Briacé to the Blanc family for their daughter Adeline. This one was also ridden by Leatitia Bernard. Laetitia Bernard gave me her very moving testimony about her equestrian experience with Oscar de Briacé (Tynagh de Briacé x Coosheen Muffin by Cooshenn Finn):

> *"Oscar, more commonly known as little Oscar, or Carosse, or Cacar, is the kindest, most reliable, and most talented pony I have ever met. He is the only one I was never afraid to ride, the one I dared to gallop with on the beach, in the fields, after Christmas meals...*
>
> *He was unstoppable at the jumps, always aimed at the fence, and never made a mistake in his first strides. He immediately understood the principle of following another horse to link up a course, I could take him on large and very windy grounds like in Cabourg, even if the guide's voice didn't reach me anymore, he always kept his trajectories, I trusted him completely.*
>
> *Together, we won several events in the French Cup for the Disabled (events between 70 and 80 cm) and did some great in Club 3 Club 2, in the years 2008-2010. Frankly, I keep an exceptional memory of him, I haven't met a pony like him since.*
>
> *I was very lucky to be able to spend time with him. He was sold to a little boy who was losing his eyesight, I remember the day they met: the little boy stuck to his leg and hugged him, Oscar relaxed and didn't move an ear, he understood everything... "*

Nelly Groene, an instructor at the Pirouette equestrian center in Couëron, regularly coaches Steeve Merlet (with Down's syndrome):

> *"Ange de Briacé does not behave the same way with Steeve as with the other riders in the ponyclub. He allows Steeve to ride safely on a cross-country course and to ride a showjumping course without outside help."*

As the Irish so aptly put it:

The Connemara pony can be maintained as a pony and ridden like a horse.

Figure 145. Laetitia Bernard riding Oscar de Briacé. Archive Daniel Chupin.

Figure 146. Steeve and Ange de Briacé. Photo Didier Merlet.

THE STANDARD OF THE CONNEMARA PONY

The Connemara pony is officially described as follows:

- Height: The height of breeding Connemara Pony is 128 cm to 148 cm at maturity.
- Colours: Grey, Black, Bay, Brown, Dun occasionally Roan, Chestnut, Palomino, and Dark Eyed Cream. Not allowed: Piebald.
- Type: compact, well-balanced riding type with good depth and substance and good heart room, standing on short legs, covering a lot of ground.
- Head: Well-balanced pony head of medium length with good width between large kindly eyes. Pony ears, well-defined cheekbone jaw relatively deep but not coarse.
- Front: Head well-set onto the neck. The chest should not be overdeveloped. Neck not set too low. Good length of rein. Well-defined withers, good sloping shoulders.
- Body: Body should be deep, with a strong back, some length permissible but should be well-ribbed up and with a strong loin.
- Limbs: Good length and strength in forearm, well-defined knees, and short cannons, with flat bone measuring 18cms to 21cms. Elbows should be free. Pasterns of medium length, feet well shaped, of medium size, hard and level.
- Hind Quaters: Strong and muscular with some length, well-developed second thighs (Gaskin), and strong low-set hocks.
- Movement: Movement free easy and true, without undue knee action, but active and covering ground.

The breed standards are the foundation, the base that must lead any breeder in all these crossbreeding projects.

There is no basic type, there is a Connemara pony.

Before I continue, let me remind you of a few basics:

BLOOD: Blood in an outdoor language is the manifestation of the real or fake energy of the pony. It can be seen in the fineness of the fabric and hair, but above all in the expression of the eyes, in the elegance of the forms, in the vivacity and grace of the movements, in the energy of the paces. The blood is an impulse[63] , that the pony has in him, that allows him to surpass himself and to give everything to his rider or his leader. The blood of a pony can only be assessed on an animal that is ridden or harnessed on repeated and prolonged efforts.

Blood is neither nervousness nor emotionality.

CONDITION: A pony's condition is defined as its state of being so well prepared that it can withstand great effort, hard and prolonged work without suffering.

TEMPERING: Tempering is the result of blood and condition.

BACKGROUND: The background is a pony's ability to withstand work, training, and strength development through blood, condition, and tempering.

I asked Hubert Laurent and Stéphane Jault to explain to me what they were looking for in a Connemara pony, beyond the official standards.

Hubert Laurent is looking for the following characteristics:

> *"The Connemara has to be a versatile pony, strong without being too heavy either, he has to have free and supple gaits (I think that the selection in France as well as in Ireland has not been focused enough on the gaits and most of the Irish breeders do not know how to emphasize the gaits of their ponies, they block heading them hard at the head level instead of presenting them with a relaxed and by letting them express themselves). What I look at first when I judge the Connemara, is the harmony, the movement, and the distinction (the chic, the presence). If he is not harmonious (for example, a beautiful forehand, but no back end...nice body, but with a short neck, a lovely head, but set too tightly on the neck, a nice body, but no underbody...), he cannot function well, he will not have the balance necessary for good riding.*

---

[63] Hypothetical fluid transmitting a force.

If there is no beautiful gait and the will to carry himself forward, he will not be pleasant to ride. I have had and produced ponies with extraordinary movements (Idénoir, his son Origan Mélody, Rock River Mélody who took part in Europe in CCE and Impérator. But these last two were unfortunately little used) however, Idénoir left his mark from generation to generation by producing ponies with true and beautiful gaits.

For distinction, the ponies with chic (Mrs. Petch puts a lot of emphasis on it) I think, often have more intelligence and blood and also they are prettier to look at."

Stéphane Jault is looking for ponies that walk. The walk is the base. The amplitude in the canter is linked to the walk. And for him the trot can improve with work:

"I need to have feedback, information, and the feeling of the riders. The presence of the breeder on the competition grounds is essential because I want to understand because I need to listen to the customers (grandparents and parents are looking for security, while riders are most often focused on reliability and performance).

The good pony must help the rider. It must be comfortable with strength. I look for suppleness with a well-stretched back to be able to repeat the efforts. The type is not enough, I want to see them in motion, and I want to observe their reactions when they are confronted with difficulties. For me, it is unthinkable to choose a stallion if you don't go and see him, touch him. You don't choose a stallion from a glossy photo or from internet. It is thanks to its imperfections that I can orient my choices. I am very critical of my animals because I have to question myself. It is the only way to progress in breeding."

I am convinced of one thing, there is no single model of Connemara pony. We are all looking for a pony to answer a specific use which for example can be eventing, driving...

The Connemara pony is hardy and versatile, so it can meet many needs. But I think that an animal of more than 150 cm is too far from the basic type. However, certain points of conformation and locomotion are frequently found in high-level ponies: Strength, amplitude and balance are major assets. If some criteria can be measured objectively (height, barrel circumference, and depth of girth...) others are aesthetic (conformation, distinction, and condition...).

I am looking for a powerful and supple pony who carries his balance on his hindquarters, who raises his withers. Locomotion at walk and canter is fundamental. In his confirmation, I look for a balance between the forehand and the hindquarters and above all a well-grafted head on a well-extended neck.

In both horse and pony breeding, the selection is based on the assumption that the probability of a performer passing on his qualities is greater than that of a non-performer. This assumption is often disproved because the ability can be hidden for one or more generations. Ability can appear and then disappear as we are sometimes reminded by the mediocrity of certain products of famous stallions.

Of course, like any breeder, I make choices. I have decided to put all my breeding stock to work. They must prove to me what they are capable of, I test them without racing to conclusions. As a breeder and a rider, I don't care about the origins first of all because I am only interested in the abilities of the pony and the feeling on his back, and when I can't ride them, I watch them work. The evaluation of the qualities of a Connemara pony is a matter of the user and the observer and not of a combination of origins, or the results in a show.

The setting up of indices, labels, and a breeding program in France are all interesting and necessary steps in the right direction, but they are only indicators that allow an estimation without taking in consideration the user's judgement.

The sporting qualities, the type, the pedigree, the track record, the character... nothing must be neglected in the search for a sire and each of these factors must be analyzed with reason without ostracism or favoritism and above all without taking into account the fashions.

All these elements are only the fruit of appreciations, objective measurements, and subjective impressions which make breeding more an art than a science.

COLOURS

For this chapter, I have taken back and updated the article I wrote for "Connemara magazine" in 1988. The origins of the diversity of colours and the evolution of the panel of colours presented between 1982 and 1988 on the ring of the Clifden show challenged me. We only saw grey ponies. The black, palomino, chestnut and cream ponies had almost disappeared.

As you read this book, you will understand that the influence of the Spanish horses and the interventions of the Congested Districts Board from 1891 to 1903 had a major impact on the evolution of the Connemara breed.

The contribution of external blood with the Barb Awfully Jolly who was chestnut, the Hackney Lord Go Bang who was bay, various Thoroughbreds, the Hunter and especially the Welsh Cob Prince Llewellyn chestnut, Movement dark chestnut, and Welsh Tommy chestnut, have marked their progeny. From 1950, the C.P.S. by its reasoned contribution of English and Arabian Thoroughbreds, a little less with the Irish Draught, allowed Little Heaven (bay) and Naseel (light grey) to type their progeny.

The Connemara pony type could not evolve without the intervention of Irish breeders who shaped a pony marked by the soil, corresponding to their taste, economic needs, and the development of this breed throughout the world.

From the studbook, it is now possible to establish the percentages of the different colours according to the volume of registration and also the year of birth.

In volumes I to VIII, some reports were made on old ponies whose coat was definitive. From volume IX, the percentages become very relative, because they are established on the report of young subjects whose colours sometimes evolved (Ex: Gold Fort registered dun and became grey). The analysis of the studbook of the mares observes a rather important diversification of colours: Grey, Black at a rate of 20% of the livestock, Bay, Brown, Dun, and Rouan. The black coat, which was very present until 1953, has practically disappeared. Since 1950, three colours alone represent 90% of the livestock: grey, dun, and bay. The data is similar for the stallions with the disappearance of the black coat.

The grey coat can without any doubt be considered the oldest and most representative of the Connemara pony breeding.

Figure 147. Some mares on the moor in 1984: dun, bay, grey, and palomino are represented. Photo Daniel Chupin.

By approving recently, a cream stallion with blue eyes, the CPBS shows its decision to revive dun. This colour is very commercial.

Hubert, unlike his usual self, is more adamant:

> "In Ireland, the fashion is for colored ponies with the reappearance of CYB[64] in breeding stock, which is a shame, especially for ponies living in the south of France. Because blue-eyed ponies often have skin problems, they are more sensitive and sometimes have vision problems. Greys on the other hand are perhaps a little too much in the majority, with sometimes problems of melanoma. It would be necessary to launch a big study on this subject to try as much as possible to eradicate the problem of melanoma by making reasoned crossings. Colours were much more varied at the time of the 1st stud-books, it is for that reason that I wanted to publish again the super article which you had written in the 1re Connemara magazine. "

Below, a diagram showing the distribution of colours of the breeders presented in classifications from 2006 to 2020.

We can see a rebalancing of colours which seems to me a very good thing, because all colours exist in the Connemara type, except for piebalds.

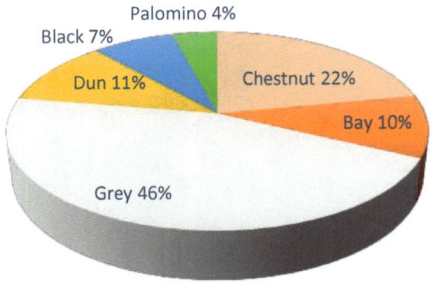

Figure 148. Distribution diagram of classified ponies' coats between 2006 and 2020. Daniel Chupin.

---

[64] Blue Eye Cream.

Figure 149. Cailin Ciuin (Abbeyleix Owen x Wireless Wave). A pony type with a dun coat is very representative of the Connemara breed. Photo Daniel Chupin.

Figure 150. Abbeyleix Dolphin at the 1984 Clifden show. Photo Daniel Chupin.

202

Figure 151. Cracker Boy Mélody, a black Connemara stallion. Photo Élevage de Séguret.

Figure 152. Callowfeenish Wave (Thunderbolt x Wirless Wave) a Bay Ticked mare followed by a filly by Tynagh de Briacé. Photo Daniel Chupin.

ADVOCACY FOR PONIES UNDER 141 CM

The Polo Pony Society was founded in 1893 to improve and encourage the breeding of high-quality riding ponies. With the Earl of Harrington as President, it seemed destined for success. The resolutions and rules developed were very simple. A height limit of 147 cm was set and animals were only admitted to the studbook after inspection. Further on, Mr. Hill remarks:

> " As one of the great difficulties in breeding Polo ponies is to keep the height within the limit, pure small pony blood, especially as foundation stock, becomes more valuable, so that the Dartmoor, Exmoor, New Forest, and Highland-bred ponies must not be over-looked, and the worth of each of these breeds cannot be well over-estimated in laying the foundation for "the breed of the future."

Concerns about pony size existed as far back as 1893.

The traditional role of the Connemara pony was that of a versatile, strong, sturdy, well-boned, and intelligent working animal. With the increasing mechanization of agriculture in the middle of the last century, the role that the Connemara pony had secured as a working animal gradually disappeared.

To adapt to the markets, the breed is moving away from the traditional type to a more "modern" type of animal, larger and lighter boned. As the breed moves away from the traditional type, valuable genes are lost.

The influence of outside blood supplies such as the English Thoroughbred has had a direct impact on the size and type of the animals. The importance of maintaining a herd of small mares under 140 cm is still a concern. There is a correlation between size and hardiness. Smaller animals survive better in an environment with coarse flora that is not very nutritious. This feeding requires a large capacity of ingestion in fodder, thus the need for a large thoracic capacity (depth of the girth passage). There is therefore a proportional link between size and depth.

Today I notice by consulting some posts on social networks that this debate is still going on. Some people openly produce oversized ponies to satisfy commercial needs. Why not, but by producing 152 cm animals they lose the essential qualities that made the Connemara ponies famous.

For Hubert Laurent:

> "I don't know if we can say that there is an ideal size for a Connemara, it depends on the use you want to make of it, I would say 148 cm for a sport pony and it's the size that everybody is looking for to compete and 143 cm for a breeder

because of the quantity of oversize we produce by crossing 148 with 148. And I think that in Ireland as well as in France we should select, promote and award especially the stallions from 140 to 144. But objectively for the use, the oversize ponies are required by the adults who want a small versatile, and rustic horse. I use and keep a lot of them at the Connemara pony-club. The C ponies are also interesting, but more difficult to sell at profitable prices.

Stéphane Jault considers that the ideal size of the Connemara pony is 145 cm, and Louis Marie Philibert also considers that the ideal size is between 145 and 148 cm, but he insists on the fact that: "Quality is not measured by the meter. We must remain vigilant because by producing stallions that are too big, it is difficult to go back. As far as I am concerned, I consider that the ideal size of a mare should be between 136 and 145 cm. For stallions, I have set myself the goal of keeping one stallion under 140 cm at the breeding farm. The second one between 145 and 148 cm.

Gill de Briacé was a grey stallion who stood 139 cm tall. He was, in my opinion, the archetype of the versatile Connemara pony.

Powerful with great jumping ability, very respectful and energetic, he was a remarkable competitor and had five riders. Practical and versatile (Show jumping, Dressage, Eventing, Hunter style, Amazon riding). His prize list speaks for itself:

- Show jumping CLASSIC CYCLE category C:

    1998: 2nd at the interregional final at the NHS, he is ranked 7th at the final in Fontainebleau (Excellent).

    2000: Vice-Champion of the 6 years old cat C.

- DRESSAGE CLASSIC CYCLE

    1998: Champion of France for 4-year-old ponies.

    2000: 2nd at the Normandy Horse Show, 10th at the final.

- BREEDING COMPETITION: French Champion under saddle and jumping skills for 5-year-old Connemara ponies.
- SHOWJUMPING PONY: 2001: 3rd French Championship C1 Elite
- EVENTING PONY: 2004: 3rd CCE C2Ponam in Châteaubriant
- AMAZON: 2005: Winner showjumping team international competition Amazon 2005 Le Lion d'Angers

Gill de Briacé was a true competitor: 29 victories and 16-second places show jumping out of 70 events. He ended his sporting career in 2005 with 2 victories and 1-second place in showjumping 130cm level.

Connemara breeders under 142 cm are the closest to the original Connemara type.

The problem of size is and will always be a concern. However, we have to admit that overall, the height is increasing. We all have the desire to produce the 145 cm pony, but this is becoming difficult because of the evolution of stallion size. The size has not only increased in stallions, but it has also increased considerably in show mares.

If you enter a 138 cm mare in a breeding show, she has no chance of making it to a ranking or a championship.

For Hubert Laurent:

> *"The problem I see now is that out of 6 stallions classified 1, five stallions are 148. There are more and more oversize stallions because they are in high demand in England, so I'm afraid that we are denaturing the breed."*

Below, you can see a table summarizing the size of the stallions retained for my analysis and the stallions classified since 2006. I took back the announced size which as you know was very often underestimated for certain stallions with maximum ratings. Some stallions were announced at 148 when they were 152 cm tall, and sometimes more. From the implementation of the classifications in 2006, the situation seems to stabilize, but here again, it is about ponies measured at 3 years knowing that they grow up to 6. I have averaged the measures by year of birth to show a trend. This trend shows a steady increase in stallion size.

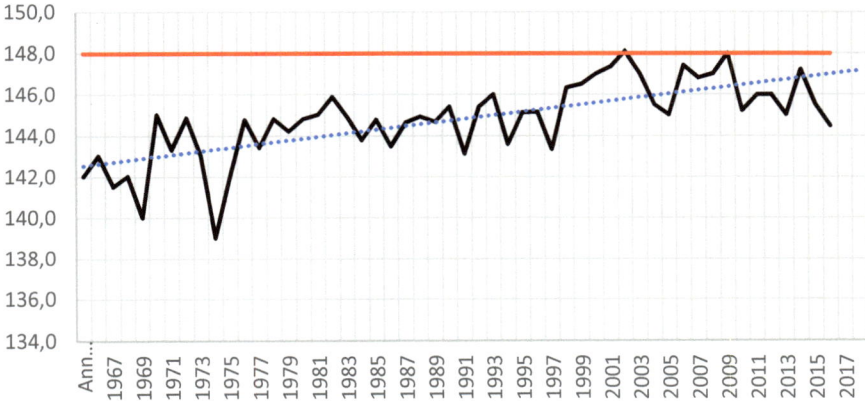

Figure 154. The curve of the evolution of stallion heights since 1960 (date of birth). Daniel Chupin.

The C ponies: 131 to 141 cm are the only solution to stay in the type. They represent what the Irish have always sought in the past to maintain the intrinsic qualities of the Connemara breed.

I am regularly contacted by parents who want to buy an oversized pony because their teenager is already tall (often about 1.8 meters). I make it a point to encourage them to put their child on a horse.

SHOWS IN IRELAND AND FRANCE

SHOWS IN IRELAND

One of the first decisions of the Irish Association was to organize an annual breeding competition. The first one was organized in 1924 and nothing, except the Covid 19, could interrupt the following editions. Despite the difficult times and during the war years, the Irish Association valiantly continued to organize this annual breeding competition, which has become an important focal point for breeders.

In the beginning, the opportunity to have one's pony inspected for registration at this event was an added incentive to attend. Over time, the annual breeding show became a "showcase" and provided the best opportunity to sell your pony at a good price. The simple fact that the annual breeding show was never interrupted was its great strength. Breeders from far beyond England and other parts of Ireland were interested in the Connemara pony and the show was a good time to visit. You were sure to see an accurate representation of the pony population, even if the prices could be somewhat inflated by the excitement of the event. It started as a small agricultural event organized by the Association to benefit the pony but also included classes of cattle, sheep, poultry, home and garden products, homespuns[65] , and more. Over the years, the ponies took over, but the home goods and crafts classes were maintained. Cattle classes were discontinued in 1957 and sheep and poultry in 1966. An interesting additional competition, instituted in 1929 and discontinued in 1956, rewarded the best-managed small farms or craft plots. The judging was done before the exhibition, with the countryside divided into eight zones consisting of two or three contiguous parishes. The aim was to encourage owners to make better use of the poor land they owned.

The first breeding competition was held at Roundstone on August 15, 1924, 180 ponies were exhibited and prizes and medals worth £60.00 were awarded.

Bartley O'Sullivan writes about the event in his 1939 diary:

> *"The wonderful popularity and remarkable success of the event was due in great measure to the personality of Father White (Roundstone was his parish and the old monastery grounds were used for the Show ground)."*

In the early years, the annual breed show was a traveling show, being held in Recess in 1925 and alternating between Oughterard, Clifden, and Roundstone

---

[65] Woolen articles made at home.

thereafter. In 1935 it was moved to Carna and held there annually until 1947 when it was moved to Clifden where it has remained ever since.

The breeders considered Carna to be the heart of Connemara and the best area for breeding ponies.

The move to Clifden was not very popular and caused unease for some time. Many breeders felt that the change was made for commercial reasons because Clifden offered more hotels to accommodate visitors and tourists. The Clifden site is now owned by the Association and improvements are made regularly.

At the 1924 annual show, the duel in the stallion ring between twenty-year-old Cannon Ball and two-year-old Charlie generated the most interest, with Charlie winning the event.

In 1925, the cash prize was increased to £70 and the number of classes was increased to ten.

In 1928 there were fifteen classes, but the number of offspring registered in the young animal classes that year was pathetically low.

In 1931, there were twelve entries in the yearling class, which must have been very encouraging. Eight were by Rebel and two by Charlie and Connemara Boy. In the unregistered and non-covered mares class, there were forty-eight entries and there were many entries in the unregistered classes until they were discontinued in 1952.

In 1933, the class was intended for "Connemara ponies ridden by boys not older than sixteen years of age. In 1934, girls were included, only to be excluded again until 1941. There was no women's liberation movement in Connemara at that time. The class was discontinued for a time, then returned in 1953 for three years, then another break, before returning in 1959 and 1960.

In 1946, Lord Killanin presented a perpetual trophy for the best-registered mare four years of age and under.

In 1949, a cup was presented to the Association by Dr. Walsh, Archbishop of Tuam, to celebrate the 25th anniversary of the show and to award the best brood mare over five years of age. It has always been known as the "Archbishop's Cup" and is a highly coveted trophy.

In 1962, the O'Sullivan Memorial Trophy was donated by Bartley's family in his memory to award the best pony in the show.

Before the advent of transportation, every pony was taken to the show on foot or horseback, no matter how many miles it traveled. Tommy McDonagh and Michael O'Neil both lived near Clifden at the time and arranged to meet on the outskirts of town to take their ponies to the Carna show in a small collective herd. The herd included mares with foals running free at their heels, yearlings, and two-year-olds who had rarely seen a halter, and probably a roped stallion at the back.

On one occasion, the "flow" in the Carna ring was criticized because it was almost impossible to find an area to show a pony on an even surface. At a breeding show, the judges must evaluate the true movement of the pony. For some years in Clifden, stallions were taken to the main street to be judged. It must have been a very folkloric sight to see the stallions and the public leave the grounds to watch the event unfold on the main road through Clifden.

Some stallions dominated the scene for almost a decade. Rebel in the 20s, Noble Star in the 30s, and Carna Bobby in the 50s. The '40s were more evenly split with Silver Pearl, Lavalley Rebel, Gil, Tiger Gil, and Dun Lorenzo, each having their moment of glory. Most of the stallions were sires of award-winning offspring during their time on the Association's list.

The Connemara Pony Show cannot be compared to any other in the world. Inevitably, some of its original charms have been lost and the specially prepared pony have replaced the ponies that used to come straight off the moors on foot.

Figure 155. The Clifden show in 1982. Photo Daniel Chupin..

Breeders who come to see the Clifden show should not forget that it was the hill and bog pony that provided the breeding stock for the studbook.

Today, ponies in Connemara do not work anymore and very few are used for sport. The competitions set up in 1924 were aimed at selecting the breeding stock. The marketing of the production was done on a herd of useful animals which sometimes worked very hard, but which had, above all to prove themselves daily. This was less the case in the 70s, and now the ponies in Connemara do not work anymore. The selection is mainly based on aesthetic criteria, often based on the results of breeding competitions.

During my last stay in Connemara, I was surprised to see important defects in the legs of many mares. Some had hollow knees and lacked bone. Breeders are starting to be concerned about this situation. I am convinced that the influence of shows has become counterproductive in Connemara. Less so in the rest of Ireland, because ponies are used for sport as in France. If the races in Connemara allowed a breeder to earn money, even during a rather short season, the disappearance of these races has allowed the development of breeding competitions called "show" in Ireland. The multiplication of prize-winning shows in Connemara allows breeders to earn money by presenting a foal. From 250 € for first place to 600 € for a Reserve Champion title. This multiplication of shows allows some breeders to earn between 1000 and 2500 € of premium in a season.

As long as the show market is buoyant, Louis Marie Philibert considers that breeders will have no reason to turn to the sport. English customers do not use Connemara ponies as intensively as in France, show ponies are sufficient for the British market.

Preparing a pony in sport requires skills, know-how, facilities, and time. It is a difficult and demanding activity, unlike the show. Maybe that's why there are not many of us.

THE FRENCH NATIONAL CONNEMARA SHOW

The first important breeding competition was the one in 1976 on the occasion of the Paris Horse Show. Louis Marie Philibert remembers:

> "This contest was initiated by Mr. Chagnaud. It was judged by Michael Clancy. For this first important contest, 4 tests were organized. A test for stallions was won by Mac Duff, the second event for stallions under 10 years old was won by Robber Boy, the third event for mares 10 years old and older was won by Fort Helen and the fourth event for mares under 10 was won by Windy Cove Chum. The Supreme Championship was awarded to Windy Cove Chum."

The National Championship were major meetings of the Connemara breed in France. They took place at Madame Morgan's property in Oursières in 1978 and 1979. I participated with my father in the 1978 National with a two-year-old filly, I keep a very good memory of it. In 1980, it took place in Comteville. There was a stallion championship in Cluny in 1981. In 1982 it was held at Le Vaudreuil where for the first time I showed ponies in hand and under saddle. Then in 1983 in Paris.

The first French Championship of the breed in France took place in 1984. From 1984 to 1993, the National took place in Tours during of the September fair.

Tours being in the center France allowed many breeders to travel to the National. In 1985 my mare Coosheen Muffin (a 138 cm mare) placed 3rd in a mare class with over 40 mares!

From 1994 to 2009, the National Connemara show was held at the Poitiers equestrian center. Since 2010 it has been taking place at the Pompadour stud on the last weekend of August.

In France, the situation and the constraints are quite different from Ireland. France being about 6.7 times bigger than Ireland, the long distances to transport and present one's pony at the National Show of the breed, located in Arnac Pompadour has a financial impact that the Irish do not have. A breeder who wants to show his broodmare will think twice before travelling 600 km. For a breeder coming from Alsace, this represents 14 hours of driving! This undoubtedly explains the reasons for the low participation of French breeders in certain classes. The judging is then done on smaller classes, but always with very high qualities ponies.

Poesie Melody, Pascal Wandon's mare, didn't just win her class at the French National Connemara, she also went on to win the best pony award at the 2017 Clifden show.

CONNEMARA PONY BREEDING IN FRANCE

UNDER THE SUPERVISION OF THE NATIONAL STUD

The Royal Studs were created by the decree of the King Louis XIV's Council on October 17, 1665, under the influence of Colbert, who was anxious to rebuild the royal cavalry, which had been decimated by the Italian wars and the Wars of Religion. Suppressed during the Revolution, the Haras were re-established by Napoleon. In opposition to the English, the Studs will favor the Arabian Thoroughbred, discovered among others during the Egyptian campaign, and will assert that the Imperial Studs will have the mission to make price stallions available to individuals to create or maintain breeds and to help breeders. According to the needs, they ensured and encouraged the production of working and war horses. Then, they took part in the expanding horse racing world. In the second half of the 19th century, the stud farms took on the role of race organization and had the monopoly of birth registration. As breeding policies evolved, they improved the saddle and army horses by using English thoroughbred stallions (Foudroyant II, Orange Peel, Furioso, Ranzau, Verdi, Night and Day, Montigny). The evolution of the need for horses gave considerable power of intervention to one of the oldest French administrations. This power of intervention made it possible to provide breeders in all the country with sport and racing stallions whose selection criteria were sometimes difficult to understand. By proposing lower stud fees (because they were indirectly subsidized by the races), the stud farm administration had a hegemonic position. After the war, the National Studs were challenged. This evolution of stallions handling, far from the regalian missions, and the budgetary restrictions of the state were going to sound the death toll of this institution. In 1982, the body of stud officers was dissolved. Little by little, private stud farms, supported by the European Commission, were less and less willing to accept the unfair competition and interventionism of the National Studs. After much turmoil, the Haras, the National Riding School, and the Cadre Noir de Saumur have merged in 2010 into the French Institute of Horse and Riding (I.F.C.E). At the end of 2014, public stallion handling stopped.

The National Studs quickly recognized the qualities of the Connemara pony, and they used them extensively to develop the French saddle pony. The over-mediatization of the stallion Thunder du Blin has undoubtedly been a profitable business for this old administration, even if this has not been reflected in the quality of his progeny. The National Studs became aware of the financial stakes of breeding sport ponies far too late.

A.F.P.C. FRENCH ASSOCIATION OF THE CONNEMARA PONY

Since 1963 several French breeders have been importing Connemara ponies. Their number increased rapidly allowing the Connemara breed to be recognized in France by the Ministry of Agriculture and thus by the National Stud. A French Connemara pony association was created in 1969. Mr. Pierre Lepeudry was the first president of the French Connemara Pony Association. Mr. Chagnaud (affix de Ravary) succeeded him. He imported his first mare in 1965, and two years later he bought the stallion Island Earl by Carna Dun from John Daly, and later Robber Boy.

In 1973, 23 breeders of Connemara ponies were listed. Mr. Alloneau (affix de La Dive), Mr. Chagnaud (affix de Ravary), and Mrs. Morgan (affix de Oursières) are the most important breeders with 10 to 15 broodmares and each having their stallion. In 1974 the Philibert family acquired Mac Duff, a son of Dun Aengus, champion stallion that year at the Clifden show. The Duff affix was born. In 1981, Louis Marie Philibert bought the first stallion to be exported from Ireland after having been a supreme champion of the breed: Fort Doolin, a son of Rory Ruadh. Garryhinch Millrace was the last stallion imported by the Duff stud in 1988. He was the supreme champion of the breed in France in 1995.

In France, the Connemara is present in all regions, and the genetic heritage has become a reference in all sport ponies.

The AFPC was chaired successively by: Pierre Lepeudry; Réné Chagnaud; Jean-François Marès; Jean-Pierre Boisseau; Yvonne de Sevin; Jean-François Marès; Audrey Dauge; Alain Perrard; Alain Debilly; Olivier Verove; Bruno Guillaume and Jean-Michel Dessagne. Pascal Wandon is the current President.

The French Connemara Pony Association developed a regulation approved by the Ministry of Agriculture. In 1970, the French Connemara Pony Herd Book was recognized and approved by the cradle of the breed and on July 21, 1997, the status of "approved association" was confirmed for the French Connemara Pony Association, by the CPBS of Ireland. The AFPC, National Breed Association (type 1901), meets its board of directors regularly to optimize the promotion of the Connemara breed. Linking all the actors of the "Connemara" world.

The A.F.P.C, French Association of the Connemara Pony (Co) and the Pony Connemara Part-bred (Copb) carry the following tasks:

- The management of the French studbook of the Connemara pony.
- The management of the French Connemara Part-Bred register.
- The management of male and female breeding classifications throughout the territory and the breeding program.
- The promotion of the breed through the web and various communication tools.
- The promotion of the breed through participation in events, various exhibitions, and sporting events...
- The organization of the National Connemara (last weekend of August)
- The training of judges for the Connemara ponies.
- International relations.

Connemara ponies are presented to a panel of judges for examination and must present a favorable veterinary certificate to be classified. The studbooks for male and female breeding stock have been divided into 3 classes at the request of the CPBS:

> **Class 1**: males (at least 3 years old) and females (at least 2 years old) breeding stock, measuring between 1.28 m and 1.48 m inclusive, having obtained a favorable opinion at the veterinary inspection and having a jury score greater than or equal to 15 / 20.

> **Class 2**: males (at least 3 years old) and females (at least 2 years old) breeding stock, having obtained a favorable opinion at the veterinary inspection with a jury score lower than 15 / 20 or with a score higher than or equal to 15 / 20, but with a size higher than 1,48 m.

> **Class 3**: foals registered at birth, ponies that have not been presented for the classification, or those that have received an unfavorable opinion at the veterinary inspection.

Partenance in a particular class is a guarantee of class criteria. You will find all the details and useful documents of these Classifications on the AFPC website.

Conduct of the classification test:

- Check the identity and size of the pony
- Free gait workshop: Each pony will be seen at 3 gaits on each hand
- Free Jumping Workshop: This is a test for males only. Each individual will be seen on 3 types of obstacles (Cross - Straight - Oxer)
- Type workshop: Each pony will be seen in a static model. The judges will detail each pony according to a grid of evaluation of the standard of the breed and they will also note the the straightness of legs and hooves standing and in mouvement.

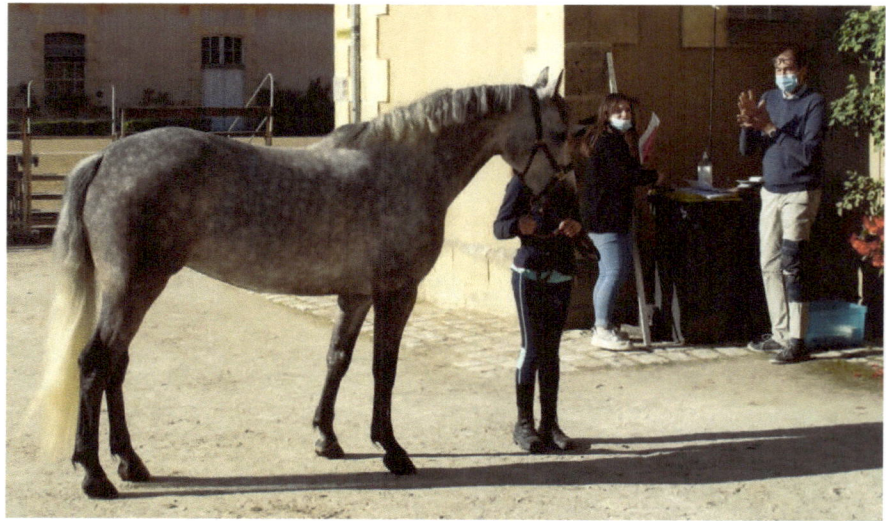

Figure 156. Fleur du Moulin d'Eau presented for classification 2021. Photo by Jeannine Marolleau.

To date, nearly 1400 Connemara ponies have been classified. 85% of the females are classified class 1 and 43.7% of the males be classified 1. Since 2006 in Ireland for a pony to be classified both his genitors must have been classified. This obligation was deferred until 2012 in France.

As usual, some recalcitrant breeders refuse to present their products to the classification. They are producing ponies that will no longer be able to access the classification process. This is unfortunate and damaging for the buyers of these ponies who, after a sporting career, will nevertheless integrate the breeding program, but will remain at the "bottom of the ladder" and will not be able to move up in the labels. They will be disoriented and will feel, rightly, cheated by the breeder.

Whatever the result of the classification, ponies are classified as 1 or 2. An animal can very well be classified as 2 at 3 years old and enter the breeding program later on because of its very high-performance level in sport. I, therefore, encourage you to adhere to this classification process which is the gateway to the PSAC breeding program.

A.F.P.C. BREEDING PROGRAM

A breeding program is being finalized. We have been waiting for it for almost 30 years. This program will be based on the already existing classification system and the program integrating sports performances. This breeding program will take into account the results in performance and breeding competitions to elaborate a database and to put forward the most performing breeders.

Others would like to go further. Hubert Laurent:

"With the help of Louis Marie, I launched the Facebook group "the Connemara pony in France, evolution, genetics, discussion forum", to try to make some things evolve and to make people aware of other subjects. Because after many years on the board of directors of the AFPC, many things have not evolved as I would have liked. There is a lack of a real selection of stallions (I would have liked to have had an aptitude and behavior tests over several days) and a policy regarding the massive imports of ordinary ponies from Ireland which have done a lot of damage to the prices we should apply and to the image of the Connemara pony."

Pascal Wandon, the President of the A.F.P.C., reveals the main lines of the breeding program he is developing with his team:

"The French Connemara Pony Association (AFPC) as a National Breed Association (NBA) has to have a breeding program. The AFPC has a mission to promote the breed, but also to inform breeders, owners, riders...

A breeding program is a tool that identifies, characterizes, and categorizes ponies to give visibility and an image of the breed at any time. It is a global and representative "footprint" of the whole French herd, but it is also a wonderful tool for a detailed analysis of each individual.

The objective is the selection of the ponies with the finality of presenting the qualities of our studbook without forgetting continued research for improvements. The objective of the breeding program is to federate, inform and transmit knowledge according to well-defined criteria. For this purpose, a study has been carried out based on the old breeding program drafts, and the different paper and computer databases... so that in the end, everything is readable and coherent for all. The breeding program uses all reliable data in both sport and breeding and is divided into 3 main parts: Performance, Type, and Breeding.

It will end in :

- *Performance labels (6 levels and 5 qualified labels: Good, Very Good, Excellent, and Elite) based on indices and performance.*

- *Type & Paces labels (5 qualified labels: Good, Very Good, Excellent, Elite) based on competition results and classification results.*

- *Reproduction labels will be made in a 2ᵉ time once each individual has a qualification in the first 2 labels.*

A special mention will be given to the multipurpose ponies (to bring to the forefront, the ponies labeled jointly in sport and breeding). The AFPC is working in close collaboration with the IFCE, the FPPCF (French Ponies and Small Riding horses Society), and Ireland so that you will soon have at your disposal an information tool that will allow you to orientate yourselves in your choices of selection of reproduction to make the breed progress in the right direction and with the research of the pony allying type and sporting capacities ".

PASTURE BREEDING OR ARTIFICIAL INSEMINATION

The choice of a stallion is always a very delicate matter, even when one has some experience. Several factors are to be taken into account: his sporting performances, his results in breeding competitions, his genetics, his inbreeding coefficient, the type of breeding used, the price of the covering, and many other reasons sometimes very irrational.

I am more and more surprised by the reactions of owners of mares wishing to produce a foal. They are astonished to see that natural covering breeding is still practiced. They go for artificial insemination because natural covering breeding scares them. They fear for the safety of their mare.

I have the feeling that the world is turning upside down. It should be remembered that the Connemara pony is a rustic animal. Like all equines, they have been breeding in freedom for 16000 years, then in semi-freedom with the intervention of man.

Until 1986, the breeding types were natural in France. There were the natural breeding in freedom and the natural breeding in hand (the stallion is held in hand during the mating).

Figure 157. Tornado de Briacé in natural covering in hand. the mare is tied up to protect the stallion and the men. Photo Jeannine Marolleau.

Artificial insemination has been authorized in France since 1986.

If artificial insemination both fresh and frozen has advantages:

- Easy to get the semen off a stallion in France or worldwide.
- Limited transportation for mares.

Artificial insemination has some disadvantages:

- The risk of the impoverishment of genetics,
- The selection of stallions reduced because not all stallions have collected semen,
- A lower success rate than in natural breeding,
- The refusal of some mares to practice this type of reproduction,
- Loss of know-how in natural coverings and techniques,
- More expensive.

I use all these types of breeding and I will continue to use them. But my experience as a stallion owner has convinced me of one thing: natural covering has better results.

This method of reproduction is natural because the stallion and the mare mate without human intervention (but not without supervision). It is less traumatic for the mare. The stallion prepares the mare with foreplay. The success rate is about 90 to 100%. It is natural and therefore more respectful of the animals.

THE FRENCH CONNEMARA ARE EXPORTING TO IRELAND

Since 1969, the date of the creation of the AFPC, the breeding of Connemara ponies has developed considerably in France. It was not until 1999 that the Irish imported the first French Connemara stallion to Ireland.

Here is the list of French Connemara stallions exported to Ireland: I Love You Melody; Gwennic de Goariva; Plume de Kezeg; Funambule II; Ice and Fire d'Albran; Too much Melody; Pumkins Pondi; Belem du Verdon; Village Sparrow; Icefyer Dansant; Pilgrim de l'Egvonne; Equiplay Melody; Atout cœur Melody; Best Shadow Melody; Thorgal de l'Aubier; Hollywood de l'Aubier; Jazzy Made Rhapsody and Banagher de Bregeon.

A presentation of 4 stallions, performing stallions or stallions having produced sport ponies.

I LOVE YOU MELODY was born in 1996 at Hubert Laurent.

Figure 158. I Love You Melody at Jimmy Canavan's house at Freneville Pony Stud Farm, Moycullen. Photo from Hubert Laurent private collection.

Reserve Junior Champion of the National at Poitiers in 1999, he was bought by Jimmy Canavan in association with his son and daughter.

This stallion has seduced Irish breeders by covering more than 70 mares per year. One of his sons, Cashel Bay Prince, made a name for himself in show jumping by winning the Clifden power event at 155 (his daughter Ardfry Skye is the 2019 European Show Jumping Team Champion), while Barana Snow, Grey Ross, Creemully Melody, and Zee Tech have emerged on the international scene.

I Love You Melody is a son of Idénoir and Equinoxe Melody by Apollon Pondy. He is a French Connemara stallion from the third generation born in France.

ICE AND FIRE D'ALBRAN, grey, 148cm, born in France in 1996 at the Albran stud (Monléon family). Grey, 148 cm, IPO 132(091) in 2003. He is the only French international performing Connemara stallion in the heart of Connemara. He is stationed at the Diamonds Equine Centre, located in Renvyle, where he covers naturally. Emmanuelle de Monléon tells us about her protégé:

> *"Ice is a beautiful, modern Connemara stallion with high-level sports genetics and one of the best maternal lines of the breed. Ice and Fire has the qualities of a true sport horse, which he has demonstrated during more than 10 years at International Pony Shows on courses at 1.30/1.35 m. Ice and Fire d'Albran was one of only two stallions selected to cross with European show jumping champion Cul Ban Mistress, who had a beautiful filly by Ice in 2017!"*

Figure 159. .Ice and Fire d'Albran in Ireland. 22 years old, ridden by Isaure de Monléon, 13 years old. Photo Élevage d'Albran.

His progeny is very qualitative: Divine Ice de Seizenn was thebest 6-year-old French pony in 2019; Blued Dew Drop IPO 145; Ready Teddy d'Albran IPO 141; Connemara stallion Blue Ice des Bretis IPO 136; Swing de l'Odet IPO 136; Aye Kiwi IPO 133; Shutterfly de l'Ourcq IPO 132; Apple Pie des Cleux IPO 131; Ace Coupier IPO 130, and Dancefloor du Cauroy IPO 158, for the main ones.

Ice and Fire is a French Connemara pony from the second generation born in France. His sire Dexter Leam Pondi is not to be presented anymore. His dame Underline of Laps is a daughter of Fort Doolin.

For the record, Ice and Fire d'Albran has Silver Shadow as a stable neighbour!

PUMKINS PONDI is a French Connemara stallion. Born in 2003 at Gilles Le Mouellic.

Figure 160. Pumkins Pondi. Photo Marguerite Brassens.

He is 150 cm tall. With an IPO 176 and an ISO 134, Pumkins Pondi is the son of Apollon Pondy and Dakota Mélody by Idénoir.

With Camille Condé-Ferreira, Pumkins Pondi won the Grand Prix of the CSIOP at Fontainebleau in 2014 and 2015, and is the only pony to have won this event two years in a row! The couple accumulated a total of ten international wins and many more at national pony shows.

Purchased by the Foley family, Pumkins Pondi joined Ireland in 2017. He continued his sporting career with Jason and then Max Foley. With the latter, he won the Irish National Championship in 2018 on the grass track in Dublin. He also won the Grand Prix at Mullingar International Horse Show in 2018.

At the age of 17, he started a second career at stud in Ireland.

His progeny in France is essentially from the Ponthouar breeding farm owned by Marie Witté.

Figure 161. Pumkins Pondi. Photo by Sorcha Foley.

GWENNIC DE GOARIVA is a Connemara stallion and French show jumping performer active in Ireland. Born in 1994 at Mr. Jacque Olivier in Lorient. Dun, measuring 146 cm, with an IPO of 144 in 2000, Gwennic de Goariva is a son of Néruda Darling and Athéna of Goariva by Lupin. This French Connemara pony is from the fourth generation born in France. He is owned by and covering mares for Shane, John, and Maeve Riordan, Lishmar House, Seafield, Donabate in County Dublin.

His progeny is emerging in Ireland with Roderg Dara IPO 146; Hugo The Boss IPO 142; Shannonside Robin IPO130.

Figure 162. Gwennic De Goariva in Ireland, at Lismar House.
Photo from private collection Lishmar Connemara Ponies.

Figure 163. Coosheen Muffin. Photo by Daniel Chupin.

What are you thinking about on this autumn morning... your distant island?

EPILOGUE

The history of the Connemara pony cannot be separated from the history of Ireland. Shaped, at the origin, by an environment and a mode of natural selection, it was on the verge of extinction at the end of the 19th century. It took the energy and determination of a few men to save it.

The mares have always been the strength of the Connemara breeding, the contribution of external blood at the beginning of the 20th century saved and allowed the regeneration of the breed while preserving the characteristics and the qualities of this pony.

If the Connemara pony has kept its soul, it would not be correct to talk about a "pure" breed, but rather of a breed with a closed studbook.

Unlike Ireland or England, we in France use our ponies for sport. French Connemara ponies are present in all sports disciplines. This is undoubtedly what allowed the French breeders to keep the physical and mental qualities inherent to the breed. The danger in Ireland is to base a breeding policy only on the show results forgetting that the Connemara pony must be useful.

France has developed a Connemara pony essentially for sport. The five blood lines are represented and we now export our products. The quality of our breeding is recognized by the Irish who no longer hesitate to import competitors and breeding stock from France.

But I think that to maintain this level of quality, the choice of our breeding stock must be based on both sporting results and results in breeding competitions. The breeding program being developed by the A.F.P.C. goes in this direction and it is a very good thing.

If the Connemara pony is now present on four continents, it owes it to its physical qualities as well as to its ease of use.

The Connemara pony remains above all the pony of the entire family, rustic, solid, kind, and practical.

This breed leaves no one indifferent, I love him for his beauty, his strength, and his courage.

MAIN BIBLIOGRAPHIC REFERENCES

Brooks, Stephanie and Mannion, Karen, *Seahorses - Connemara and Its Ponies*, Pisa, Litografia Varo, 2002.

Dossenbac, Monique and Dossenbac, Hans D. *Horses of Ireland*, Paris, Éditions Payot, 1977.

Feehan, John, *The Book of Aran: The Aran Islands*, Kinvara, Tir Eolas, 1994.

Joannon, Pierre; Pyle, Fergus; Veber, May; Gauthier, André; Salles, Catherine, *L'Irlande*, Milan, Librairie Larousse, 1981.

Joannon, Pierre, *Irlande, Terre des Celtes*, Rennes, Éditions Ouest-France, 1999.

Joannon, Pierre, *L'Irlande ou les musiques de l'âme*, La Gacilly, Édition Artus, 1989.

Joannon, Pierre, *Histoire de l'Irlande et des Irlandais*, Perrin, 2009.

Joynt, Ernest, *Histoire de l'Irlande: Des origines à l'état libre*, Nouvelles éditions bretonnes, Rennes, 1935.

Lyne, Pat, *Shrouded in Mist*, Leominster, Orphans Press,1984.

Macmanus, Seumas, *The Story of The Irish Race: A Popular History of Ireland*, New York, The Irish Publishing Co,1922.

Maxence, Philippe, *Ireland 1916: The Spring of an Insurrection*, Versailles, Via Romana, 2015.

McCormick, Finbar, *The Horse in Early Ireland*, Belfast, Queen's University of Belfast, 2007.

Neville, Grace, *France-Ireland: The Story of a Centuries-old and Still Present Friendship*, Cork, University College, 2018.

O'Brien, Maire and O'Brien, Conor Cruise, *A Concise History of Ireland*, London, Thames & Hudson, 1985.

Petch, Elizabeth, *Connemara Pony Breeders' Society 1923-1998*, Clifden, Litho Press, 1998.

Uris, Jill and Uris, Leon, *Ireland: A Terrible Beauty*, London, Corgi Book, 1984.

Wodham Smith, Cecil, *The Great Hunger: Ireland 1845-1849*, New York, Harper & Row, 1962.

TABLE OF ILLUSTRATIONS

230